Aoife Barry is an Irish journalist, broadcaster and writer living in Dublin. She is a former assistant news editor at TheJournal.ie and appears frequently on national radio. Her writing has been published by the journals *Banshee* and *Thi Wurd* and featured on *Sunday Miscellany* on RTÉ Radio. This is her first book.

SOCIAL CAPITAL

Life Online in the
Shadow of Ireland's Tech Boom

Aoife Barry

HarperCollins*Ireland*

HarperCollins*Ireland*
2nd Floor Macken House
39-40 Mayor Street Upper
Dublin D01 C9W8
Ireland

A division of
HarperCollins*Publishers* Ltd
1 London Bridge Street
London SE1 9GF

First published by HarperCollins*Ireland* 2023

1

A catalogue record for this book is available from the British Library

ISBN: 978-0-00-852423-4

Typeset in Minion Pro by Palimpsest Book Production Ltd, Falkirk, Stirlingshire

Printed and Bound in the UK using 100% Renewable Electricity
at CPI Group (UK) Ltd

To Kieran

Contents

WHO'S WATCHING WHO?

TRUTH AND LIES ONLINE

GHOSTS IN THE MACHINE

TECH AND THE CITY

Snapshot of a Life Online

You're eight years old and the telephone in your house is the most important communication device around. The information you get comes from the radio, TV, books, your parents, friends. You're too young for newspapers, and anyway, they're just too big to read. You know that in the evening the TV newsreaders with serious faces and padded shoulders will tell you what's happening in the world. Right after the Angelus rings out at 6 p.m., the important news will come.

Ireland has its first woman president. The big pop song that year is called 'Shiny Happy People', but the news is filled with sad stories, and words you like the sound of: Birmingham, Gorbachev, Dubrovnik, Maastricht.

You don't know it, but a thing called the World Wide Web has recently been invented, meaning computers can now communicate with each other in a new way. The word 'web' makes you think of spiders and the glistening threads they entwine: beautiful, but with a dark purpose woven through them.

2001

You're eighteen and about to do your Leaving Cert exams. You're sure that every job you apply for as an adult will require telling an employer your results. You know the internet exists. For a while, you could only use it at a friend's house. You'd eat Pringles and then wipe the milky potato dust off your hands to type 'chat rooms' into Alta Vista. But recently your family got a computer and put it in the kitchen. Now you can go online in the morning, the evening, and after school. It has a noisy modem, but you don't mind the sound because it feels like you're entering a portal to somewhere new and exciting.

There is an incomprehensible amount of information online, but you just search for photos of the grunge band Silverchair, or visit chat rooms. You talk to faceless Australian men who email you afterwards. They write 'LOL' a lot and you wonder why they are telling you they love you.

You send your first email with an attachment and wonder how many hours it will take to arrive. Last year was the millennium. You had secretly wished the Y2K bug would strike all computers at the stroke of midnight, just to make things exciting. But nothing exciting happened.

2011

You've started working at a digital-only news publication which would not exist without the invention of high-speed broadband and Wi-Fi. Your smartphone lets you go on the internet whenever you want. You no longer have to fight with your sisters and brother at home about using the telephone and cutting out the internet. But all new things soon become quotidian, so this phase has stopped feeling exciting. It feels normal.

Your social life is recorded and catalogued through Facebook. It's the latest in a string of websites that have become central to not just your social life but your way of thinking about yourself and the world. First there was MySpace and Bebo. Before them were the forums. Online, you can read people's words and feel moved or appalled by them; you can share moments of connection; you can feel part of a fandom. You wonder, though, about the negativity that can seep in – the complicated characters you bump into online who make you feel on edge, or weird. It feels a small price to pay, though, for all of this novelty and possibility.

You used to write a music blog, but now you only blog occasionally because you've joined Twitter, which is a site made up entirely of status updates. It sounds laughable, but the whole world happens on there.

The country is in a recession and people have been emigrating to as near as London and as far away as Australia. Some of your friends work for the companies who run the biggest internet sites in the world. Everyone working for Google seems to live in apartments right by the office. The jobs there are like jobs from the future: free food, free gym, free beer, nap pods.

In a year's time, you will start getting emails from someone with the initials BOD. You don't know them, but they will follow you around the internet, emailing you comments, sending you photos they took from your social media accounts. You will think, is this just what it's like to be online? Before the decade's end, you'll discover you're not the only one who's been getting emails from BOD.

2021

You wonder if this will be the year you finally get control over the time you spend online. Sometimes it feels like if you're not on social media, you might as well not be alive. Your phone goes everywhere with you, like it does for everyone. People don't joke about 'smartphone addiction' anymore.

The internet is for arguing with people about who offends who most over what. People who are seen as caring too much online used to be called 'snowflakes', as if they were so fragile, they could melt. Now sometimes people wonder if everyone cares too much, if there are just too many opinions jostling for space on social media. Reading the online discourse gives you a feeling of cynicism that sits like a jagged rock in your stomach.

Twitter is now one of the most influential and infuriating websites in the world. Facebook is a shrine to your youth and you avoid visiting it as much as you can. You're living through a global pandemic. At the start of it, you received messages from strangers forwarded to you by friends, warning of lockdowns and telling you to stock up on food. You see lies and mistruths spreading across social media and WhatsApp, stories about 'plandemics' concocted by shadowy government figures and billionaires.

People cope with the pandemic by filming themselves dancing on a new app, TikTok. You open TikTok and flick through videos about losing weight, teenagers dancing, jacked-up young men talking about ways to cook oats and make sourdough. You're told that the app gets to know you so well that eventually it will show you exactly what you want to see. You only use it intermittently so it doesn't get to know you well enough to do that.

New legislation is brought in so people can be prosecuted for cyber-bullying, or sharing nude photos without consent. Both of these things happen online all the time now.

BOD, the emailer, has been jailed for harassing you and five other women online. He is released after three years. His emails changed how you interact with the internet forever. You wonder, if everyone who'd been harassed online retreated, who would end up making the internet their home?

You watch as influencers influence, war breaks out, people fight, memes are made, tech billionaires toy with their power, and life goes on.

4

Introduction

We know that life moves fast on the internet, but sometimes its changes can be so swift, they are discombobulating. As I was putting the finishing touches to this book, Twitter – one of my most-visited social media sites, and one of the world's most controversial apps – appeared to be undergoing an unexpected and shattering revolution. Things had already been changing in recent years in the world of social media. Facebook had been the first such site to herald a new evolution of online communication, an American website set up by nerdy Harvard students which went global. It moved relationships online beyond the innocent days of MySpace, Friendster and Bebo, and into a more exciting, interconnected world where social media was soon less of a choice than a necessity. While the early social media sites were platforms, Facebook showed that they could build themselves into infrastructure: essential for people, businesses, celebrities, politicians, and families.

This was inspirational to a generation of young, enthusiastic and power-seeking tech entrepreneurs, and Silicon Valley was the incubator for attempts at following Facebook's lead. Two major creations that emerged to capture global attention were the photo-based Instagram (later bought by Facebook) and microblogging site Twitter. They blossomed to the point where, like Facebook, they became embedded in everyday life. Collectively, these three companies – alongside the behemoth YouTube, the youth-oriented app Snapchat, and the hugely popular site Reddit – showed that the internet was a place where clever people could set up websites that would do more than connect people. In this new frontier, the founders could become billionaires; their sites could have cultural, political and social power; their origin story could even be turned into a Hollywood movie, as happened when David Fincher made *The Social Network*, about Facebook.

But every story, every narrative, has to have its points of conflict, its moments of peril. These had been occurring quite frequently for Facebook in particular, with a series of crises and controversies dogging it for a number of years from the mid-2010s. Even if Twitter and Instagram weren't saddled with as much constant criticism and scandal as Facebook, they too were the focus of concern over how they moderated content and what their impact was on their users. By the cusp of the 2020s, the carefree early days of social media felt like a moment of collective naivety – were we all really so stupid as to think that these sites and apps, connecting so many strangers around the world, and helmed by extremely rich tech bros in love with capitalism and at home in the corridors of power, would not lead to issues on both individual and societal levels?

Us users, devoid of real power when it came to what these sites, apps and companies could do, had to grudgingly accept that social media was not created simply to allow us to catch up with news or private message crushes: these sites were set up to make money, and our every click, like, and friend request was a coin dropping into a CEO's source of income. We had to realize that nothing, indeed, was free, and that we were the product. By the late 2010s journalists, academics and intellectuals were teasing apart exactly what that meant. How could we keep hooked into the internet, and all of the useful, titillating and life-changing content it provided us, while being cognisant of what it was taking from us, too? Books like Shoshana Zuboff's *The Age of Surveillance Capitalism* showed us exactly how our data kept companies like Google and Facebook making money; *The Shallows* by Nicholas Carr asked the uncomfortable question about what on earth the latest iteration of the always-on internet was doing to our brains.

These questions, and their varied answers, fermented away for a few years. Then came the early 2020s. While Facebook was the main site that kept getting into trouble, a change of ownership at Twitter showed that there might be an appetite out there among users for serious change when it came to how they interacted on social media. The future for this arena was looking rough, and none of the questions created by its existence were being answered – they were just being joined by even more thorny queries. When I started to write *Social Capital* in 2021, Twitter wasn't having a good time, but I wasn't to know it would be the site to show what sort of social media future people desired – and how hard it would be to reach tech utopia. The site was, by this time, known by many of its own users as a 'hellsite'. It had started off as a place to gather and share short, pithy posts, called tweets. Twitter had a similar origin story to Facebook, Instagram, et al.: a group of forward-thinking tech-obsessed men had created a new way to communicate online, and became rich while doing it. It was a symbol of the possibility of tech ideas, of disruption, of levelling the world of news and connection.

When I first joined Twitter, just like all the other social media sites I'd joined over the years, it had felt intimate and even cosy. There were distinct communities, and I was part of 'Irish Twitter' from 2008 on, a self-defined community of people who lived in or were from Ireland. Things felt local, but that feeling of locality gradually faded as the years went on and celebrities, brands, news outlets, politicians, trolls, and corporations realized that broadcasting your thoughts on Twitter had heft and power. It became more than a place to just share your thoughts. Like Facebook, it had shown the power of the internet to connect people. But unlike any other social media site, it had really shone at moments when it mattered to have people openly sharing their experiences, like during the Arab Spring and Black Lives Matter protests, the MeToo movement and the invasion of Ukraine. On a smaller level, it became an essential site during hyper-local events like when Storm Emma hit Ireland. It let people post about personal, sometimes even inconsequential things, and have them become meaningful by being read and responded to by other people. The 'main character' on Twitter changed day to day. Sometimes its high points, where it felt like everyone on there was talking about the exact same thing, had one leg in absurdity, like the day everyone was tweeting about David Cameron and a pig, or the weeks of arguments over whether a dress was blue or not.

While Facebook was groundbreaking in how it connected people on a grand and intimate scale, Twitter seemed to be the dream of the internet come to life, where anyone from anywhere could post anything at any time and there would be someone to witness it. It built on what the previous social media sites had created, and through providing an open forum for dialogue and shared experience, it began to give people a voice that could be easily amplified. That in turn brought about actual change, as Twitter allowed users to communicate directly with politicians and powerful people. Voices that weren't normally heard could be shared on the site in a different way from other social networks. Companies and brands had to reckon with instant customer service feedback; countless news stories were broken on there.

But within a few years, Twitter had become a site with global reach which was owned by a company that was struggling to make an acceptable profit. The user experience was becoming uncomfortable. Ads cluttered Twitter feeds; negative and abusive comments could be sent easily; moderation had to be ramped up but never felt sufficient. The atmosphere on Twitter both reflected and heightened the darkness of the world outside, as Trump's election, Brexit, the pandemic, the invasion of Ukraine, the climate crisis and multiple other major news events were broadcast, outlined, discussed and debated on there. Misinformation sprung up easily. Scrolling through Twitter began to feel like self-harm of the mental kind. It genuinely made people feel bad. But it was too hard to stay away. The whole world seemed to be happening in its 280-character slots (even though if you weren't on Twitter, it didn't really matter – it was in many ways its own bubble). We needed to know what was going on, and we could find out right there. Every last disturbing thing.

Then came Elon Musk. The South African billionaire, who always seems to wear the smirk of someone who knows he has more power and money than you, was riding high on the success of his company Space X, and the mashup of success and criticism garnered by his electric vehicle company Tesla. The ebullient Musk was prone to making dashed-off major pronouncements on Twitter, but in a tone that could be read as 'Just joking!' if he changed his mind (which he sometimes did). When he announced he was going to buy Twitter and change it for the better, it seemed like a stunt. But he made the purchase – before rapidly trying to reverse his decision. Eventually, he was forced by a court into completing the sale, for $44 billion.[1] The next thing Twitter users knew, a guy who often posted uncredited memes, and who was sympathetic to conservative and right-leaning viewpoints, was the new boss of the place where they spent much of their internet time. Within days, Musk had fired half of Twitter's staff, including staff in Ireland, and was making plans to monetize membership of the free site.[2] The symbolism of a billionaire buying a company, sacking its board, and then setting fire to whatever he disliked was a stunning display of late-stage capitalism and techno-dystopia.

Days after Twitter's layoffs were announced came layoffs at Meta, Facebook's parent company. More layoffs followed at other important tech companies. The veneer of steady progress and power on the tech world's reputation was starting to tarnish. As soon as Musk was confirmed as Twitter's new owner, my feed became populated with people waving goodbye, pledging not to forget the good old days. The genuinely emotional reactions – people were angry, sad and nostalgic – put paid to the old criticisms about social media only being a place for sharing photos of your lunch, or posting solipsistic updates about your boring life. Yes, users did both of those but the threat of things ending showed that people got something from Twitter; they made proper friendships and relationships, they cared about what happened there. People tweeted about leaving Twitter, or at least contemplating leaving it. Some were packing up their thoughts and moving on to new digital locations which they hoped weren't run by a billionaire running riot. I was sceptical about their claims, given Twitter's power, but thought it best to sign up to at least one alternative to secure my user name.

I joined Mastodon, which was having such a heavy influx of new members that it had to undertake funding drives to keep up with the demand. Mastodon is made up of servers which are independently owned and run. As Mastodon explained on its Twitter account while trying to entice people to dump Musk's new playground: 'Why choose Mastodon? Because it's decentralized and open-source, it can't be sold and won't go bankrupt. It respects your privacy and gives control over the network to the people. It's a product on top of a protocol, the way Twitter should have been.'[3] The world of servers and decentralization can sound like confusing jargon, but essentially it means that on Mastodon you can choose distinct and discrete communities to join – each one on a different server – so although there can be some crossover between servers, there will never be a truly unified experience, unlike on Twitter, where the more members it gained, the more it felt like a global market. Mastodon claimed to have a better way of solving one of social media's biggest problems, moderation, by making server owners pledge to undertake 'active moderation against racism, sexism, homophobia, and transphobia'. But as membership grew, it was clear the same types of moderation issues might end up plaguing Mastodon servers too.

On Mastodon, I was handed something I hadn't experienced online in many years: a blank social media slate. I was a newborn. But as I clicked 'follow' on people's accounts, and watched my follower count rise, I realized that the slate had already been half filled in. It was déjà vu: I spotted many of the same names and avatars as on Twitter. The vibe was like Irish Twitter in the early days, when it was less populous and people felt the stirring excitement of novelty, mixed with the feel of an internet forum or bulletin board in the Noughties. Back then, we felt like the online space in which we spent time was intimate and private, within our control. But it also held huge potential, both for individual users and the space itself. It felt like new ground was being broken just by being there.

So it turned out, then, that the future of social media was the past. Twitter's new evolution, with a suspicious 'baddie' at the helm, seemed to be forcing a revolution. It was making people think about how they were spending their time on social media, jarring them out of their routine and making them face up to questions that had been niggling at them. People were asking what the ideal social media experience was, and whether it was possible to even get there. While people had often threatened to leave, or did leave, Facebook during its moments of crisis, this felt different. Now, there were genuine alternatives – like Mastodon – to retreat to. Twitter users were rising up and choosing to go somewhere else. And they were choosing to go backwards.

The online locations they wanted to step into were not radical, newly imagined websites that had crashed the code of old. They aimed to do things like we used to back in the early days of the internet, only a little simpler. Mastodon was not concerned with making things go viral, or enabling users to become famous. It wanted to dampen down Twitter and Facebook's habits of shouting out opinions and racking up the shares and followers. *Hush now*, it seemed to say to its members, *let's just take things slow.* It appeared to want to foster consideration and contemplation, two words which seemed anathema to online life in 2022.

Looking back over social media's previous two decades, I was not surprised to see people deciding to turn back to what they once knew, to when there were fewer people around, less noise. To when an online space felt personal and humble. What working on this book has shown me was what I had suspected: that life online had meant holding onto intertwined threads that users were desperately trying to unpick. They hadn't even spotted how they were coming together, as they were spun by every keystroke and like. The threads were made up of a feeling of excitement about a means of expression and connection; the joy of learning new things and finding kinship; the exasperation and anxiety as more negativity, trolling and targeted behaviour emerged on the sites they used; the desire to be on the very sites that had started to repel them, as they provided essential and enlightening information. All of the biggest social networks

11

were having and creating problems of their own. Twitter had just forced people to face up to things suddenly.

By 2022, Facebook, once the star of the social networking scene – the big brother who made it possible for website founders to become genuinely powerful people whose creations could both entertain and corrupt – was a damp squib, lost in a sea of irrelevance and mistrust. Long buried in the digital graveyard were the simpler days of Bebo and MySpace. Instagram, owned by Meta, had evolved from a photo-sharing hub into a commercially oriented site of influence, though its users still clung to it like an old life raft that could puncture at any stage. People had embraced messaging apps as new ways of connecting, like WhatsApp (owned by Meta) and Telegram. YouTube still had a mysterious monetization policy and an irritating algorithm, but pumped out new vlogging stars easily. And bulldozing through it all was TikTok, the Chinese-owned app that was chaotic, addictive, and scaring its competitors witless.

It was not a surprise to see that in order to find some calm amidst the digital chaos, to step out of a social media world that was barrelling on faster and faster without a thought for its members, users were stepping backwards. They were deliberately aiming themselves towards a new-slash-older version of the social internet, a small-scale one which promised less virality and novelty. But I wondered to myself, given all that had gone before, how much of the past online we are doomed to recreate. Although it seemed that sites like Mastodon were aware of what had gone wrong, they were also trying to deal with managing millions of members, and in doing so would face some of the same issues that faced the commercial behemoths. But the newer independent sites had the gift of awareness, which the earlier internet pioneers didn't have.

What the ground-breaking internet voyagers did have was hope. Back in the Sixties and Seventies when the early internet ideas were being dreamed up, it was a time of cultural and political change. Anything was possible: you could push back against old ideas and traditions, and begin to dream up something fresh. The internet had its roots in the New Left and counterculture movements that emerged in the US, which espoused a new way of envisaging the world and people's relationship to it.[4] As Tim Berners-Lee recalls in his memoir *Weaving the Web*, the internet pioneers believed an egalitarian web of information could be created, and that humans would do good with it.[5] Or at least do something interesting with it, if they couldn't be good. Today, we talk about the beliefs of these pioneers as if they come from an ancient era, but they were experimenting with brave ideas less than half a century ago.

Those ideas born in the US were disseminated across the world. Here in Ireland, men and women set up internet societies and gave away CD-ROMs in the Nineties so that others could experience the wonder of the internet too. Even though some people didn't understand what they were doing, these enthusiasts did it because the net meant potential for a new world with new rules. But they have had to watch as their dreams warped into a hallucination of sorts. The spirit of the early days of the internet was 'frontier stuff', Niall Murphy, an Irish internet pioneer, tells me. He has an entire website dedicated to the history of the Irish internet, from the first service providers in the Nineties, to the college societies that birthed a generation of internet evangelists, to the first online Irish businesses.[6] When it comes to the power of the internet to bring change, he describes it as being a wedge for Ireland loosening out of the inflexible place it was in in the Eighties and Nineties, opening the country up to the world. 'It's access to another world in a very real way,' he says of going online. But while the internet in Ireland grew up in a country that was itself growing up economically, Murphy saw that as things got bigger online, that didn't mean they would get *better* online – they might well get worse. It was understood in those early days that people wanted community, and tech enabled them to gather together. It was about the individuals, not necessarily the internet providers and website founders. 'But now, the situation we're in, I feel the companies have inserted themselves into the human impulse to communicate,' Murphy says. 'And that impulse is turned on itself.'

Today, we're never without self-consciousness because of social media, something he thinks is not only damaging, but wasn't foreseen at the time that he and his peers were listening to the not-so-dulcet tones of dial-up. While the early days of the internet were about expansion, he describes the most recent years as being about shrinking possibilities and control.[7] He doesn't regret his role in it, and says the people who built the infrastructure – whether due to ignorance, utopian outlook, or just because they're human – weren't thinking thirty years ahead. They simply weren't to know where their creations would take them. I doubt they could have imagined the journey a site like Twitter or Facebook went on, and all the gold and mud that would be churned up by their evolution. 'I wouldn't make the mistake of saying the builders are unsullied by the consequences of their actions,' says Murphy. 'But I would say, if you go back to the pioneers and ask "did you intend all of this?", they'd say no.' They surely would not have envisaged that their work would have led to powerful social networks with millions of members and ties to politics and influence, and that this could all start to disintegrate as the users grew unhappy with what had been created for them.

Back in the Nineties and early Noughties, the internet could be dipped into. You were in control of how far you went. But within a handful of years, going online was like being half submerged all the time. It became an effort to wade over to the riverbank and drag yourself out. The stories of people who have experienced both the joys and harms that being online has had to offer since social media emerged in Ireland are the heart of this book. It's not a story of good versus bad, or an attempt to get you to log off and reject social media entirely. It's an exploration of what it is to be a person online right now, taking in some of the major internet moments in Ireland to illustrate what we've experienced and what we have – or haven't – learned from it. One of the fascinating things about the internet is that each of us has our own singular experience of it. Each of us has our own personal social media feed that we consume; each of us reacts differently to what we see. It's impossible to capture the experience of everyone online, but what we can do is look at the instances that point us in the direction of the greater stories we can tell about what social media has meant – and means – to us in Ireland.

Our location is significant, too. In Ireland, we have come to embrace the tech company as a sign of progress. The setting up of European and EMEA headquarters by the biggest tech companies here – Meta, Twitter, TikTok – meant a boost for our corporate tax accounts and for employment, in a country that had come through a damaging recession. As the chosen one, Ireland could be proud of the impressive message this sent out. As long as these companies remain here, social media users in Ireland will always have a special tie to the companies whose platforms they use. We can see the impact of them physically, in the transformation of the Silicon Docks area of Dublin. We can understand the positive impact of the employment they have provided. And we can see, too, how these companies need to feel happy in Ireland to keep that 'special relationship' going.

In this book, I will look at how social media is now a place of influence, where you can become a brand yourself and start a career based on just being you. It's a place where users follow the lives of everyday people, and where apps have as a result begun pushing users to shop as they scroll. That influence has brought issues for the influencers as well as their fans, leading to a backlash in 2018 which changed the game for Instagram in particular. I look too at how anonymity, an integral part of life online, has become a fraught topic in the discussion of the future of social media. It enables cyberbullying and harassment, has been linked to the deaths of young people, and it has allowed the worst sorts of harms – racism, homophobia, transphobia, sexism – to ferment across every social platform available. And yet it has also given people the freedom to be themselves, and to discover a new way of expression, a sense of liberty.

During the pandemic, we could turn to our favourite apps to soothe us. We could share photos of our sourdough starters and watercolours, and reach for Twitter to find out the latest on Covid-19. But we could also find in plain view tweets, videos and posts containing odd and disturbing misinformation, while people used messaging apps like WhatsApp to ensure that this misinformation reached as many people as possible. It was a flashpoint in what's going to be an ongoing battle for social media platforms. Meanwhile, in the background of everything have been the ghostly figures of the social media moderators, trying to clean up the sites and keep us users safe. But the impact on these people and the work they do in the dark is only just becoming public, and some of them are locked in court cases over jobs they say caused them mental distress. In the tussle to keep the internet safe, people are suffering.

Threaded throughout this book are my own learnings, as a 'very online' person who worked for an online news outlet and who has adopted many new major social media trends as they emerged – only to find myself, in 2019, questioning what it was all about, and why I wanted to have a voice on the internet. That was the year a man was jailed for the online harassment of me and five other women. I write about my experience for the first time in this book, teasing apart what can lead to such a thing happening, and whether there is a solution to online harassment beyond incarceration.

The book ends where, in a sense, it begins: the area known as Silicon Docks, in Dublin, where the offices of the major social media giants are based. As I take a walk around this part of the city I live in, I reflect on what its many changes tell us about Ireland's past, and its future, and speak to the people who have witnessed its transformation. As 2022 has shown, the world of social media is now a rocky one, both in terms of the infrastructure online and in the real world, and the sites we've become attached to are at the whim of billionaires. We don't, really, have much control over what CEOs in boardrooms decide to do with their products. But as users, we have control over some things: our behaviour online, and how much of ourselves we are willing to give these apps and sites. As we figure out our personal relationships with these social websites, the stories I share in *Social Capital* can help guide us towards a future we want – and one we most certainly don't.

INFLUENCE

Can't say it enough! You are not too old and it's not too late.
Follow your heart, chase your dreams, make it count.
Happy Saturday ladies, have a good one.

*

I used to be scared about getting older but levels of
my give-a-fuck-o-meter decrease with each passing year,
I'm actually kinda excited.

*

Are you even on holidays without a last minute dash to ____
to grab the last (but best) bits! Can you believe each
of these outfits are under €100! #iworkwith

*

Feeling fresh after my facial – it just makes your
skin glow. You can get it with a massive discount on the deals
I have with them & use my code for further discount!

The Protest

On an unseasonably mild November day in 2021, a small group of people could be seen rounding the corner onto Kildare Street in Dublin's city centre.[1] Kildare Street is a quiet home to the country's seat of power, and the group made their way towards the heart of it, the Palladian-style Leinster House. There, Ireland's TDs and ministers work, gathering three days a week for sittings of the Dáil, in an eighteenth-century building that was once the home of the Earl of Kildare.

On a typical day, you'll see suited men and women walking in the area, on the way to nearby offices; snap-happy tourists wandering up to Stephen's Green park; or commuters waiting for one of the raft of buses that stop by a tree-lined area. But sometimes the gates at Leinster House become a place of protest, and it was to them that the small group was heading. The protests can be varied, and photos of them are often shared on social media. Usually they show similar things, mainly people holding banners and signs. But occasionally the photos go viral, like one taken at a protest against the introduction of marriage equality. The image was of two men, one holding up an anti-same-sex-marriage oven glove.[2] (Same-sex marriage was later approved by referendum.)

That November afternoon, as the group neared Leinster House, I could see they looked very different from the usual protesters, even the ones toting oven gloves. For starters, all were wearing white plastic masks covering their faces, which had arrows and dotted lines on them, the sort of marks that a plastic surgeon would scribble in a movie to show a patient what beauty they intended to carve into their face. It looked like an eerie vision coming towards me as I watched on – part Halloween, part *The Skin I Live In*. Making things even more odd was that two of the group were pushing a metal cart, carrying a person wearing a mask and a white bodysuit. She was clinging on to the bars, peering out, while holding a ball and chain with the Facebook logo on it. Passing cars slowed down as confused drivers took in the scene. These types of protests can vary in size and audience, and when the masked group arrived there were already people protesting on the same turf. I anticipated a standoff, but as the newcomers set the brake on the metal cart, the others shuffled off.

Alongside the now departing protesters was a small collection of journalists like me, and some politicians. We'd been given advance notice of the event by Uplift, a non-profit Irish 'people-powered campaigning community' that describes itself as being run financially 'on fivers and tenners'.[3] When the group took off their masks, they revealed themselves to be teenagers, wearing Doc Martens and jeans, checked shirts and woolly jumpers. Behind those menacing masks were the bright faces of teen girls who had travelled from Schull Community College in Co. Cork to Dublin alongside Uplift. They had a message for Facebook and Instagram, and for Minister Catherine Martin, whose department oversees online regulation issues. The teens' demands weren't small: they wanted an urgent inquiry into Facebook, and for Facebook whistleblower Frances Haugen, who had recently gone public about what she discovered while working for the company, to speak before the government. They also wanted Facebook to be publicly questioned by a government committee.

Listening to the students that day outside Leinster House, I thought about how, unlike me, they did not know a world without the need to have a presence online. When they were born it was the mid to late 2000s, when social networking was getting embedded into the online world. They grew up alongside smartphones; some no doubt had owned one from a young age. As teenagers, they never knew a time without having to create their own online profiles, without sending Snapchat snaps, or posting Instagram stories; without watching what other people were doing on the internet and how other people looked and lived on there, and feeling the itch to compare. They would never have known the mental blank space of not having to be on an app, or having to know it even existed. I thought back to my own teenage years: the comparisons to my friends, the worrying about what boys thought of me, the learning about the adult world and all that came with it from magazines and friends.

It was an imperfect time, one which left me and my peers with our own hang-ups. But socially, we felt free – my generation could live our lives through two-hour phone calls, notes passed in class, and Friday night meet-ups. For all of its trials and stress, it was a time – in comparison to now – of great freedom. Because the world had changed since I grew up in the Eighties and Nineties, with things feeling, as they tend to do from generation to generation, a little more dangerous as we became more aware of our collective vulnerabilities, these teenagers had a less free life in some ways compared to me and my peers. Untethered by mobile phones capturing our every move, us internet-free teens were able to ramble about without eyes on us, without being contactable by parents or followed by big tech. We didn't have to express ourselves in a digital space, and though we worried about how other people perceived us, we could live in partial ignorance about that. We didn't have to curate what we looked like, or try to create a persona away from our real-life entities. Photographs were printed and put in albums, not in a digital repository for anyone to judge them.

Still, I could see how these students had a wonderful opportunity for freedom thanks to the internet that wasn't accessible to young me. While I dipped into chat rooms and forums, they had a huge, layered, colourful world of information and interconnection that they could dive into. They could go down rabbit holes on Wikipedia; go gaming on Twitch with a friend in another country; access niche servers and fandoms to obsess about K-pop musicians. They could glide up mountains of information about music, art, history, science; they didn't have to scrabble around for knowledge. But once the internet became more accessible, my generation could choose whether or not to opt in. These teens risk social alienation if they choose to opt out. Even if they eschewed all of this new internet culture, they could never quite escape it because being online is now part of the greater culture. Would this group of students envy me, knowing of that freedom – that as much as social media had grown swiftly, I'd had some space without it? Listening to them speak, I suspected they would.

They were very aware of the risks and dangers of social media, and were angry about it. One of the students read out a letter calling for the Irish government to commit to stronger rules and laws that 'minimise the harm caused by Facebook and other global digital corporations', specifically referring to the Online Safety and Media Regulation Act and the European Digital Services Act, which were being worked on at the time as lawmakers fretted over how to deal with the impact of social media. They wanted the ministers they directed the letter to – Catherine Martin and Robert Troy – 'to rein in Big Tech's abuses while defending people's fundamental rights', like the right to free speech. I wasn't sure who penned the letter, the girls or Uplift staff, or perhaps both, but the wording was strong. They wanted the government to 'ensure that people can use digital communication platforms without being reduced to products in an insidious surveillance economy'.

These students had travelled all the way from Schull, a journey which takes at least four hours. I didn't think I'd have been able to find my way to Leinster House at their age. Back then, my few journeys to Dublin were centred around going to eat in Eddie Rocket's with my Gaelic football team (I was a terrible player), or trying to navigate the overwhelmingly busy city streets, choked with traffic and people and always impossible to remember how to navigate on return journeys. The young me, outgoing as I was, wouldn't have believed I had the right to go all the way to the capital and attempt to speak to politicians.

Yet here these teenagers were: not cocky, but informed and angry. They were no doubt influenced in part by young activists online, who have been teaching us older people the value of knowing your own voice. They couldn't have escaped the work of climate activists like Vanessa Nakate and Greta Thunberg, or students like Emma Gonzalez as they spoke out against appalling US school shootings. Some of the students no doubt followed Instagram accounts dedicated to sustainability and anti fast fashion, run by young people appalled at the throwaway attitude of their parents' generation. For every cause, there is a young person online expressing their anger about it. The world they live in may see their every move online surveilled, but these Schull natives also knew the internet gave their voice a platform. Thanks to Instagram posts and stories about Black Lives Matter, or tweets about Traveller rights, or snaps about someone's experience of sexism, they could learn about the way the world could injure people, and how to fight back against it.

The teens' main concern was the impact social media algorithms were having on how they saw themselves. When I spoke to them, they had that teenage shyness that can be switched off when needed, but overtakes when you're put on the spot. They told me that they felt the companies – Facebook and Instagram – were profiting off the insecurities that their apps instilled in young people. They wanted change, but they didn't trust the sites to regulate themselves. It was up to the government to protect them, they told me. They described knowing people who had been on social media since primary school. They had seen ads for diet pills online; heard conversations about cosmetic surgery. They felt that the message on social media being given to young girls was that if they don't look a certain way, they're not good enough.

These conversations were familiar to me, as they were similar to concerns I'd shared with my own friends as teens, though we worried about them in the context of print ads and magazines, which were easier to escape from than the internet. When my friends and I talk today about the problems caused by 'idealized' images, we're usually referring to images online. Yet what the teens were concerned about wasn't just to do with how social media presented body image. It stretched further than that, into how apps like Instagram in particular enabled and encouraged people with the most influence to share dangerous or troubling ways of living

23

and appearing. How influencers could once make money shilling 'detox tea'; how 'what I eat for X calories a day' videos were trending on TikTok and Instagram reels; how easy it was to watch Instagram videos of Botox being administered; how the algorithm frequently pushed weight loss ads into feeds. Behaviour and beliefs were normalized before the teenagers even got to see them debated.

As an adult, I can roll my eyes at the 'how to lose belly fat' reels that keep popping up on my Instagram feed, and try to defend myself mentally against their impact. Any issues I have with my appearance are because as a young teen I was totally undefended against the toxic messages I was shown about idealized bodies, in an era where 'heroin chic' was en vogue. But I wasn't confronted with this content daily, on a device I kept in my pocket. I wasn't bombarded with often quixotic ways to appear and live the way a young person on Instagram or TikTok is today. I felt for these young students, and for how the barrage of troubling content must have become like a form of visual tinnitus, constantly there and never without impact, but something they had to learn to live with.

The teens hated the way the apps encouraged comparison, making them feel like there was something wrong with them for being who they were. They spoke about the 'beautiful women that are pushed to you as the beauty standard', and how that altered what young people thought about themselves. They were concerned about the way these sites allow users, through filters or apps, to manipulate how they appear, and how that sets a whole new beauty standard. They wanted more education on filters (which had initially been created to make photos on Instagram look arty, like 35 mm film), and what they can do to your self image. The teenagers didn't see Facebook doing any of that education, they said.

'We're here today because we want to protect young people like myself from Facebook profiting off the insecurities that they instilled in us,' one teen told me. 'We can't let Facebook do it themselves because they are making so much money off this, they won't stop, so it's up to the government to protect us now.' Another teen said they were annoyed that they had to protest on a school day, missing class 'because these people running Facebook can't be arsed to protect us'. The irony, of course, was that Facebook and Instagram provided these teens with a space to share their own voice online, but didn't provide the ears to listen to their complaints. 'We have to be up here when we should be in school, we should be learning – instead we have to ask them: Hey, can you do something?' said one student.

But Meta – which owns Facebook, Instagram and WhatsApp, and which tends to try and swallow up its competitors, or design very similar features to them – was not set up to protect teenagers like these young people from Schull. It believes it is a platform, not a publisher. It provides a space for expression, not a solution to the issues that expression creates. The company talked a good game when asked about the protest, sending me a statement that said it never allows content that promotes or encourages suicide, self-harm or eating disorders, and pointing out that in the last few years it had updated its policies to ban even more content. Meta agreed that the internet needs regulation, the spokesperson went on, but it wasn't going to do that itself, because 'rules established through a democratic process could add more legitimacy and trust than rules defined by companies like ours alone'. It was waiting for regulation from the same people these teenagers were appealing to.

If Meta wasn't allowing certain content, then why were teenagers having to protest outside the seat of parliament? One answer is the obvious one: it's not always the so-called 'toxic' content that has a toxic impact. What passes for acceptable, positive, or even promoted content on Instagram, Facebook, TikTok, Snapchat and Twitter can still have a negative impact on users. All of those posts that promoted a certain way of looking or living might appear innocent in isolation, but added together could become a source of pressure and angst. It's easy to ignore one post telling you to calorie count in order to look a certain way, but seeing many of these posts in your feed becomes a trend, and can make young people in particular wonder if they should be doing the same.

Three months before the students' protest in Dublin, a former Facebook employee in the US, Frances Haugen, leaked internal documents that she'd gathered in her time there to the *Wall Street Journal*.[4] Haugen was an intriguing whistleblower, because she wasn't calling for Meta to be burned to a smouldering lump of congealed plastic and wires. Instead, she felt that the company could improve things from the inside. The documents showed, for example, what the company discovered when it undertook studies over three years on how Instagram was affecting its young users.

According to one internal presentation, when it looked at teens who reported suicidal thoughts, 6 per cent of American users and 13 per cent of British users traced this issue back to their use of Instagram. When it came to body image, 32 per cent of teen girls surveyed said that when they felt bad about their bodies, using Instagram made them feel worse.[5] It wasn't just an issue for girls – 14 per cent of boys in the US said that Instagram made them feel worse about themselves. Not all teens are harmed by using Instagram, the company found. But still, the data spoke for itself – there were significant numbers saying they were being impacted. Haugen told the US Congress that Facebook knew how to make its apps safer, but wouldn't, 'because they put their astronomical profits before people'.[6] She was highlighting that social media platforms are companies, set up to make money ahead of anything else. They weren't set up to be safe spaces.

Instagram's head of public policy, Karina Newton, retorted at the time that the *Wall Street Journal* story focused on a limited set of findings and cast them in a negative light. But the company stood by the research, and didn't try to claim the stats were incorrect. Instead, it said that the findings demonstrate Instagram's commitment 'to understanding complex and difficult issues young people may struggle with' and also inform the work Instagram does to help teens experiencing those very issues.[7] [8] Instagram pledged to respond to the findings and see what it could do better. The leaked information confirmed that Facebook and Instagram couldn't claim to be ignorant about the negative impacts their products had on some of their users. The question next was whether their attempts to remedy this would work.

A month after Haugen released the documents, Facebook changed its company name to Meta, and introduced the world to the notion of the virtual reality Metaverse. If it was an attempt to distract the world from Haugen's revelations, it wasn't going to work, not least because Haugen went on an extensive press tour about her findings. You could only hope someone with power at Meta was listening, if they weren't too consumed with the multibillion dollar idea of holding virtual reality meetings populated by avatars of their workmates.

I was captured by this new wave of punching back at the tech companies that have become so fiercely embedded in our lives, at how both young teens in a small Irish town and a whistleblower working within social media itself were going public about their worries. There had been growing waves of pushback during the years, and they had only gotten bigger every time they re-emerged. They were particularly big after troubling controversies, like the Facebook–Cambridge Analytica scandal, where it emerged that a consulting firm had been able to harvest Facebook user data and then sell that data on to be used for political advertising. After whistleblower Christopher Wylie went public in 2018 about how easy it had been to collect the data via an app, Facebook users were left feeling vulnerable and hoodwinked, and the company had to go into immediate damage limitation mode.[9] It was fined in the US and the UK, and called before the US Congress. That was one of the worst moments for Facebook, and deleting your profile on it felt smart, even if many people claiming they would didn't follow through. There had been calls for people to delete Facebook over the years since then, with the hashtag #deletefacebook going through various phases of popularity. My own Facebook use had dropped drastically, but that was just more due to changing habits than anything else.

Seeing the teenagers' protest made me realize that it wasn't just adults like myself, who had experienced life before social media, who were a mix of curious, appalled, and helpless over the impact these social networking apps were having on our lives, and how much time we spent on them. No matter what age you were, you could begin to sense something was off. Things were moving along at quite a clip too, as a year after the teens protested, Twitter was taken over by Elon Musk and lost half its staff, and Facebook also went through a round of job cuts, after over-betting on its pandemic-era growth. The companies that were once the golden children of tech were starting to struggle, and this was making their dedicated users question the nature of their relationship.

But these were companies who had inserted themselves into our lives with ease, because we'd welcomed them in. Their products had become more than just tools that we used during our downtime. They had become the means for people to gather huge influence, to create careers, to transform themselves into, in the words of the prescient 2005 UK sitcom *Nathan Barley*, 'self-facilitating media nodes'. Meta-owned Instagram in particular had given people a new means of wielding influence, and this influence – held by individuals, brands, and celebrities – online was a large part of what was troubling these masked teenagers as they protested outside Leinster House. They were able to point to the trend of influencing, and its impact, as a major reason why they were feeling ill at ease over what they saw on social media. And in turn, they were bearing witness to how the swift growth of influence online was being matched by rules that were being made up as things went along. They were appealing to the companies directly because it seemed like the companies didn't know how to handle what had been going on, and that, away in their glass-walled offices, they weren't hearing what ordinary people were saying.

But there was a reason why these apps were so popular, and why people wanted to use them to build an audience; why they wanted to post about their diets, or fashion hauls, or pets. The teens felt particularly aggrieved over how the apps and platforms affected their body image, which was a legitimate and ongoing worry. But the world of social media is a big and broad one. While the growth of influence online was causing some people to feel unhappy and pressurized, it was also enabling other people to find liberation. Social media was continuing a long tradition on the internet of allowing people to etch a space for their own identity online.

The I in Everything

I

The internet has given us a blank space onto which we can project a vision of ourselves. As the writer Jia Tolentino puts it in her book of essays, *Trick Mirror*, 'the internet brings the "I" into everything.'[1] Writing online, you can become the focus of your own world, and by sharing your life you can draw others in: people who empathize with you, who want to learn from your experiences, who want to be like you, or who are just nosy. The first personal websites were about detail and banality: Ranjit Bhatnagar listed what he ate for lunch every day; Justin Hall shared quotidian details of his life. They understood the internet could be a digital version of the writing of the French novelist Georges Perec, whose inventories of items and occurrences became fascinating once written down for public consumption.

Long before the Schull teenagers grappled with apps, in the Nineties and early 2000s there were sites which allowed people to write personal diaries, like LiveJournal, where you could be as private or public as you wished. Build-your-own websites like Geocities allowed people to create web pages where they could post online diaries, the 'weblogs' which became 'blogs'. Blogger, Blogspot and WordPress – easy to use, free sites – subsequently encouraged the explosion of the blogging era, offering personal stories a bigger moment online. (In 2004, 'blog' was the Merriam Webster word of the year.) Blogger was created by a young American tech entrepreneur Evan 'Ev' Williams, who believed in blogging's democratic power. It was open to anyone with an internet connection. You didn't need an audience waiting – you could foster one yourself. You could publish without needing permission. He sold the site to Google, when it spotted the potential in blogging too, but soon left the company. Just a few years later, he became one of the founders of Twitter.[2]

By the mid-2000s in Ireland, saying you had a blog marked you out as an online hipster. But blogging was embraced here because bloggers could see the personal and political power it had. Ireland even had its own blog awards, whose demise signalled the dissipation of blogging's cultural power. I set up my first blog in college, and updated the site in breaks between lectures in the computer lab in the Boole Library in UCC, using basic HTML to add features like a coloured background or shimmering font. Every time I wrote a small bit of code, I felt a little thrill. I rediscovered my very first blog a few years ago. At the time I thought it looked slick, but through a 2020s lens it is very much of its time, with a cut and paste, photocopied feel to it. I loved that little site, writing my updates about my college radio show and posting playlists. I felt that if someone from outside my community found it, it would make my show somehow more real.

After the initial radio show blog, I started one dedicated to music. Then a few years later I moved on to food blogging, which was in particular vogue thanks to people like the late Julie Powell. Her blog about a year spent learning to cook from Julia Child's classic *Mastering the Art of French Cooking* later inspired a movie starring Meryl Streep. My own blog was less adventurous, even though I called it 'Adventures in Veg' – as a new vegetarian, I wanted to meet other people who had a similar diet, to take the edge off the nerves around going down this new epicurean road. Blogging wasn't just about the individual; it was also about establishing a community. That community could be small – at the height of my blog's 'popularity', I had a small handful of regular readers – but it all counted. If you were lucky, or more likely hardworking and determined, your blog could grow popular enough to turn you into an early version of an influencer. Powell wouldn't have called herself anything of the sort, but her blog could be read by anyone in the world, and influenced many others to start writing about food. She helped to start a trend just by following her instinct, and being willing to write about the tough parts of her life.

Though the word *influencer* only emerged with Instagram's rise, the very first 'influencers' were bloggers. In my world, they were women's lifestyle bloggers. I typically found myself reading US-based blogs, like the one by 'mommy blogger' Dooce, or Ree Drummond's 'The Pioneer Woman', because with them the scale was always bigger and more exotic than anything I could post about. The most popular of them knew how to cultivate an envy-worthy life from the get-go, unlike those of us who wrote 'Hello, world!' in our first blog post. There was even a fascinating coterie of Mormon mommy bloggers in the US, who were young and married with lots of children. They didn't talk about religion, but their church-approved blogs injected an unexpected sense of youth into Mormonism's image.

Lifestyle bloggers walked so that today's influencers could run, but they weren't as different to each other as we might like to imagine. Lifestyle blogging started off with few barriers to entry, but soon there were professional standards to uphold, and expensive digital cameras to buy. During my own food blogging days, while posting to 'Adventures in Veg', I attended workshops on how to style food images, and made friends with fellow food bloggers who dedicated hours of hard work each week to testing recipes and responding to comments. We understood that we were part of a community and that it was good to have standards, to network and to provide something of value to our readers. I learned first-hand how much hidden work went into building an audience and making your blog posts stand out.

Most of us in the Irish blogging world put in the work even if we didn't have extremely popular blogs, because much of the value in blogging

31

was the community and self-expression. But we knew that in the wider world there were the mega-bloggers – the ones who struck big deals with advertisers for sponsored content, monetizing their work. In Ireland, the biggest bloggers got book deals or made career pivots. In the US, Ree Drummond, aka The Pioneer Woman, who wrote recipes and blogged about her marriage to a ranch owner in Oklahoma, got her own TV series. At one point, Reese Witherspoon was supposed to star as Ree in a biopic about her life. Blogging was social media influencing's less glamorous sister, but while it could turn ordinary people into celebrities, it was Instagram that helped Irish people reach bigger audiences and have an even more immediate impact. The possibility for success grew even larger once that app came around.

The golden blogging era is now over. Though people still write and read blogs, they don't have the cultural hold they once did. We can blame social media for that, and specifically Twitter, which disrupted blogging before Instagram came to steal its crown. Twitter was initially called 'microblogging', a phrase that highlighted how it wanted to steal some of blogging's success, but also how tweeting could take less effort. Why bother to write a 1,000-word post, complete with photographs, when you could write something that (in the early days) only needed to be 140 characters in length but could be seen by thousands? Twitter capitalized on people's latent laziness.

In the early 2010s, people who might previously have set up a blog began to migrate over to the latest sites and apps. Yet while it was Twitter that had positioned itself as a natural follow-on from blogging, it was Instagram that became a home for those who might ordinarily have penned a blog and built a following. It prioritized images, rather than snappy messages. Kevin Systrom and Mike Krieger, who founded Instagram in 2010, believed in the power of a good photograph. They wanted users to share photos that were important to them, and provided filters to give them the grainy, nostalgic look of 35 mm or 120 mm film. Instagram and another app, Hipstamatic, were at one point the symbols of a 2000s hipster obsession with analogue technology, beloved of moustachioed Brooklyn dwellers and skinny-jean-wearing Dubliners alike. Even after Instagram was bought by Facebook, Systrom and Krieger fought to keep the app true to its original premise: the meaningful sharing of images. But the app couldn't avoid being swallowed up by Facebook/Meta's worldview of heavy growth, ultra-connection among users, and commercialism. Like Evan Williams leaving Blogger to Google, Systrom and Krieger eventually left Instagram in Facebook's hands.

After Instagram was bought by Facebook, it became a new way for people to share the details of their lives, whether it be an account dedicated to a pet, a nerdy examination of cult films, or precision coffee brewing. There was an intimacy to Instagram that was reminiscent of blogging. By putting hashtags on your photos you could collect followers, and stay true to the early internet dreams of interconnection. As Sarah Frier writes in her book *No Filter: The Inside Story of Instagram*, 'Instagram's early popularity was less about the technology and more about the psychology – about how it made people feel.'[3] You could easily scroll through people's Instagram pages and get a sense of who they were through how they presented themselves via image and text; whereas with Twitter the emphasis was in short declarations. Facebook was still in the background, ever-present in its authority and legacy, and it too had provided a home for figures to become popular and influential. But Instagram changed the game.

Until around 2015, the word 'influencer' wasn't in everyday parlance, but Instagram helped cement the term. Influencers aren't a step down from celebrities; now they can be celebrities too. Every trend on Instagram has created its own group of top influencers, be it the fitness trend, make-up artist trend, or body positivity trend. In order to create a brand, people have to be aspirational in some way, and Instagram provides the platform for influencers to promise us something. It exploits our attraction to aesthetically pleasing images. Users can become like digital magpies, spotting the sparkle in images of beautiful bodies and objects. When I look through the people I follow on Instagram who aren't people I know, I can sense that aspiration in terms of the values

I hold, or want to hold. I don't care about signifiers of wealth, so I don't follow people who boast about what they spend money on. I don't like following diet-related content. I tend to follow people who promise a sense of 'realness'.

But as much as I think I'm following a lot of 'real' people on Instagram, I know that to be on there is to curate and create a vision of your life, and to be validated in that vision by people's likes and follows. Even the most 'real' person I follow is moulding an online version of themselves based on what their followers, and potential followers, want, tweaking their content based on the feedback they get. Having your own Instagram page does not automatically mean you have to put every last unvarnished detail of your life on there. But there is also a sense that on Instagram you have to present something that shows what you think others want to see, even on a small scale. I would rather die than post a crying selfie on there, but for some people, salty tears are their brand.

Back in the early days of Instagram, there was no algorithm to help things go viral. The staff handpicked profiles to highlight on the app's blog. By choosing who they wanted people to 'discover', they were directing thousands to specific accounts, and what the company highlighted as attractive became a North Star for users. Businesses realized that a stylized photo could do the marketing for them for free, and created Instagram-worthy backdrops and decor. Individuals could see what content – of theirs and others – resonated with people more, based on metrics like photo likes, and that began to influence what they posted. In those early days, there was no oversight over things like brand partnerships or paid deals. Us users didn't always know if what we were looking at involved money changing hands, or if the person we followed really was a big fan of the product they were pictured simpering over.

While growing Instagram, its founders understood that getting celebrities on board would give it some cachet. At first it was a new way to appear 'real' online, but soon celebrities – and brands – began to understand the power of Instagram not just to document and share, but to sell. It could be used to hawk products and sponsorships in a more natural, homespun way than appearing in an actual ad, and you could get almost instant feedback on what worked. The Kardashian–Jenner family are some of the most powerful Instagram users now, making millions from their posts. Rather than team up with other brands to sell things, they soon realized they could become the brand themselves. Even if something they post isn't technically an ad, everything they feature is promotion for their multiple product lines, like Kim's shapewear line Skims, or her sister Kylie's eponymous beauty line, because the individual members of the family have turned themselves into products. They have taught wannabe influencers how Instagram can seamlessly cross the lines between personal and business. Instagram responded in kind by making it easy to sell items through the app, adding a shop feature, which legitimized and normalized self-branding.

Ireland is a small market, so while we don't have the equivalent of a Kardashian family here, the successful influencers can make good money. The ones who make the most are the influencers who have leveraged their social media presence to create a solid brand, one which gives their followers products they associate with their idol, and which taps into that aspiration of being as good/beautiful/successful as them. One of the best examples of an Irish influencer who has made the most of the internet's transitions is Suzanne Jackson, aka SoSueMe. She started blogging while working as a radio station receptionist in 2010, migrated to Instagram and Snapchat, and went on to hook in such a rapt following that she was able to create her own brands SoSu (make-up) and Dripping Gold (tan products). By 2015, five years after starting her blog, SoSu had three employees, and Jackson was doing 'workshop tours' where people paid €75 to get her beauty, blogging and fashion advice. That same year, she told the Irish website *The Daily Edge* that if she mentioned a product from any brand, it could sell out within a day. She also said that some of her fans would cry when they met her.

Her Instagram page these days is filled with photographs of her doing workouts to grow her 'peach' (bottom), looking glamorous on nights out, or spending time with her dogs. She appears as content and glossy as you'd expect from someone whose life has been on an upward trajectory since those early days blogging. In December 2019, she thanked her followers in an Instagram post as she reflected on how her life had changed in ten years, describing herself as going 'from being on the dole queue to owning multiple million euro businesses'. In 2020, profits at her company Cohar Ltd increased by 29.5 per cent to €2.12 m, which followed profits the previous year of €1.64 m, journalist Gordon Deegan reported in 2021.[4] She currently has just under 300,000 followers, and in the summer of 2022 the thirty-seven-year-old stepped down as CEO of SoSu and Dripping Gold. It wasn't because it wasn't doing well – profits were increasing and she was able to bring in a new CEO, enabling her to work on building a new brand.

Another Irish influencer who was canny enough to expand beyond her Instagram account is former model Pippa O'Connor, who like Jackson has her own brand, focused on the fashion and wellness space (she has more than 400,000 Instagram followers). Revenue at her Poco brand increased by 6 per cent to €2.7 million in 2020, even with the pandemic being in full swing.[5] Both O'Connor and Jackson are influencers who have had the savvy sense to follow the online trends as they evolve, but also understand that it isn't enough to tie their earning power to their Instagram account. By leveraging their own popularity to create companies and brands that are based on their reputations but can reach people on shop floors, they are able to step away from selling themselves based on how much of their lives they give away online, and instead focus on growing their companies. When Instagram's popularity wanes, they might decide they don't even need it anymore. But most of all, to other influencers and potential influencers, they are examples of just how good things can get.

II

The early days of influencing were all about instinct: learning on the fly about what followers wanted and what they didn't. Both Suzanne Jackson and Pippa O'Connor had to build their brands on their own, tweaking their approach post by post, item by item. Now, influencing is such a popular career path that you can do a course on social media influencer marketing in Ireland, run by Coláiste Dhúlaigh College of Further Education in Dublin. It's an easy course to make fun of, and even Lorraine Harton, who set it up, can see how people might judge it. 'At the time, I had a very stereotypical view in my head of what a social media influencer is,' she tells me of her initial thoughts when asked to set it up. 'Like a Kardashian; not even as business savvy as a Kardashian. I just had a very vapid, superficial image in my head. And I really didn't like that word [influencer].' But on reflection, she realized she was being judgemental. After looking into the work that goes into influencer marketing, and meeting the people who signed up, she could see the value and potential in the role and the course.

On their first day, the students are told to watch the Netflix documentary *The Social Dilemma*, which is about the addictive nature of social media, and listen to *The New York Times* podcast 'The Rabbit Hole', which is about the impact of the internet on people and how they behave online. It's like being made to read the side effects pamphlet in a box of medication before taking a pill; the students are armed with the worst possible scenarios before they set out on the course. Their tutors are from film, media and journalism backgrounds. They teach the students about the ethics of journalism and how to apply it to their work; what type of content they want to make, the motivations behind it, what the repercussions could be. The students learn how to make video and audio content, how to edit and shoot and make a storyboard. They learn about each individual platform and its specific audience. They learn how to create a logo, and use Photoshop and Illustrator to create graphics and assets.

Harton says that YouTube is the top site that her students want to focus on. In a way, YouTube requires a lot more of you than almost any other app. It can take hours to stitch together a good TikTok video or Instagram reel (something people realized when Instagram changed its algorithm and forced people to make more video content), but there aren't the same expectations that these videos will be well produced. It's typically the message that's more important than the medium with this lightning-fast video content. It's how funny the videos are, or how meaningful, or gross, or informative. In an interview on the official TikTok website, Lagomchef, who has almost 765 k followers and makes cheeky, saliva-inducing food videos, said, 'I love the raw, immediate nature of TikTok. I spent a lot of time on Instagram curating my feed and my content ideas with not much joy! With TikTok I feel it's way more accepting of unpolished videos.'[6]

On YouTube, the way the message is presented can be as important as the content, even though the videos can be hours long. The influencers on YouTube know they are in huge competition with others to get eyes on their videos, which is why you'll see thumbnails promising the SECRET to something, what NOT to do, what TO DO immediately, or how to TRANSFORM your life. What can look very easy – plop yourself in front of a camera and open your mouth – can have an intense amount of planning and money behind it. The illusion of ease no doubt fools some people into thinking they too could be a YouTube influencer if they just tried, like someone claiming their child could be as good an artist as Jackson Pollock. That's one of the greatest tricks influencing has played on people: making the audience think that it's simple and easy, when it takes a level of energy that some of us just couldn't give. There is big money to be made on YouTube – popular YouTubers, like US vlogger and personality Emma Chamberlain, and Mexican singer Kimberly Loaiza, are said to be worth tens of millions. The top YouTuber at the moment is MrBeast, who makes millions from his online persona and ventures – which even includes a 'ghost kitchen' that sells burgers, as well as videos where he gives away thousands of dollars to strangers. But in turn, he invests millions into his high-concept videos. You get what you put into YouTube.

The influencer marketing course attracts a varied group, Harton says, and isn't about taking an ego trip. 'There weren't many people coming in going, "Oh, I think I'm great and I want to promote myself online."' The second year of the influencer course saw more mature students join, and some didn't actually want to promote themselves. Instead, they wanted to do social media management for brands. 'I think the younger ones, they're used to broadcasting everything online, and it has become a lot more normal,' says Harton. 'And then the more mature students who come in, they'd be a little bit more self-conscious, I'd have to almost encourage them to put themselves in front of the camera.' The older I get, the less I want to put myself online. I know I'm not alone in feeling that way, having talked to other millennials about it. Because our generation hasn't grown up having to be face-forward online, it's an extra burden and can feel mentally draining as well as exposing. We can also betray our age easily. The 'millennial pause' is something that older millennials find themselves mocked for online. It's a split-second pause at the beginning of videos that's a hangover from when it took apps a moment to begin filming.

The very first class in the course is on finding what makes you stand out. 'To be a good influencer, you need to find your niche,' Harton tells them. 'And then the idea would be that you connect with people enough that you'll get brands on board, because that's how you make money.' If you don't want to partner with brands, or are very picky about who you partner with, you can create and promote your own brand. (And if you don't do your research, you can betray the fact you'd never normally use the product, or you could partner up with a corporation with dodgy values). There are multiple ways to play the influencer game, and just because partnering with brands is the most common one, it doesn't mean it's the most satisfying for influencers or followers. But it's certainly the most common.

Harton says she's noticed that the younger students effectively 'live' online: 'They're getting their news, they're getting their information, they're getting everything online.' There was much spluttering when it was reported in mid-2022 that Prabhakar Raghavan, a Google senior vice president, told a Forbes conference that Google's studies showed 'something like almost 40 per cent of young people, when they're looking for a place for lunch, they don't go to Google Maps or Search. They go to TikTok or Instagram.'[7] Some claimed this meant these apps were the new Google, but to me it showed that the youth trust what they're recommended by *people* online. They want to find guidance from a real-life person, not a faceless search engine. With so much content and information – not all of it correct – proliferating online, a personal tip has value, hence the popularity of influencers.

While she's enthusiastic about all of the positive things she's seen her students achieve from being online, Harton has become aware of the negative sides of social media itself. 'It's so easy to get addicted to it. That's the scary thing about it. So we'll have a lot of conversations with the students about that,' she says. Her students tend to be good with boundaries – between what's life online and what's life offline. Given that the younger millennial and Gen Z generations grew up immersed in an always-on internet culture, it makes sense that they would be able to create a boundary between digital and real life in a more meaningful way than me and my older millennial generation. Or if they don't create a boundary, it could be that they accept the now essential role of the internet in a way those who lived without it don't. The anguish that being online causes us older adults could be not so much down to how often we're online, but how bad we feel about it. We might be doubling down on feeling bad by judging ourselves for doing exactly what the creators of social media platforms want us to do. Another factor in the ability of young people to cope is that – though millennials in particular might not want to admit it – what we think is 'cool' online will most certainly not be seen as cool by people younger than us. We might be turning them off copying our online behaviour simply by undertaking it. Some might turn away from the anguish because they see what it does to us.

Thomas Arnold started posting videos to YouTube as a young teenager, inspired by some of the big stars on that platform like Shane Dawson (an American who started off making sketch comedy videos, but who by 2020 was courting controversy over comments he had made in the past) and video game streamer, PewDiePie. Arnold's first videos were about cricket, and as they performed well it encouraged him to move further into video production. He was a co-founder of the GOAT House, a house where Irish TikTok creators lived for a period of time in 2020. These days he runs a video production company, but for a number of years he uploaded three videos a week to YouTube, then TikTok.

Arnold is twenty-five now, and says that after all of his time creating content for the internet, he doesn't view any online content as 'real'. 'What I mean by that is: it's all made up, it's all just people wanting to get clicks on a thing called the internet,' he says. 'Most content is not the same as everyday life – it's just emotions. It's dreams. It's dreams and stories.' He's not saying this as criticism, but as fact. What we put online isn't an exact reflection of how we live our lives, as there is a creative element to how it is portrayed. That's why he's in visual media after all: storytelling. It's why he loves watching movies, and making videos himself. 'It's escapism, really,' he says.

He says that the version of him in his videos is 'an exaggerated form of myself'. He compares it to how we might talk to our parents one way, and our friends another. 'YouTube, or any form of social media, is a performative art,' he explains. 'Because if it wasn't a performative art, then by that logic, I should be able to film you breathe and that should be entertaining, because that is technically real. But nobody wants to see that. So I've always been aware that I am a character of myself, I guess, but that's perfectly fine.' He doesn't mind because he wants the viewer to be entertained, to be educated, to be inspired. He grew up in a world where the internet already existed, and was aware of its possibilities from a young age. I suspect this is why he doesn't tie himself up in knots over what being online 'means', which in turn frees him up creatively.

Arnold says that the world of being an influencer is not as glamorous as people think – it's just a job, at the end of the day. Though influencers might be making thousands of euro a month from their content, their expenses can include buying clothes and props for a photo or video. Being aesthetically pleasing means the chance of more likes and engagement, and bigger opportunities for monetization in return. 'It's all a big competitive game of getting enough eyeballs on your content so that people will pay you,' says Arnold. 'If you're not willing to compete the same way people compete in business or compete in sports, then you're going to have a hard time succeeding in the business.'

Irish podcaster, writer and former journalist Rosemary Mac Cabe began her foray into Instagram and Twitter while working at *The Irish Times*. Her first taste of a bigger audience came after she tweeted about travelling when the Icelandic ash cloud led to cancelled flights across Europe in 2010. Her tweets helped her get to 10,000 followers on Twitter, which was a sizable number at the time. Then she joined Instagram, her audience followed, and she started to make enough money from part-time influencing that she could give up her magazine job. She did freelance radio and TV slots while working with brands on sponsored grid posts, stories, and YouTube videos.

In the early days of creating paid-for content, Mac Cabe found that some companies misunderstood the value of her work. When she turned down one company after they offered a €200 voucher as payment, an employee responded that it would have only taken Mac Cabe ten minutes to post the content. 'I wrote back and said: but it's taken me eight years to get to this number of followers. I've put work into this,' replied Mac Cabe. The offers did get more professional, and for a time she worked with an agency. Most of the bigger influencers work with agencies, so don't have to deal with brands directly. But there's not a huge amount of transparency regarding the prices people are paid for influencing work. Back in 2016, I wrote an article looking at this topic, and found it was common for popular influencers to be paid up to €3,000 for a post. In 2016, the world of influencing was so new that people were surprised to see that influencers could command hundreds of euro for a grid post or video, never mind thousands. Some influencers have been transparent about what they earn – Nicole O'Brien, a Cork woman who appeared on Netflix's *Too Hot to Handle*, told the *Irish Examiner* in 2021 that she earned $4,000 from one sponsored post.[8] But unless you hang out with a lot of other influencers, you don't really know what other people are charging, Mac Cabe says.

Rosemary Mac Cabe describes a 'weird type of ownership' between influencers and their followers. 'Your followers think they're your customers, when actually they're not spending any money. Time is money and attention has value, and I understand that,' she explains. 'But I think there's a weird sense of entitlement that people get when they follow you online that maybe isn't necessarily warranted, or earned.' She found that the more followers you get, the more demands people make on your time. She once put up a photograph of her kitchen and got a message asking her to rate the pros and cons of the coffee maker behind her. There's power in influencers' opinions, and that's why followers ask those kinds of questions – and brands know this. The growth of the influencer marketing industry has been huge: it's more than doubled since 2019, and is worth $16.4 billion worldwide.[9]

But the industry wasn't insulated from the effects of Covid-19. Almost overnight, influencers found their livelihoods threatened. Immediately, some kinds of content were impossible – travel bloggers were instantly shifted into a new reality – and other kinds were insensitive. The needs and desires of followers changed rapidly. While the world was on lockdown and people were dying, the typical influencer tropes of presenting an envious life, and selling something while you're at it, looked gauche and inappropriate. Brands and influencers had to cancel ad campaigns and partnerships, or pivot into new ways of presenting themselves and selling. Some fitness influencers, for example, started hosting online classes, offering content for free on their page. Other influencers had to pivot to entirely new forms of content.

But the fact that there are questions about what influencers earn shows that a level of transparency is demanded of them that we wouldn't demand from other workers. It betrays the belief that to be an influencer is to not be doing 'proper' work. The melding of personal and business also means that there can be blurry lines around when influencers have posted something and been paid for it. Today, you can expect some transparency when you see sponsored content produced by an influencer, but it took a while for this to become routine. The questions around monetization and transparency came to a head in 2017, when the Advertising Standards Authority for Ireland (ASAI), an independent self-regulatory body set up and financed by the advertising industry, got so concerned about influencer marketing that it started monitoring accounts.[10]

At that time, a troubling amount of influencers were – accidentally or otherwise – not always tagging branded content. The ASAI wanted influencers to be more honest, and brought in guidelines around adding hashtags like #AD (advertisement) or #SP (sponsored) to ads or sponsored posts. People can report questionable content to the ASAI – given the sorts of things I'd seen myself on Instagram, I wasn't surprised to read one complaint in 2021 that found an influencer had put the word #AD on her posts . . . in white text, on a white background. But while the ASAI can order ads to be removed or never run again, there aren't any legal ramifications. Often by the time the complaint is processed, the ad is gone anyway.

It took until 2018 for the ASAI to uphold a complaint about sponsored content posted by an influencer. An ad from Rosie Connolly – who has almost 400,000 Instagram followers – for Rimmel foundation found her slapped on the wrist after Rimmel acknowledged that her paid-for posts on the product had been filtered with an inbuilt camera feature. There hadn't been an intention to mislead, but it didn't 'reflect [Rimmel's] values'. The cosmetics company put strict rules in place for future Instagram collaborations, and promised to stringently monitor all paid posts. Under the ASAI rules, the onus was on the advertiser – not the influencer – to make sure the rules were followed.[11] There have been multiple complaints about other influencers in the years since, even with all of the guidelines being brought in.

Three years after the measures were introduced, the ASAI asked people what they thought about influencers. Only 7 per cent of the respondents said they had trust in what influencers post. Over half (51 per cent) were concerned by a lack of transparency in influencer marketing, while 42 per cent believed influencers to be more responsible with advertising than they were in 2018. It also found that 59 per cent of people considered influencers who don't seem authentic to be 'annoying', while 57 per cent get annoyed at seeing too much sponsored content.[12] In those few years, behaviour by influencers and attitudes towards them had evolved, and a lot of it was down to a backlash in 2018 which pushed the rumbling discontent to the surface.

The Backlash

I

Siobhán O'Hagan was leaving a gym in Chiang Mai, Thailand, in 2018 when she got a notification on Instagram: Bloggers Unveiled has mentioned you. 'Oh, God,' was her first thought, she tells me three years later, her hands covering her face in mock horror. 'I'm still shaking thinking of it.' It's just before Christmas when we talk. She's in a Dublin apartment, but usually she lives in Bali. Her Instagram photos – her name on there is OhFitness – are bright and colourful, showing her in sunny climes; lifting weights in the gym; sharing her secret to being happy with your body (finding activities you enjoy); eating pizza; and standing on the edge of a pool, the pink and gold of a Bali sunset glowing behind her like a Turner watercolour. If there's an attitude she projects across her feed, it's happiness. She has a clear sense of identity, with her red hair and smattering of freckles.

When I think about how Ireland's influencing scene has grown, and its various phases, I always land on 2018 as its most significant year. This was the year that set influencing on the trajectory that it's been on since, not just in terms of the type of content people aspire to produce on Instagram, but what followers have begun to expect from creators. In its 2018 roundup, Instagram said that the year showed 'that sharing love and

45

kindness is still a top priority for the Instagram community', because so many people used heart emojis and love heart stickers. The year's trends included ASMR (autonomous sensory median reaction) videos of things like soap-cutting and slime popping, which are said to promote positive and relaxing feelings; the K-pop band BTS's fans were the top fandom community; people were using the app to share thoughts on the movements #MeToo and #TimesUp. But over in Ireland, some people were starting to become unhappy about what influencing meant, and how the creator–fan relationship was working, and their feedback was not sprinkled with happy emojis.

A scepticism had slinked into some quarters around influencer brand deals, missing sponsored hashtags, filtered images, and rumours that some people were buying their followers. Not long after the ASAI appealed to influencers to be more careful about their sponsored posts, a page called Bloggers Unveiled started calling people out. Bloggers Unveiled wasn't the only 'callout' page to focus on Irish influencers, but it was one that got a huge amount of attention. (Another, Bullshitcallerouter, appeared at the start of 2018 but only lasted a few months.) It took just eight months for Bloggers Unveiled to become one of the most talked-about pages in Irish Instagram circles before it crashed and burned amid claims of bullying and questions over the identity of who ran it.[1] By the time it closed down, it had over 223,000 followers and had posted more than 240 times. For some users, it was a reckoning; it was about time that a page like Bloggers Unveiled swept under the Instagram rug and made influencers accountable for what they were posting.

Siobhán O'Hagan knew that Bloggers Unveiled shared images of influencers who appeared to have photoshopped their bodies to look smaller, or who seemed to 'forget' to acknowledge they'd been paid to post content. The page could tag the influencer involved, making them immediately accountable and sending other users their way to comment on their posts, or private message them. It was clearly inspired by sites like Estée Laundry and Diet Prada, two US Instagram pages that held beauty and fashion brands to account. But being Irish, it didn't aim for the big brands – it went local, focusing on the small yet well-followed and lucrative pool of Irish influencers. Bloggers Unveiled positioned itself as the new sheriff in town, there to drag the guilty out into the light, and make them pay (or at the very least, lose followers) for what they'd done. But for those in the firing line, the alleged infractions weren't always what they were made out to be.

I'm curious about O'Hagan's approach to the likes of Bloggers Unveiled, because I know that she's faced bullying and trolling online, and I've seen a multi-page thread about her on one particular gossip forum, with strangers tearing apart every imagined 'flaw' of hers. She set up her account while studying to be a personal trainer. While her peers were getting business cards printed, she believed that the way to go was social media. This was in 2015, right before Instagram influencing was a big thing in Ireland, so many of her classmates thought her idea wouldn't catch on, she says. She'd post workout tips and tricks on her account, and she followed different fitness trends, like bodybuilding and CrossFit. Within a few years she was selling personal training programmes through her account, having built up enough of a profile to set up her own business. Being so aesthetic-led, Instagram is a natural home for fitness influencing in particular – the proof is in the pudding, or in the photo of the tanned and muscular body.

O'Hagan says she's never had a strategy, but has been able to understand what people on Instagram want. She learned that Monday was a good day to post motivational posts about weight loss or training, because people tend to look for that sort of information at the start of the week. She discovered that her photos of hungover McDonald's meals would be more popular than a lean chicken breast, as it was more 'real' than what fitness influencers typically post. Understanding that Instagram is an image-driven platform was one of the ways O'Hagan was able to grow her following, but she could also see how that could be problematic. She knew that she would sell her business more if she put up photos where she looked 'a little bit leaner', as people wanted to look like her. 'It's one of those sad realities,' she says. But she no longer feels that she has to post lean pictures in order to get more followers, and has also evolved when it comes to her own training. 'I thought it was normal to structure your day and your life around getting as lean as possible,' she says. 'It's only looking back now that I realize there's so much more to life."

The irony is that when she did put up videos or posts giving personal training advice – as opposed to just aesthetic posts – she'd be criticized in the comments. It was easier to stick to the bikini photographs, which didn't get the same type of criticism. 'Even now, I want to put up helpful content but it's not worth people criticizing it, so I'll just put a picture up of me in a bikini and I'll say "sign up to my programme" – which is not ideal,' she says. A post advising people to look after themselves at Christmas and not feel pressured to diet got 1,000 likes, but a reel of her in a mini-skirt around the same time got about 8,000 likes. She has a sanguine attitude about it. 'If that post only got 1,000 likes, that could be fifty people that you helped a little bit,' she told herself, whereas in the early days of Instagram the lower numbers would have discouraged her. Instagram gives instant feedback, but that feedback isn't always what influencers expect. Listening to O'Hagan's story, I can see how people could get trapped between what they feel is the most useful content to put up, and what gets a good reaction. You could end up being forced into a corner based on what you're seeing in the comments. O'Hagan has found her own way around what works, but that's not easy for everyone trying to make it on Instagram.

While some influencers were accused of photoshopping in thinner waists and lying about cosmetic work, it was a post about how she stretched her hips that drew Bloggers Unveiled to O'Hagan. She had shared a post about hip stretches, and in the video she was wearing branded MyProtein clothing. There was nothing to do with the clothing in the video, and the outfit she was wearing was old and not for sale. But she is a paid brand ambassador for MyProtein, so when she's paid to post about its products, that's supposed to be declared under ASAI rules. The fact she was wearing the branded gear, even though she wasn't advertising it, drove at least one person to send the post on to Bloggers

Unveiled, hoping they'd caught her out. People started commenting about her on the Bloggers Unveiled page, 'saying "yeah, never liked her. Classic O'Hagan, has always been really dishonest". They were voicing their opinions in the comments. It was vicious,' she says. If this had happened to me, I'd have signed out of Instagram and wondered which of the nearest bodies of water I should drop my phone into, but as the comments streamed in, O'Hagan sat back and assessed how she was feeling. 'To be honest, at the time I was in a really good place. Mentally I was okay. I was able to take it.' Friends were telling her to turn off her phone, but she decided to stay online and reply to the comments, to tell people that she hadn't tried to dupe them.

I didn't follow Bloggers Unveiled but might as well have done given how often I visited the page out of nosiness. I didn't even follow most of the influencers it posted about, but there was something initially satisfying about seeing people being called out for not disclosing ads, or for some sort of subterfuge. It shattered the carefully curated image that influencers had put together, revealing how underneath it all they weren't what they were saying they were. If you had suspicions that Influencer A's skin looked too good, seeing her – and it was mostly women featured on the page – being accused of filtering her photos felt like some sort of justice. But it also felt grubby. Some accusations, like in O'Hagan's case, were skirting a very thin line, or were untrue. Others felt petty and mean – like the photos of Suzanne Jackson and Rosie Connolly before and after they were 'insta–famous'. Yet what Bloggers Unveiled was doing was speaking to a feeling that what was on Instagram might be presented as real life, but it wasn't necessarily truthful. And if the platforms themselves weren't going to hold people to account, the users would.

Still, the page didn't analyse why high-profile users might want to filter their images or get cosmetic work done. It didn't look at how Instagram is an aesthetically driven platform with image-led trends, and that some influencers might have felt pressurized to look a certain way in order to fit in with what was popular. It didn't highlight that while some followers wanted the creators to show they had flaws, to admit you have flaws could get you more criticism. If a grey hair was visible in a video, you could be sure you'd get a DM informing you. If you had spots, it was either seen as a political move in reclaiming acne, or proof you weren't wearing the right make-up. Though Bloggers Unveiled and its ilk did the necessary job at that time of bursting the boil that had been festering, it didn't stop to examine how the app itself had not anticipated where influencing was going, so was having to deal with everything in real time.

It was often the low-hanging fruit that was being grabbed, a symptom of social media's habit of encouraging instant emotional reactions, because thoughtful responses and debate can take too long in its fast-moving world. There is often no room for nuance in arguments or conversations online, which is why it's easy to jump to conclusions or make presumptions. If it *feels* like something is off based on a single tweet or Instagram post, then people will assume that's the truth. So when there are big issues to be discussed, like some influencers and brands not being very honest in how they promote products after money has changed hands, or whether the item they claim to have bought is actually a free gift sent in by a PR company, that conversation could become very black and white, with goodies on one side and baddies on the other. At least Bloggers Unveiled got things into the open – I can't imagine what the backlash would have been if all that annoyance and suspicion kept growing for another few years.

The posts on Bloggers Unveiled did encourage some people to alter their behaviour. One influencer with 130 k followers took weeks off the platform after being accused of editing images. When she returned, she thanked people for their constructive comments – but also said she had received messages telling her to kill herself. Even though Bloggers Unveiled wasn't sending its followers to post death threats, it couldn't control what people did once they landed on the profile of someone it highlighted. A writer for the website Lovin' Dublin shared her experience of being wrongly accused of lying about getting extensions for a promotional article about a hair salon, saying, 'It's one of the most talked-about accounts in the country and it's a shame that some people believe everything that's posted on it.'[2]

While Bloggers Unveiled was calling for Instagram influencers to be on their best behaviour, whoever ran it wasn't transparent about their own identity. It would have been risky to say who they were, but it didn't look great considering the page was positioned as a place of truth-telling. From early on in its life, amateur online detectives scoured the internet for proof of who the person behind Bloggers Unveiled was. Whoever ran the page – be it a person or persons – wasn't backwards in coming forwards with their accusations, which made some people all the more eager to figure out who they were. Rumoured identities were reported on Twitter and Instagram, and an Instagram page called BU-Revealed was set up in July 2018 that claimed it would be revealing the name of the page's owner, but in the end it didn't provide much insight. People might throw a name into the ring online as a way of feeling like they were taking part in moving things forward. There were a lot of people on both sides who wanted to know who Bloggers Unveiled was, so a few names were batted around as suspects, often due to past behaviour online. People dug into certain users' previous posts and messages, to see if they'd left clues. But while this might be helpful, it could also potentially damage the person's reputation despite having no basis in fact. A blog was set up in August 2018, naming a woman who it was claimed was Bloggers Unveiled. The same woman, Ramona Treacy, went public, telling *The Irish Times* that she was not Bloggers Unveiled – and that she had received threatening messages and had gone to the Gardaí after she was told 'may your ovaries rot from the inside out'.[3]

Bloggers Unveiled's mystery owner eventually called time after less than a year. Their final message in August 2018 read:

Things have taken a nasty, toxic, vindictive and unhealthy turn. This page is not something I want to be involved in anymore. I'm removing myself from all of this. The baying for blood makes me sick. What a shame that it had to come to this. I feel bad for everyone in this clusterfuck that has been created, but I do not want someone's blood on my hands. Thanks once again and take care.[4]

II

Though callout pages haven't totally disappeared from Instagram – Estée Laundry and Diet Prada are still popular – things have shifted in how Irish influencers are criticized online. Just like how some people turned to server-based, old-school social media sites after Twitter was bought, forums have become a particularly important place for analysis and discussion around the behaviour of influencers. Knowing what can go on in forums, and the cover of privacy they give people, I wasn't that surprised to see people turn to them. There's something about the older way of doing things online, the forum-based approach, that is appealing when you want to talk privately or semi-privately. But because these forums are privately moderated – or even unmoderated – sometimes almost anything can be said on them.

Over the past few years, a UK forum called Tattle Life (aka Tattle) has become much feared by Irish influencers. It's just one of many forums online where people can criticize or gossip about influencers, or have their say without fear their comment will be deleted (as it might if they comment on the influencer's profile). Because Tattle is one of the biggest ones based in the UK, it's found a home for people aiming their spears at Irish influencers; the Irish influencer world is very small compared to the UK, so fans are often in both countries. Tattle calls itself a 'commentary website on public business social media accounts', though not all of the people featured on it make a living from posting online. It says it allows commentary and critiques of people that monetize their personal life as a business. 'We have a zero-tolerance policy to any content that is abusive, hateful, harmful and a team of moderators online 24/7 to remove any content that breaks our strict rules – often in minutes,' the site says. That comes as a surprise when you read the content on the forum.

Some of the people discussed on the site are high profile, like UK TV presenter Stacey Solomon, but you don't have to be famous to feature on Tattle. Some of the most busy discussion threads I've read on there are about online figures (mostly women, but a few men are featured) with niche followings. On Tattle, once you're on social media with the clear intent to gather followers – particularly if you're obviously getting something out of it, like free gifts or sponsored items – you can have a discussion thread set up about you.

One of the influencers on Tattle who comes in for a huge amount of criticism is UK-based Mrs Hinch, whose chirpy Instagram updates about how she cleans her – already sparkling – home made her a social media star. There are hundreds of threads about her. Once one reaches its 1,000-post capacity, it is closed and a new one opened. The threads about Mrs Hinch are not kind. At one point, people were trying to figure out if she'd given birth to her second son but was lying about still being pregnant. Whether the people being discussed are famous or not, the thrust of most conversations on Tattle is negative. One day I saw discussions about an influencer's weight; another influencer's parenting style; and posts mocking a popular fitness professional's drinking habits. The titles of the discussion threads have a certain tone, filled with in-jokes:

Abs are fake, boyfriend's a flake, are her subscribers even awake?
Influencer extraordinaire, reopened New Look with nobody there.

The Tattle website is a vortex; each visit spins you around in a tunnel of criticism. I felt perturbed at what I was seeing, at the volume of negativity, the granular level of the discussion, and the assumptions made so readily. Members often egged each other on to believe certain theories, fancying themselves as digital Columbos who could casually skewer an influencer who was a wrong 'un. During the Covid-19 pandemic, some posts called out influencers for allegedly breaking Covid-19 lockdown rules. On Tattle, the members could keep people in check, and they knew that in some cases the influencers were reading the forum to see what the absolute worst feedback on them was. Perhaps it was a coincidence, but Tattle members shared examples of where they felt their complaints had had a result, where influencers had altered content or deleted it after it had been discussed on the forum.

Siobhán O'Hagan knows there are people on Tattle who hate her, and that they say all sorts of things about her. 'It's awful. I just have to protect my own mental health so I just don't look at it,' she says. But she has empathy for those who are on the site. 'I was living the dream in Bali while Ireland was in lockdown – I can understand how people might have wanted to be angry at me,' she says. Tattle has been called 'the most toxic place on the internet' by the *New Statesman*, and since 2019, there's been an active petition in the UK called 'To Close The Forum Tattle Life'. Over 67 k people have already signed the petition, which was created by former YouTuber Michelle Chapman. Chapman says on the petition page that though Tattle is supposedly a place for people to leave constructive criticism, she's had her looks, health and more spoken about in 'derogatory' terms. 'This can't go on. This is affecting myself in a very big way and many others too,' she says. One of the comments on Chapman's petition retorts, 'If you don't want people to comment on your life don't put your life out there for consumption.'[5]

In the late 2010s, Instagram influencer Clemmie Hooper, who posted about her family under the name Mother of Daughters, got tired of reading the comments about herself on Tattle. She created a profile on the forum under a different name, presumably with the belief that she could change opinions from the inside. But the subterfuge became consuming and soon she found herself on the verge of being caught out. To throw people off the scent, she started commenting about others close to her on Tattle – even making negative comments about her own husband. In the end, she still was unmasked, and had to release a statement in 2019 when the story reached the newspapers. 'I regret it all and am deeply sorry – I know this has caused a lot of pain,' she said in a statement. Reading the comments had made her feel 'extremely paranoid and affected me much more than I knew at the time', which drove her to do what she did.[6] I know a few people who have threads on Tattle about them, and all of them do not look at the site. Some get friends or family members to keep an eye on the threads, in case the comments cross a certain line, although there's no guarantee that there will be a positive outcome if they have a complaint.

There will always be places online to talk about the people who make their living from being on social media, but some places take their criticism to an even greater extreme. Cian Griffin runs the popular Instagram page Gaylgeoirí, which combines queer and Irish language culture. It's really funny, and even though it might sound niche, in actuality it attracts people from both inside and outside the LGBTQ+ and Irish-speaking communities. Griffin started the page to promote a radio show he did with a friend, and when his friend moved to Canada he kept the page going. Over the Covid period, he amassed a following as people looked for something fun and positive to distract them.

He lives a lot of his life online, as he's a social media manager in his day job. He is a true digital native, which means that he is experienced not just in how to express himself online, but also in how to navigate dealing with toxic messages and responses. Though his page is an overwhelmingly positive place, it is not free from negative feedback. From him, I learned that there are forums where people target certain influencers and agree to get a group to flood their comments and private messages. During the pandemic a stranger messaged him to say someone had been posting about him on one of these forums. 'The hate that was coming through [as a result] was ridiculous – I was getting death threats in DMs, hundreds and hundreds of comments on my posts, just hate . . . it was so disgusting to see, and nothing was done,' he says.

Because he is experienced with being online and running the account, he's able to have a balanced attitude towards it – it can't be easy, but he says that 'if what I'm doing is triggering bigots into spiralling online, then I'm happy'. A large part of this is because he also has pride in his visibility as a gay man online and recognizes that it is meaningful and influential, and can have genuine impact. He doesn't want to let criticism affect this visibility and in turn affect others. 'The younger generation, especially those who are queer and not out, they can see I'm not bothered by it,' he says. 'That I show it's okay to be gay: life as an out and proud person is so much better than they could imagine.'

Negativity and toxic behaviour can also move into the real world. As Rosemary Mac Cabe grew her following and sponsored content, she started attracting more negativity. She'd keep an eye on forums where she knew people were discussing influencers like her to see what was being said. 'I would not be the type of person who would never Google themselves,' she tells me. So she knew when people had started talking about her. 'Some of it was good, and some of it was, "Oh my God, she's so smug. I can't stand her. I don't know how she got to where she is. She's the least fashionable fashion writer I've ever seen", she says. While nothing she read was 'hugely life-alteringly bad', the accumulation of all of these negative comments started to affect her. Then an incident outside her own house forced her to question whether it was all worth it.

The sight of balloons is usually a sign of celebration, but when Mac Cabe found a bunch of them taped to her front door one day, they signalled something sinister. A note was attached to them. 'They'd written something like "Rosemary Mac Cabe, you're a Thalidomide-looking gowlbag", she says. The note was worrying and offensive, but at the time she was able to rationalize it, presuming that it was someone who had recognized her door from her social media accounts, and played a prank while coming home from the pub. 'I genuinely don't believe that that was the action of somebody who was targeting me, or stalking me or wanted to hurt me,' she says now, at the vantage point of a few years. But at the same time, she was freaked out.

Mac Cabe had already been second-guessing some of what influencing required her to do. When she posted about brand promotions, she worried if it would look odd to post about a serious topic on her Instagram stories, followed by an ad. As an influencer, she was able to get feedback on her performance in real time. Immediate responses – a comment, a DM, finding a thread on a gossip forum – can assess influencers' worth, ability and impact. In turn, Mac Cabe had been feeling the pressure of having to be palatable for brands, only presenting a sunny, consistent image that could make products look good.

She eventually decided she wasn't getting enough out of influencing to stick at it, though she has dabbled since in some sponsored content. She also changed her tack on Instagram. 'It really made me be a little bit more protective of my own space,' she says. She retrained as a personal trainer before moving to the US, where she lives with her husband, stepsons and son. Her next route was one that's become available in recent years to people who want to monetize themselves online, but don't want to exclusively work with brands, and a sign of where influencing is moving towards. Mac Cabe was able to monetize both a podcast she hosts with her sister – 'Not Without My Sister' – and write about her life via the membership platform Patreon.

I don't have an interest in being an influencer, but my two younger sisters both have sizable followings on Instagram, one as a travel blogger/business owner and one as an author, so I've had a second-tier view of that world. My sister Stephanie Barry-Woods is an influencer who has a business and Instagram account under the name StephMyLife. A former software developer who worked for a financial company in London, she and her husband left their jobs in the mid-2010s to pursue their dream of travelling the world. Like all dreams, it hasn't always been easy, but Stephanie's decision to grow her following on her StephMyLife page enabled her to change careers entirely, using her new skills to become a travel planner and blogger. When the pandemic happened and travel was immediately affected, she was able to use her tech knowledge and experience to start her own company providing accredited website development training courses.

Stephanie didn't set out to be a traditional influencer, but in internet parlance that's what she'd be referred to given her following of over 81,000 people. She originally set up her personal Instagram account in 2013, and when she went travelling in 2016, she wanted to see if she could grow her following and find a way of earning money through working online. The influencing scene wasn't as big as it is now, particularly in Ireland, but she could see that there was potential to find a niche. Back then, you needed to have 10 k followers to share a link on your Instagram stories, and thus be useful to your followers by linking them to interesting content or to your own website or blog. To get to this figure, she began building an audience through posting photos, information and videos as she travelled. Once she could share links, she could direct people to her own website, where she shared information on how to travel on a budget. That soon grew into helping others plan their own trips.

Her following got a major boost towards 10 k when she was tagged by another influencer in a photo. As she met more influencers and was tagged in their photos, the number crept up and up. Given her content was of sunny beaches and faraway countries, and that she was living other people's dream of giving up the day job and following her desires, people were also drawn to her account to see how she did it. But as her follower number grew, she learned that things are a little different when you have more eyes on your Instagram page. A bigger audience meant more feedback. In the early days, she could wake up to five replies to an Instagram post, but almost overnight that grew to fifty which helped her make more connections on the app. But it also meant more time spent replying, and knowing that the feedback and questions might not always be what she wanted to hear.

Thanks to being featured on other influencers' pages, her following exploded around 2018, at the same time Bloggers Unveiled and its ilk emerged. 'As a result, there would tend to be a lot of DMs when I posted about things, asking were they sponsored, or just saying "I hate sponsored posts, I love that you don't do them", she told me. Though she didn't find anything wrong herself with sponsored posts or affiliate links (where the influencer gets a very small percentage cut of what a person buys through a specific URL), it contributed towards her going out on her own, and not relying on brand partnerships to make money.

What she learned too was that there can be a different attitude towards influencers in Ireland compared to other countries, and this fed into those messages she got in the early days. 'In Ireland, it's accepted that you're going to get negativity if you're doing sponsored content,' she says. 'In America, some people now pretend to be sponsored by companies, because it gives them clout.' But in Ireland, in some quarters there can be an attitude that influencers have 'notions', and are getting things they don't deserve. That, says Stephanie, can undermine the fact that influencers work with brands because the brands are able to advertise through them to thousands of people. It's a commercial partnership, but a tiny proportion of the money earned from sales is going to the influencers – it's the companies who get the bigger chunk of the pie. Instagram has enabled her to create her own career, without needing a boss's permission. She can pursue whatever new idea she comes up with: 'I can have an idea tomorrow, and I can turn it into something and put it out there to the world. I can market it and see if people like it. The freedom to do stuff like that has been really cool.'

I know myself that I can find the tone of some influencers' stories and posts to be overly chirpy or positive. In the past couple of years, I've also noticed that some of the biggest female lifestyle influencers in Ireland won't even say much in their posts – they might share a glamorous or candid photo accompanied by a short description, or just an emoji. Talking to Stephanie, I understood why that might be. While followers might want influencers to be 'real' and show them what their life is like, that can be a fraught one for influencers. You need to be careful about how you approach your videos and posts. 'You get the same energy back that you put out on posts and stories,' she says. 'So you have to be mindful of that.' That can be as simple as not overtly complaining about your job as an influencer, or showing your life to be slightly nicer than it might be every day. She found that if a post or video has a negative edge, the same energy would be present in the replies she would get to it.

That extends to when she goes through tough experiences. 'Instead of posting in the middle of it and saying "this is happening right now", I'll take some time away from my account, wait until it's resolved, then come back on and explain what happened,' says Stephanie. That's not because she wants to hoodwink followers, but she has learned – through experience and advice from more seasoned influencers – that it helps to be able to present the entire narrative to followers, so they know the situation has been sorted out. Presenting them with an issue that's ongoing can be confusing. It can also lead to an increase in negative comments, beyond what she would normally get. Just like offline, she knows that she will be some people's cup of tea and not others' – that's just part of being human. But the difference online is that you can get all of that feedback in one go, and it's hard to escape it. 'I should be able to show up as myself,' she says. 'But I also think that I shouldn't have to deal with opening my phone and having people criticize my life, my relationship, my voice, my appearance. And if I can do very simple things just to stop that coming in, I will do it.'

In the four years she's been seriously pursuing making her living online, she's seen influencing morph into a fresh version of itself, driven by the newer generations trying it out. As younger people started to earn money through Instagram, they brought with them a fresh way of looking at things, she says. She has noticed that Gen Zers are usually fine with being called 'influencer', and are not ashamed of the term. They have also started using the term 'content creator', which puts more value on their work. It doesn't have baggage for them. They also don't tend to look as much for approval, which she says shows in how they don't broadcast the negative comments they get on their feed in the same way older influencers were used to doing. A bigger change, though, comes in how much of their lives they are willing to put online. 'A lot of younger creators just don't put their personal lives on there anymore,' observes Stephanie. 'They are able to separate work from their Instagram. Their followers don't know what their living room is like, or what their relationship is like. They are able to compartmentalize things. Their social media presence doesn't have to be their whole life.'

This observation is interesting as it shows how the early influencers, or people with large followings on Instagram, leaned into the emphasis there was then on sharing every element of a person's life. Their 'realness' and willingness to broadcast everything bought them followers, because we want to know about how other people live. Influencing was a wobbly career option, and so people did what they could to solidify it. But now that influencing has weight, the new generation don't have to go the same way – they get to benefit from the advancement of the job without having to sacrifice privacy. They can gather followers through showing one aspect of their lives, based on their interests, knowledge or skill, and focus on that rather than having to show off any other elements of their day-to-day. When she tells me about this, I think about the people I follow for their niche content – like the philosophy expert who analyses the Kardashian family, and the artist who makes ceramic models of supermarket groceries – but who rarely share details of their private lives. Because social media is so trend-driven, with people following what they see other people doing and iterating as they figure out what works, this new approach is bound to rub off on longtime influencers. Stephanie says it has definitely helped many creators place value on their work. 'It just came to a point where creators began thinking they were done with feeling anxious around how they are perceived. They would try to make the best decisions, and wouldn't feel obliged to defend them to everyone,' she says.

Some might call what happens on Tattle or with influencers 'trolling'. Today, trolling is a blanket term that can be used to refer to all sorts of bad behaviour online, from people deliberately being mean, to users derailing conversations or just saying something stupid. But it can also refer to messages or comments – that by saying something overtly negative you are 'trolling' the receiver. This sort of behaviour is built into internet culture. Before there were trolls there were the 'flaming attacks' of the Nineties, where people would post personal attacks against people they disagreed with on forums and groups. Flaming on sites like Usenet built the model for 'trolling' as we know it, according to a 2014 history of trolling by Ashley Feinberg on Gizmodo. The first mention of 'trolling' as we know it was in 1992, on a Usenet newsgroup.

These days, we often refer to any negative behaviour as 'trolling', though sometimes the behaviour might seem negative because we just don't want to hear it. But when you have tens of random people sending you negative messages, that feels like an influx which you have no power to stop.

Social media apps enable this to happen by their very design. The ability to see a stream of comments or messages is great when you know most of them are positive, not so much when you fear what they could contain. The platforms have introduced new tools, like multiple inboxes, to try and reduce this, but that's still not really enough to remove the problem.

'On social media we'd had the chance to do everything better, but instead of curiosity we were constantly lurching towards cold, hard judgement,' writes Jon Ronson in his 2015 book *So You've Been Publicly Shamed*, which looks at what happened when ordinary people found themselves going viral online, accused of doing something offensive or wrong.[7] Typically, the nuance in the situation disappeared in the resulting online scrum, and people's reputations and careers ended in the time it took to send a tweet. 'Every day a new person emerges as a magnificent hero or a sickening villain,' says Ronson of the social media world.

Little has changed from when he wrote his book, which indicated that the same impetus that sends people to tear apart influencers on Tattle is what leads to public shamings on Twitter or Instagram. It's what encourages the setting up of pages like Bloggers Unveiled. People do it because they believe they must hold someone to account – and they don't necessarily think about the impact on the person they're talking about. Online, there are things that people should be held to account for. But on forums like Tattle, it isn't always egregious wrongs that are being discussed. It can be petty, small incidents, the equivalent of a bitching session that involves more and more and more people.

Because of the problems inherent in being on an app which enables people to become influencers, some users are finding new ways to gather together a community. These new ways remove the instantaneity that's part of social media apps, protecting the creator a little bit more. Two of the most popular sites for doing this are Patreon and Substack. Patreon is a membership platform which allows people to pay for regular content from creators – they can pay a few euro a month, or pay an annual amount, or else pay per post. Rosemary Mac Cabe was a Patreon member and has since migrated to Substack, a similar newsletter-based membership platform, where people can pay $6 a month for weekly and monthly personal writing from her, as well as community features, or pay $60 a year for the same (which works out cheaper). Supporters can sign up for a free monthly newsletter, but paying is the only way you'll get access to her community and subscriber posts. Sites like these are a form of patronage that give power back to the creator – it means they don't have to appease a brand with their content, and can have full control over what they release. It can feel more intimate, and a slower way of communicating.

On Substack, the posts themselves arrive in people's inboxes as well as being posted on a specific webpage, in a hark back to the email news-letters of the early internet. This allows people to produce exclusive content, and receive feedback from a community whose members want to pay for what they read. It means the writers know that people value their words. It also removes things from the social media public square, adding a layer of protection. 'It does feel like the old days when you just had your own little community online, and it didn't feel like anybody else could infiltrate it at any second,' one woman who writes a beauty newsletter on Substack told me. 'With Instagram, I just started resenting the fact that I felt like I had to romanticize my life and post about it all the time,' she adds. Instead, she doesn't have to follow trends on her newsletter, and can be fully directed by whatever her passions are. She says that young millennials have had to give away part of themselves online for many years, and are feeling the backlash. 'They've shared a lot of their lives, and I feel like there might be a turn away from sharing.' With newsletters and patron sites, the sharing is on different terms to a social network. They're not without their issues though: Substack has found itself criticized for the content of some of the newsletters it hosts.

The turn from some users towards these sites shows that while people still have an interest in writing and creating content publicly, and creating a community around them, they might want to avoid the influencing funnel. Eschewing the more traditional style of influencing is not an indication that people don't see value in having a presence online, or fostering a following. It's showing instead that where there are more curated, individual and (seemingly) safer ways of putting out work and building an audience, people will take a chance on them. None of these new modes are without issue, but all offer opportunity. But even as they move away from the Instagram model, these types of sites and their users have learned a big lesson from influencing – that there is always a price to pay when we put ourselves at the centre of the frame.

NAMELESS, FACELESS

Do you like turtles?

*

Sorry to say, but Michael was talking to me at the fair
and he said you guys were an awkward couple because
he was embarrassed to be around you.

*

Do you try to look ugly or do you always look like that?

*

You have no right to say that about a beautiful girl like her.

*

Mass media is knocking on wrong door. It is necessary
to go deeper and to find a root of a problem.

Anonymity

I

'On the internet, nobody knows you're a dog.' So goes a *New Yorker* cartoon drawn by Peter Steiner in July 1993: a monochrome sketch of two pets having a conversation while sitting at a computer.[1] Steiner told a *New York Times* interviewer in 2000 that he hadn't been aiming to do any 'profound tapping into the zeitgeist', but his sketch has had longevity because it's an adage for the digital age. When it was first drawn, it reflected the sense that the internet allowed people to experiment with identity, and over the years the cartoon has been used to illustrate the changes in this area. In 2015, another *New Yorker* cartoon riffed on the original, with the new caption reading: 'Remember when, on the internet, nobody knew who you were?' In November 2022, in the midst of Twitter's Elon Musk drama, the latest version said: 'On Twitter, nobody verifies you're a dog.'

The internet pioneers believed in the power of anonymity. They believed in people being able to express trust online. The two weren't mutually exclusive. Anonymity took the pressure off. It allowed users to enter the online world under a chosen name, which tied into the hopefulness about participating in an exciting invention. It also helped people be playful, or mischievous. When the world of the internet was smaller, the problems

67

created by anonymity and pseudonymity were small. But as social media grew, and captured the attention of people across generations, the issues caused by anonymity and pseudonymity were thrown into relief.

When I first joined chat rooms and forums in the late Nineties and early 2000s, there wasn't a question of using my real name. Of course I wouldn't use it. I knew I was entering an unknown landscape, where no one knew me, and where I didn't know anyone either. It also seemed to me that the whole point of being online was not necessarily to be yourself, but to extend reality in order to create a persona, whether hugely different to you, or just you with a mask on. Being online was gamifying life, making you the main character in a choose-your-own-adventure being written with every tap. While I wish I could say I created an entirely new character to step into, in reality I just wanted to be a cooler version of myself. In the late Nineties, I'd usually go for a name inspired by whatever band I was a fan of at the time. I still use the pseudonym 'sweetoblivion' on most platforms, which I adopted back in college (robbed from the title of a Screaming Trees record). Maybe it's a way of hanging onto my youth.

Choosing a new name offered a sense of privacy, a sense of image control. Even in the early days, I knew to an extent that I should try to protect my identity online, not least because I was young and female. I knew from the attempted cybersex in some chat rooms that even indicating I was female (never mind a teenager) was like a red flag to a hormone-raging bull. In wider society, a young woman was at risk of sexual harassment, and soon I knew it was possible online too. Anonymity could protect me in some ways, but it could also encourage other people to do whatever they wanted.

Moving into the 2000s, the relationship between social media and anonymity started to fracture. Social networking sites began encouraging people to be who they were online, in order to better connect with others. My peers and I didn't stop to think about what giving out our real names, photos, dates of birth and school details told the owners of the websites we signed up to. The sites didn't feel like they had huge reach, beyond our circles – certainly nothing like the reach they seem to have today – and after all, we wanted to connect with our friends. In addition, we didn't realize we were products, and that our information could be used, sold and traded. In the excitement about this brand new world, there didn't seem to be time to examine what it all meant.

What we were most concerned about was how to personalize these new online spaces. The two biggest sites for my era were MySpace, which came first in 2003, followed by Bebo two years later. Of the two, MySpace had the bigger cultural impact. Everyone's first friend on MySpace was Tom, the founder Thomas Anderson, forever immortalized in his profile photo wearing a white T-shirt while smiling genially over his shoulder inside a classroom, a whiteboard behind him covered in illegible symbols. But we wanted more friends than Tom. We wanted real people to be impressed by our posting about bands and our 'top eight' friends on our page. The amount of deliberating I did over what I put on my MySpace page, and what that said about me, was substantial, if embarrassing. Like interior decorating a room with IKEA furniture, your page would retain an eerie sense of similarity to other pages. But still – it was all yours.

After MySpace came Facebook, where we were not just asked but required to give our real personal details. Even more so than on the other sites, you had to be who you were to collect friends on Mark Zuckerberg's creation. Something changed with Facebook; part of it no doubt was down to the intentions of Zuckerberg, who was constantly making adjustments so that users would want to use the site more. Those of us who joined in the early days will remember every little change that took place – when we used to post on people's Facebook 'walls', and when the homepage feed was a chronological record of what people were saying, and not a melange of ads, sponsored content and updates you don't care about.

Because Facebook crossed the age groups, it became a website that meant more than just somewhere to connect with people. It's almost hard to describe it, but it became important to how people lived. Instead of talking to people in 'real life', you could invite them to events via the site; Facebook Messenger became a separate product as people used it instead of texting; you could make your relationship genuinely 'official' on there. For a time, Facebook felt as real as real life. After a night out, you would upload photos to a photo album as a record of what happened. It was where you updated people on the minutiae of your days, and Facebook status updates could be used to say something meaningful or even revelatory. Celebrities and well-known people joined Facebook because it gave them a space to share their opinions – and have people argue in the comments. It seems strange to recount that there were days where it felt like something was missing if I didn't check Facebook. Now, it holds none of that power for me.

In large part, that's due to Twitter. The site brought with it a shift in revealing identity, harking back to the chat room era. It backed things up slightly, reintroducing pseudonymity as an acceptable way of being online. When you joined Twitter you soon noticed that not everyone used their real name or photo. It wasn't necessary to say who you were, and once you didn't come across like a 'Twitter egg' (if you didn't change your profile photo, that was the default image), it didn't really affect how you could connect with people. The early days of Twitter saw us using the site as a depot for Facebook updates, oneliners and non-sequiturs. But gradually, real conversations started to happen. Twitter stripped things back compared to Facebook: no need to upload photos. Let the words do the talking. Connection seemed to occur in a purer, more distilled way.

It was always known that under the cover of a pseudonym, people can say or do what they want. But when this starts happening in larger numbers, and it becomes part of life online, the pitfalls of anonymity and pseudonymity start smacking users in the face. For some people, there is now a jadedness and suspicion about anonymity and how important it is online. Without revealing who they are, people have felt free to say whatever they like. But at the same time, spend time online and you'll witness plenty of people willing to say and do what they want under their own names. I've read abusive tweets from people with 'football fan and dad of three' written in their Twitter bio, under a photo of them with their smiling children. The cognitive dissonance it takes to send a racist tweet while proclaiming you're a proud father is quite something, but that's the internet for you – some people don't feel like it's the real world. And yet the consequences are very real. Having an implicit trust in your fellow users is not part of being online these days. There are too many things that have happened to make us distrust the strangers whose posts we see, as well as the owners of the platforms we use.

When you experience trolling or abuse online, it can give you a new perspective on what anonymity on the internet means, and what should be done about it. Cian Griffin, who we met in the previous chapter, runs an Irish Instagram page called Gaylgeoirí. 'Social is my main source of news, entertainment, the main tool I use for communication. It's so ingrained in my day-to-day, and it's also my real life,' he says. 'I think just having your own space to create and connect with your friends virtually is such a cool thing.' He turned into a content machine during the Covid lockdowns, posting a meme a day, bilingual spoken word poems, and song parodies as Gaeilge. But for all of the goodness he sees online, he also sees the bad sides – the toxic content, the hateful comments, the death threats in his inbox. That's why, he tells me, he favours people having to say who they are online, even though he feels he personally can handle the hate when he gets it. 'Weekly, I get DMs from faceless, empty, anonymous accounts, telling me to kill myself or that I'm an abomination, or that I'm a disgrace to the country, or that I'm a disgrace to the Irish language community or GAA community,' he says. 'People are so comfortable sharing horrible, horrible sentiments online under the guise of anonymity.'

He believes if people had to give their real names, this sort of behaviour would be reduced. 'Less people would be comfortable sending abuse and hate if it was necessary to have your passport or driver's licence or something else attached to create an account,' he says. He knows it wouldn't deter the hateful behaviour entirely, but thinks it would remove 'a massive, massive chunk of the people creating accounts to literally send hate'. Instagram influencers like Griffin know to dread a message from an account with no profile image and a handle like 'joebloggs28372626'. It usually doesn't bode well. But that doesn't mean 'MaryAnne75', with the image of her and her kids as her avatar, isn't popping in to say something rude. Griffin says people turn to anonymity because they know that their opinions aren't widespread: 'They know that society doesn't agree with them. So they don't do it on their personal accounts: they create these fake ones to be able to spread the hate.'

Though he's not bothered by personal attacks, as he's comfortable in his skin and proud of his sexuality, Griffin worries about younger people online, and how they might deal with anonymous attacks and abuse. 'Thinking back to myself at that age, I would not have been equipped to deal with the hate I get now,' Griffin says. 'It's terrifying how easy it is for people to literally tell someone to kill themselves. I think it really needs to be addressed by the platforms.'

II

The British author Barbara Pym died in 1980, so it was a surprise when she started tweeting. The woman calling herself 'Barbara J Pym' on Twitter had a fierce interest in Irish politics and journalism, and very strong – and controversial – opinions on some of the high-profile people involved in it, particularly the Republican party Sinn Féin. She was part of the Irish Twitter political commentary sphere, whose members chew over granular discussions about government parties and their personalities and policies. I'd occasionally see her tweets being retweeted, but I didn't follow her.

In May 2021, talk of Barbara Pym was suddenly all over my timeline. It had emerged that a person behind the account was the Irish journalist and columnist Eoghan Harris. Harris was known as an uncompromising and opinionated writer, hence his column in the *Sunday Independent*. He had a long history in Irish journalism and in Irish politics too, including time as a senator after being nominated to the role by Bertie Ahern. His is a voice that has been much listened to, and much read. People knew about his political opinions, particularly his strong criticism of Sinn Féin.

He didn't appear to be someone who would need to broadcast anything anonymously, not with a profile like he had.

But he did. When the Pym account was suspended by Twitter for breaking 'platform manipulation' and spam rules, eight other accounts were banned at the same time. Though they were linked to the Pym account, Harris maintained they weren't run by him. Instead, he said that he was one of seven people operating the Pym account.

Once unveiled, Harris stayed true to form and did not remain silent. In a radio interview with Sarah McInerney on RTÉ *Drivetime* on 21 May, he said that there was nothing irresponsible about the account, and that the six others involved – historians, business people and trade unionists 'of the older generation' – did not want to be named. (It was later said in court that Harris was the sole operator of the site, contradicting this comment to RTÉ.) He had wanted the space so he could address topics in Northern Ireland that he couldn't address in his column, particularly reaching out to Protestant and Loyalist young people, he said. 'I felt I needed that outlet,' he told the presenter.[2] Asked why he didn't just set up an account in his own name, he said it was because he needed the assistance of other people to do it, and that the group wanted to operate under a pseudonym. McInerney told Harris she'd had to mute the Barbara J Pym account herself, due to personalized and abusive tweets about her.

Journalist Aoife Moore tweeted: 'This account sent me sexualized messages about whether Mary Lou McDonald "turned me on", the size of my arse and called me a terrorist from the month I started at the *Examiner*. Since then, I've had to go to counselling and the guards.'[3] The account had replied to a tweet of hers about Sinn Féin leader Mary Lou McDonald by asking 'So that's what turns you on?' Harris later said that the comment had no sexual connotations. Moore, and another journalist, Allison Morris, took a defamation case against Harris.

Harris wrote a letter to *The Irish Times* which said the Pym account was not a trolling account, and that 'any tweets I sent to women journalists were neither sexual nor abusive but political in aim'.[4] The *Sunday Independent* in turn said that what was posted on the account went 'far beyond' fair and reasonable comment. Harris's contract with the *Sunday Independent* was terminated immediately, his editor describing his actions as a 'betrayal of trust'.

Others spoke out about the impact the now suspended anonymous accounts had had, and the type of commentary that came from them. Francine Cunningham, who is married to Peter A. Vandermeersch, CEO of Mediahuis Irl, which publishes the *Sunday Independent*, detailed on her blog how one of the other suspended accounts, @WhigNorthern, made untrue comments about her, first by name, then by pseudonym, calling her 'Lady MacBeth'. When Cunningham noticed that the 'Barbara J Pym' account was liking WhigNorthern posts about her, she wondered who Pym was. 'Looking at her Twitter profile, she looked like a vivacious, middle-aged woman from Northern Ireland. I didn't know then that instead of a woman from Northern Ireland like me, "she" was an older man who had never lived in Northern Ireland, along with assorted others who still refuse to put their name to their words,' wrote Cunningham.[5]

In the Pym case, the revelation that a well-established journalist was involved with a pseudonymous account came as a shock to many in Irish Twitter circles. But in reality, anonymity can be attractive to anyone, even those with a platform. The Pym case showed that there can be limits to public platforms, that even if you have a newspaper column of your own, it might not be sufficient. You will still undoubtedly have more to say. That might be down to the constraints of the platform, or a word count limit. But it might also be that what you want to say could not or would not be printed in a newspaper. That your tweets could go beyond the bounds of what is considered fair comment.

What the Pym case shows is that while social media accounts appear to offer a space for 'free speech' in a so-called public square, that speech is never without impact. The civil cases taken over the tweets are ongoing, but they show just how strongly those targeted felt about what was said. A limit had been reached. And yet, what Harris was doing might have annoyed his employers, but it wasn't against Twitter's rules to set up the anonymous account.

The Pym case was unusual in that the identity of one of the people behind it was revealed as soon as Harris was asked by his editor what was going on. In most cases, it's a long, drawn-out journey to find out who is behind an anonymous account, with no guarantee of a result. In October 2019, someone set up a new account on Instagram called Pallaskenrymemes. During its ten-day lifetime, the account published 52 posts with photos and images that had text over them, and while the photos looked like they were stock images, the text was linked to people and events at Salesian Secondary College in Limerick. It was essentially a meme account, not set up in any official capacity by the school, even though it used its address, crest, name and website URL.

It was obvious once people saw the content (not to mind the name, which specifically included the word 'memes') that it wasn't official. The posts referred to staff members' weight, sexuality and personal appearance, and commented on the cost of food on campus and other parts of school life. There wasn't any sign as to who had set it up, whether it was a student or a teacher, another staff member, or someone totally unconnected with the school. A judge later said that it was 'inconceivable, given the coarse and vulgar content of the posts, that anyone viewing the user account would mistake it for an "official" school account'. The school got a solicitor to message the owner, asking them to delete the account. Whoever owned it deleted what they'd posted. Then the password came into the school's possession, sent on by a student who said they had been given it anonymously by a person operating Pallaskenrymemes. Now the school was able to log in to the account.

It discovered that twenty-one of its students had been messaging whoever was running it. The school asked Facebook Ireland Ltd for the owner's details, but the company said that it couldn't disclose this without a court order or request from the Gardaí.[6] The next step was court. To unveil who owns a social media account you need a court order called a Norwich Pharmacal order. It originally didn't have anything to do with the internet, and came out of a case brought by a UK company over unlicensed shipments of an antibacterial product. The order means that in the case of alleged wrongdoing, a defendant (who's not accused of any wrongdoing) can be compelled to disclose information to identify a third-party alleged wrongdoer. Basically, you're asking someone to tell tales about the identity of someone who you think did you wrong.

Norwich Pharmacal orders can be used to make social media companies reveal who is behind accounts. The broadcaster Miriam O'Callaghan used one in 2022 to discover who was behind scam ads that had been running on Facebook alleging she had left her RTÉ job and started selling beauty products.[7] In Parcel Connect vs Twitter International Company in 2020, the High Court told Twitter to reveal the identity of whoever was behind an account that parodied the name of parcel delivery company Fastway Couriers. The parody account, called Fartway Deliveries Ireland, had been replying to people's queries about items by saying things like their parcels had been 'left in caves'.[8] It was suspended by Twitter, but not removed, and Fastway had to go to court to try and find out who was behind it. The High Court order was successful.

But, as the Salesian case shows, a Norwich Pharmacal order won't automatically be given. The school said it wanted the details so it could deal with the individuals through a disciplinary or pastoral response. The judge found that the fact the information wasn't being sought for the purpose of legal proceedings was 'significant'. He also said there is a strong argument that people using a social media platform anonymously have an expectation that their identity won't be disclosed without their consent. 'This is subject, of course, to any countervailing public interest in the disclosure of their identity,' he added. The Charter of Fundamental Rights of the European Union gives people a right to respect for their private life, a right to the protection of personal data, and a right to freedom of expression, and the judge said this presented a potential obstacle when it came to granting disclosure orders. In the end, he referred the case to the European Court of Justice, to answer questions like if the rights people have under the charter imply a right to post material anonymously on the internet. But the case was struck out, without answering that question, in June 2021. The school didn't get its order in the end.

A case in 2012 in Northern Ireland showed how revealing someone's identity online can even pose a danger to them. In XY vs Facebook Ireland, a man brought a case after his image and name was published on the page Keeping Our Kids Safe From Predators. He was a sex offender with multiple convictions. The Facebook page was set up in 2012, and the man said that after his photo was published on it, he was threatened that he would be burned out of his rental accommodation. He was in fear for his safety, and believed if the material continued to be published it would only be a matter of time before the threats materialized into an attack on him or his home.[9]

The judge said that the contents of the Facebook page constituted unlawful harassment of the man, and posed a risk of infringing his rights to freedom from inhuman and degrading treatment, and his right to respect for private and family life under the European Court of Human Rights articles. An injunction to remove the page was granted. The XY case showed how, while social media is a great place to raise awareness of an issue because of how much reach it has, there are individuals at the other end of that who might suffer, even if there might be public interest in that person having previous convictions.

Identity can be used as a weapon online in other ways. The use of 'doxing', or sharing documents which reveal a person's identity, has been used to target scammers but also to turn innocent people into targets. It has its roots in the long history of hacking and hacktivism, but came to wider attention during Gamergate in the mid-2010s, when feminist activists online were harassed en masse and in some cases doxed, their addresses and personal details put online. Doxing like this can mean serious danger. Identity unmasking has been done by the media too – like when the founders of a mysterious NFT collection, Bored Ape Yacht Club, were named by Buzzfeed,[10] and when the person behind the very controversial Libs of TikTok account (which was later temporarily suspended by Twitter due to its content) was identified in the *The Washington Post*.[11] In these cases, there was a public desire to know exactly who was behind these accounts, given their power and reach.

It can cost in the region of €10,000 to take a High Court case to be granted a Norwich Pharmacal order, if you do want to find out who has been sending you hateful messages. 'This takes us back to the old saying that the doors of the High Court, like the doors of the Ritz, are open to everybody,' T.J. McIntyre, Associate Professor at the Sutherland School of Law, University College Dublin, tells me when I ask about his thoughts on this topic. He also points out that there can be long delays in getting access to data held by firms in the US, even where those firms have an Irish presence. The high cost of seeking the order means that access to justice is unfairly distributed, he says. 'It's a problem because it means that the tool becomes one that naturally lends itself to abuse by people with money who are seeking to shut down investigations into the wrong-doing, or even people who just don't like being criticized,' says McIntyre. Plus, there could be a risk to those who are going to be 'unmasked' by the order – they might be a whistleblower, for example.

McIntyre, who is the chairperson of the organization Digital Rights Ireland, has been writing in defence of online anonymity for over a decade, but says that the debate hasn't moved on in that time. He says there are still people, policymakers in particular, who have very little familiarity with the internet and are wedded to what he calls 'very failed notions' of how to deal with problems like anonymity online. McIntyre doesn't believe that making people use their own identity online would automatically force us all to behave better. Look at Facebook, which has a real name policy. 'That has done precisely nothing to deal with the problem of abusive behaviour,' he says. And yes, after seeing countless petty arguments and horrendous comments written on Facebook, I get what he's saying here.

He doesn't agree with the idea of bad behaviour online being caused by anonymity. When people are abusive, 'they're abusive under their own names just as often as they're abusive under pseudonyms,' he asserts. He says this is borne out by the few cases where people have been prosecuted for online abuse – it tends to show that very often this was being done through online identities which reflected their real names. In the summer of 2020, Twitter started rolling out a feature where AI could pick up if a tweet was potentially harmful or offensive, and the user would be asked if they wanted to send the tweet.[12] That didn't stop some people from posting whatever they desired.

Why does T.J. McIntyre think anonymity is important? He says it's better to take this question and flip it: to ask, 'Why are there reasons why it's important to stop other people tracking and monitoring what you do online?' 'That's most obvious if you think about vulnerable groups,' he says. 'You can think about LGBT people generally, or people who might be the victims of harassment if their identity becomes known.' He says one of the problems with 'real name policies' is that they can expose people to the threat of harassment or even physical harm in the real world.

McIntyre doesn't believe the push for real name policies has any momentum at the moment, and says it would be very difficult on a practical basis for any Irish government to introduce. But he does say that we might see schemes for verifying identities being introduced in some way. These schemes tend right now to be connected to keeping children away from certain content online, by verifying their identity in order to verify their age. In practice, this would mean seeking identification information from all users on a platform, which could be done by, for example, requesting their passport details. Age verification online is included in the UK's proposed Online Safety Bill. 'There's a risk you might see something similar taking place in Ireland in that context, rather than directly in the context of real name policies,' says McIntyre. But he believes the effect of this could be dangerous for some people. Plus, we've already seen from the Facebook data leak in 2021 that if you give information to a social media company, that doesn't mean it's always going to be safe.

One way of allowing people to have a public pseudonym is called a 'digital identifier'. This identifier would be used to authenticate a person's identity, as people would have to provide ID information while signing up to a social media service. They could then be pseudonymous when posting. It's something that comes up when I talk to a senator, Fianna Fáil's Malcolm Byrne. He was at the protest by the young students outside

Leinster House in late 2021, and was also involved in the drafting of the Online Safety and Media Regulation Act.

This topic isn't abstract to him. He's been trolled online, and has even been impersonated on Facebook. When he reported the impersonation to Facebook, he says it told him the page didn't go against its community standards. He and friends kept reporting the page, and it eventually disappeared. He's also been subjected to anonymous homophobic abuse online. Even though he understands why some people need to be anonymous, the difficulty for him is where anonymous accounts are set up deliberately to do harm. So he favours the idea of a 'digital identifier', as he doesn't see a reason why you shouldn't have to identify yourself when you sign up to a social media account. It could be done through a digital intermediary, that would hold the information, rather than the social media site holding it.

For some inspiration on how to deal with identity online, Byrne turns to somewhere unexpected. 'I have a friend in tech who always says to me: If you want to know what's going to happen in social media and tech, look at porn. And he doesn't mean actually looking at pornography. What now happens with Pornhub, and increasingly with a lot of porn sites, is if you want to post something on it, you can do it – but you have to identify yourself first.' There are undoubtedly people who would agree with the idea of digital identifiers, but feel very uncomfortable about the idea of a social media platform holding that information. Byrne points out that social media sites already have access to a lot of data about users. Think of everything you've put online: your date of birth, age, college, marital status, parental status, employment. And that's aside from all the other titbits of personal information we drop in our tweets and posts. Byrne argues that whatever flaws there might be in a government holding people's identity information, 'at least there is some hope of control', as the government can only use it for certain purposes. 'But you hand it over to private companies, that gives them enormous control,' he claims. That's not an argument everyone would agree with. Even if people didn't want to hand over private personal information to a social media company, that doesn't mean they would be happy handing it over to the government either.

Anonymity is a complicated beast, with complicated opinions surrounding it. The behaviour it can encourage can be horrific, but without anonymity many social media users would be forced to stay silent. We see this in the story of Aoife Martin, whose individual experience of anonymity highlights the protection and harm it offers people. As we'll see, anonymity can bring liberty – and it can leave you open to abuse.

Aoife Martin's Story

You can 'know' someone for years online, and yet never have met them in real life. When I speak to Aoife Martin, it's our first time chatting face to face – although, thanks to the pandemic, we're having to do it over Zoom. Still, she is very familiar to me, with her curly hair and expressive eyes. We know each other from Twitter: we'd both joined at around the same time, but Martin has been online a lot longer than me. She was there in the nascent days of Usenet, which was an early form of bulletin board system set up in 1980, before the internet even went public. Usenet has (it's still around) different 'newsgroups' dedicated to different topics, and you need to install a special provider to access it. Martin was on Usenet years before many of us were frittering about on forums, mainly visiting film and book newsgroups. 'It was just somewhere where you could talk to like-minded people,' she tells me. It was an eye-opening place too, with porn and kink newsgroups being just the tip of the content iceberg (some of its newsgroups are moderated, some aren't). 'If you wanted to find something bizarre, you just had to look,' she says.

She used her former name back then, mainly because she just frequented arts-related forums. As the other social media sites emerged, despite being an early internet adopter she didn't find herself attracted to using them. She thought they were probably just for teenagers. She even resisted owning a smartphone for years. But then she joined Twitter around 2010, and immediately saw what the fuss was about. She was back in an online space similar to the Usenet days, where she could share anecdotes and passions with people who liked the same things as her. It was also on Twitter that she was able to make a pivotal decision about how to represent herself online.

Twitter was a space where she could be herself. On there, she was a woman called Aoife Martin, with an animated avatar. But in real life, she had joined Twitter before she had come out as transgender and transitioned. The site became more than a place to send tweets about what films she was watching or books she was loving. Instead of being an archive of status updates, it became the space 'where I could just be Aoife, and not have anybody question that'. From the very beginning, she used the name Aoife Martin on Twitter, but didn't tell people she was trans. Not being out in her real life meant Twitter was somewhere she didn't have to worry about identity. It was a space to take some of the pressure off the rhetoric of being 'in the closet'.

But that freedom wasn't always freedom. She never posted photos of herself. 'When people said, "let's meet up", I always said no, I can't. I would resist any sort of real life interactions,' she says. She also hadn't joined Twitter to find other trans people, and hadn't, up to that point, felt a sense of community with other trans people online. She was walking her own path on the internet. It hadn't even crossed her mind that there would be a thriving trans community on Twitter, but there is, as she later found out. Meanwhile, she was meeting new friends virtually and growing close to them, chatting over direct messages (DMs). In the space between offline and online life, real relationships could take root. 'The people I made friends with when I first started tweeting are still my friends now, they are the people who stuck by me,' she says. They were the people she first came out to, over DMs. It didn't matter that they hadn't met in real life. There was an implicit trust there.

Coming out on Twitter wasn't easy, and it wasn't a one-off thing. 'Any time I come out to somebody, it's always slightly terrifying,' she says. 'It's less terrifying now in that I don't care what people think. But back then, it was slightly terrifying each time.' Telling her close friends on the site was the first step, the second was saying it publicly on Twitter. She knew she could let people assume she was cisgender, but she wanted to tell people she was trans. When she eventually did make her public announcement, she immediately shut her phone off. Later that day, she got the strength to look at her notifications and found that the response was overwhelmingly positive. 'I've been very, very lucky in that respect,' she tells me. I remember the day she announced she was trans: the lovely replies to her tweets, the feeling of a group of strangers wanting to make another stranger feel loved just as they are. Those moments happen less frequently on my timeline these days, but back then genuine moments of connection felt very possible.

The ability to sculpt her own identity on Twitter helped Martin to live as herself in an online space, eventually allowing her to become herself outside of it. She feels being able to be anonymous and then choose when to speak about her identity on Twitter helped. 'It probably gave me the courage to eventually come out and transition, in that it gave me that space I needed to know this was the right thing I was doing,' she says.

Twitter provided Aoife Martin with a berth to rest into being herself. But the site is also where she has endured abuse and toxic behaviour from strangers and anonymous accounts, usually solely to do with her identity. If anonymity is a blanket, one side is comforting and soft, protective of those under it; the other is harsh and prickly, with harmful hands reaching out from beneath. She's blocked thousands and thousands of accounts, after having read 'horrific stuff' said about her and other trans people. When we chat, her account is private. As trans and non-binary people have become more visible in society, owning their own space, they are being exposed to more online abuse. Putting up a shield against this abuse can mean, for some vulnerable minorities, going back into a metaphorical closet for safety.

But visibility of any minority is important for both its members and the wider community (online or not), as it helps people learn about others. Social media has given people across the gender spectrum a podium from where they can educate strangers, either through sharing information or just through living their own lives. One of the most popular Irish Twitter users is Panti Bliss, the drag persona of gay rights activist Rory O'Neill.

Look through her replies on Twitter and you'll see fans and supporters sharing their thoughts on trans rights, Panti's performances, and life in Ireland in the 2020s. But amongst the positivity are replies that question her stance on trans rights, or make fun of her identity or opinions.

Visibility can have a cost. In 2019, a survey by Ditch The Label and Brandwatch which analysed online posts over 3.5 years for transphobia found that out of 10 million posts, 1.5 million were transphobic.[1] To show others what's happening, some people share the transphobic tweets and posts, knowing that otherwise people won't realize the scale of it. Aoife Martin used to use social media to call out transphobic behaviour – and says it's people's right to do this if they wish – but stopped doing it a few years ago. It was, in the end, amplifying the behaviour. She does, however, share infographics and information on trans rights and trans lives.

In her experience, transphobia online has gotten worse. 'It's going to continue to get worse as the world teeters towards oblivion. I just can't see it getting any better,' she says. She had hoped that as more conservative, alternative social media sites began springing up, like the US-based sites Gab and Parler, and Donald Trump's Truth Social, it might pull people from sites like Twitter, if they had joined to spread anti-trans or anti-LGBT views. But so far, that doesn't seem to be happening. The main social media platforms have the power to make viewpoints spread far faster than these apps, and crucially, they can be spread to areas where those who oppose them reside.

Added to all this is the fact that in the 2020s the discussion around trans issues has been growing online. While more trans voices are being heard, the topic has also been the focus of critical opinion pieces, which can be shared online too. Prominent Irish voices both in support of and questioning transgender lives can be amplified and shared in a few clicks. Irish Twitter overlaps heavily with UK Twitter, and there is an at times fractious British-based discussion around questioning trans identities which has started to seep into Irish online culture. (In Ireland people can self-declare their gender under our legislation, but that's not the case under the UK's gender recognition act.) While being online means people can discuss trans rights and gender identity as is their right, it means that trans people just trying to spend time online are being forced to watch their identity being argued over. The topic is not oblique to them. It is their actual lives that are being debated.

Martin has a love-hate relationship with Twitter in particular. 'For as much as I despise it, Twitter has been enormously beneficial. It gave me a voice where I never had a voice before,' she says. When she was first on Twitter, she didn't have ID with her name Aoife Martin on it. 'I wasn't legally Aoife Martin. So I suppose we could consider me anonymous in that respect,' she says. Some people who are trans need to be anonymous online, as it is the only place where they can be themselves. In the debate around whether social media sites should verify the identity of their users comes the question about what happens when your official ID doesn't match up with how you are living. In Ireland, since 2015 people have been able to legally change their gender, thanks to the Gender Recognition Act (and Dr Lydia Foy, who took a case in 1997 which ultimately led to the passing of the Act years later – she was the first person in Ireland to receive a Gender Recognition Certificate).[2] [3]

If we want to move away from anonymity online and towards keeping people safe by revealing identities in some way, it might seem straightforward on the outside to require people to show ID with their gender. But it is not the case that all trans people follow the same process and timings when it comes to applying for a Gender Recognition Certificate, which allows them to apply for a new birth cert. The internet can provide a safe space for people to explore their gender before they make any official decisions – or they might not want to make an official decision at all. The online world has long been a place where people can be creative with their gender and sexual identity, in the knowledge that anonymity gives them a safe space for exploration and epiphany. It's also a place where you can find out more about what it is to be trans, whether you are part of the community or not.

Requiring people to show an official ID before they join a social media platform could lead to a number of issues. For one, if their gender on that ID is then reflected somehow in their online profile, that could be problematic and an untrue representation of who they are. Secondly, that ID might have a trans person's 'deadname' on it – the name they previously had, which in the case of trans people is offensive and upsetting to use. They might not want to provide that information, given that it doesn't reflect the real them. This could be traumatic for them, and could force them offline. When your passport, driving licence, or your birth cert is a reflection of who you are, then you might not have an issue with it being used to verify your identity online. But it is not such a simple thing for some people, and can lead to fear and shame around what their ID says about them and what it could mean for their expression online.

There is no one answer to what would keep every social media user safe, which is why it's important that decisions aren't made around this issue without a multiplicity of voices being heard. Given her experiences, Aoife Martin would be wary of putting the issue of anonymity solely into the hands of Ireland's politicians, particularly as she says they often see online criticism as abuse, when some of it is very valid. This could indicate they would be most likely to bring in stringent rules around anonymity, believing it to be a protective move, rather than exploring the many consequences of it.

Because it's so easy to share and amplify opinions on social media, trans people can easily see abuse, even if it's not aimed at them. When Martin talks me through the abuse she's experienced, it shows how difficult it is for some people to simply exist online, and why they might feel protected by their own anonymity, but at risk because of others' anonymity. She has even seen people tweeting her deadname, which is worrying as she chose a new surname to protect family members. In isolation, some posts about and to trans people online might look pretty harmless. 'But it's the drip, drip, drip. It's the constant attacks and remarks and various things that are said about you,' says Martin.

After all she has experienced, she is careful about what she posts. 'It's made me censor myself, which is a little worrying,' she says. 'And there was a time where it didn't bother me. But as I've gotten older it bothers me more and more.' Even if she posts an opinion about something – like an opinion about a book or film – sometimes she ends up deleting it because she can't handle people replying to her, even if they're being positive. That's not always because she is trans, but because the volume of negative responses and assumptions online have ramped up in recent years. I don't get targeted for my gender identity on Twitter, but like Aoife Martin I know that feeling of flinching when I post a tweet, wondering what issues people might find in it. Outside of any specific communities being targeted, because Twitter has grown so much you don't have just your pals in your replies anymore. Strangers can find fault in whatever you post – and tell you. So I can understand how much more amplified that feeling is for her. Sometimes just the act of putting a tweet out into the world feels uncomfortable, because it invites comment, and asks for eyes to read it.

Aoife Martin has reported lots of accounts over the years because of abuse, and some have been suspended. But by the same token, she's reported tweets and got a reply from Twitter a few days later to say they found nothing wrong with them. 'I'm thinking, "right . . .",' she says, raising an eyebrow. 'I think Twitter would have to get lots and lots of reports before a human will actually take a look at something and decide whether it needs to be removed.' So there is no guarantee that if you're targeted – for any reason – that you will feel safety is within reach. She points to how long it can take platforms to remove abusive accounts, even ones involving high-profile names. 'They're not going to give a shit about some little LGBTQ person with a few hundred followers,' given this, she says.

We could see it as luck that we live in an era where we can hash out and tease apart complex issues around identity with strangers and friends online, learning and growing from the encounters. But when your identity is the focus of that debate, being online can feel like an unsafe and unwelcome place to be. As Aoife Martin's story shows, there is so much goodness and support to be had on social media. But you never know what sort of behaviour you'll come up against online, and how that might affect you. To be online if you are in a minority can mean having to be constantly on the lookout for abuse, depriving you of an uncomplicated experience.

HATE AND HARM

Hey @Twitter, I reported this tweet earlier and you said it wasn't racist. Can you explain to everyone how this isn't racist? This is racism 101! I'd say I'm surprised, but I'm not. I'm saddened.

*

I reported this racist tweet as well as many others.
Quite demoralising that such an obviously racist
tweet is deemed acceptable.

*

Is Ireland the most woke country in Europe? I think it might be.
If woke ideology takes the GAA the battle is over here.

*

Ireland is officially God forsaken. It's MSM are vehemently
antiChristian & communist in ideology. It is a globalist,
woke, progressive, wasteland. The govt is now desperate
to subject children to porn classes.

A New Way to Bully

I

When the iPhone was launched in 2007, it was aimed at adults. So too are today's most popular apps. But in reality, children and teenagers don't have many barriers stopping them from joining most sites and apps, even with age limits in place. You can just lie. It's easy to forget that the internet isn't an adults-only bar – 48 per cent of eight-year-olds, 45 per cent of nine-year-olds, 55 per cent of ten-year-olds, and 96 per cent of thirteen-year-olds are active on social media in Ireland, according to recent research by CyberSafeKids.[1] Young people often hang around in the same spaces as adults: the same research found that YouTube, TikTok, WhatsApp and Snapchat were the most popular sites among those children, in descending order. This is the world the young teenagers I saw outside Leinster House grew up in. It's not like the childhood I had, where I experienced the introduction of digital technology as it happened. It sounds quaint to recount, but I remember the first mobile phone I saw, a big bulky brick of a thing. The first mobile phones my friends and I owned were given out for free when we opened new bank accounts while starting college. I remember the first text messages we sent, which had oddly truncated words to save space. The generations that came after us were born into a world with all of this technology already cemented into the way we live and work, and it was constantly evolving as the years progressed.

Today's young people and adolescents are digital natives in the true sense of the word, who played as babies with toy mobile phones and computers, and as toddlers fumbled with their parents' smartphones while watching YouTube videos. They learned how to pinch-zoom into images and how to press play on a video, just as they were learning how to put the right shapes into the right slots, and how to spell the word 'cat'. Technology isn't an optional add-on to their lives; it's a crucial part of growing up. It also provides their parents with a sense of safety as their children get older. Knowing that your child has a phone (at whatever age you believe appropriate) means you don't have to wonder where they are or if they can contact you in an emergency. That sense of safety has to be balanced, though, with the fact that parents now have to figure out how to allow their children access to these essential devices, without having the devices control them. 'Screen time' and 'parental controls' are now as big a part of the parenting lexicon as 'weaning' and 'toilet training'. And as their children age into their adolescence, they will learn about forming relationships online, and how to deal with the same things us non-digital natives suffered while growing up: cliques, arguments, feeling left out. They might also have to deal with cyberbullying, knowing that while their offspring might be at risk in the classroom, just as my generation was, they are now at risk online too.

When I was in my first year of secondary school, a classmate started throwing orange peels at me during lunch breaks. I can't remember how many times it happened, but I do remember her face as she sat near the grey metal lockers at the back of the classroom, throwing the slimy peels my way. I remember too what it felt like to pretend that I didn't care, to ignore it, or try to make a joke out of dodging the orange and white missiles. Those sorts of incidents always stay with you. The cringing mortification you feel; the sweat that gathers at the back of your neck. You wish that one person's actions didn't have such an impact. The fact you care makes the bullying feel even worse.

In a CyberSafeKids survey, 29 per cent of the children said they had experienced online bullying. It could take various forms – being kept out of messaging groups was a popular one, as was being sent hurtful messages. The bullying was often a secret that the children carried around with them – over a quarter who had been bullied didn't tell anyone about it. The number of children reporting cyberbullying has grown as the use of devices (not just smartphones, but game consoles and any other way children can access the internet) has grown. Ten years before the CyberSafeKids survey, in 2011, there was research done by Cotter and McGilloway which showed that 17 per cent of twelve- to eighteen-year-old Irish students reported being the victim of cyberbullying at least once.[2]

During the pandemic, people were drawn to the internet to escape the unsafe world outside. The internet was so essential during the first year that the Central Statistics Office (CSO) found that in 2020 there was a decrease in the number of people who had never used the internet; It dropped from 11 per cent to 8 per cent. In the sixteen to twenty-nine age group, the vast majority of people (96 per cent) used the internet daily in 2020, and when it came to students in particular, 97 per cent of them used the internet daily. In fact, it was students who were the most frequent users of the internet that year.[3] But for all the escapism the internet gave young people during the pandemic in particular, cyberbullying continued. There was a study called KiDiCoTi: Kids' Digital Lives in Covid-19 Times that came out in 2021, which found that 28 per cent of children and young people reported being victims of cyberbullying during lockdown, while 50 per cent said they had seen others being cyberbullied. The younger they were, the more likely they were to have been victims of cyberbullying.[4]

When young people do their own research and talk to their peers, however, the results can be surprising. Five hundred teenagers in Mayo answered questionnaires sent to them by the Mayo Tusla Youth Advisory Committee in 2019 about their social media use, and their answers showed that, for some of them, social media could be a lifeline. Some did feel under pressure to use it, but 87 per cent of the teens overall said they felt happy using social media. Some of the teens had an interesting insight into the topic as a whole. One of them wrote, 'Social media is a tool. Like any other tool in our life it can be used for both good things and bad things. I personally believe that healthy social media use should be emphasized as opposed to demonising its entire existence.'[5]

A decade ago, social media had found its footing. In 2012, Facebook reached one billion active users; Twitter had 100 million users posting on it; and Instagram was bought by Facebook that year. Social media had 'come of age', as a Neilsen report trumpeted.[6] Looking back at 2012 in social media roundups would bring a tear to the eye, with all their mention of celebrations after Barack Obama's US presidential victory; the important citizen journalism shared from Syria; and the Curiosity Rover announcing its arrival on Mars via tweet. But while we were discovering the possibilities for a globally shared experience online, families were starting to speak out about the harm that was being experienced by young people. Cyberbullying was covered extensively in the media as a result.

Students spend a lot of time on their phones, which is not a surprise given that your phone can be used for messaging, posting, searching for information, reading, and many more things. Online and offline life bleed into each other, and this is reflected in how cyberbullying occurs – Brian O'Neill and Thuy Dinh of TU Dublin said in 2015 that, compared to face-to-face forms of bullying, 'the boundaries between the roles of victim, perpetrator, and bystanders are less easily drawn in online bullying.'[7] [8] Some of the cyberbullying being called out was directly connected to anonymity, which took advantage of that nebulous criss-crossing of connection.

In the early 2010s, sites became popular which were about exploiting the utopian dream of anonymity to allow users to ask other users questions. The idea behind the sites was that with anonymity automatically allowed, people might be freer to ask things that they wouldn't normally ask, while the answers might be more revealing. It could be seen almost as a rite of passage: young people learning about what others might say when there's no chance of knowing who they are. But a cursory look back at the internet's history, and the history of human behaviour itself, will show that people are willing to be badly behaved even when their name is known. Having a site built around anonymity aimed at young people meant it didn't take long for people to use it to bully and troll.

The impact of these Q&A sites was even darker than people could have imagined. By 2012, there were a number of high-profile deaths by suicide of teenagers in Ireland and other countries that were linked to online abuse and bullying on these anonymous sites. The Q&A site which came under the most pressure globally was called Ask.fm. Young people loved Ask.fm – in 2013, over half of its 65 million users were under eighteen, *Business Insider* reported. I didn't join the Latvia-based Ask.fm, but did join a similar site, Curious Cat. It was fun at first, but I started feeling dread when checking out the questions, and left the site shortly afterwards. You might hold your palm above a lit candle for a thrill, but experience will show you not to stick your hand into the flame. Any adults on there might have had the knowledge and inner strength to help them step away when things got iffy on these sites. But part of growing up is to test boundaries, and to learn difficult things about life and how people will behave, through first-hand experience. As a consequence, it wasn't a surprise that teenagers stayed on these sites even with the threat of bullying. It's also understandable they were drawn to a site where, unlike Facebook, their parents probably weren't hanging out.

In 2012, it was reported by the *Irish Examiner* that the deaths by suicide of two young Irish girls – Ciara Pugsley (fifteen) from Co. Leitrim, and Erin Gallagher (thirteen) from Co. Donegal – were linked to cyberbullying on Q&A sites. Their loved ones spoke to the media about their concerns around the impact of anonymous websites, with Ciara's father Jonathan calling in the *Irish Independent* for legislation to be introduced to tackle cyberbullying. 'Among the messages [she] received were that she was depressed to attract attention, that she was fat, and that she had no respect for herself' the *Irish Examiner* wrote in an article about Erin Gallagher.[9]

95

A number of innocent girls accused of bullying Erin were themselves cyberbullied, the *Irish Independent* reported. There were also reports in the UK and the US on teens who had taken their own lives due to online comments, with fears rising that Q&A sites were putting children and teenagers at risk.

It is difficult to report on cases of youth suicide, as there are clear and specific guidelines in place for the Irish media, which include that a means of suicide should never be reported, and neither should details of any notes left at the scene. There has to be sensitivity around what is reported, and particularly on definitively saying what caused the person to take their life. There can be complicated, multifactorial reasons behind suicide, and guidance would caution heavily against saying that these anonymous question sites were the sole cause of the deaths. But parents were distraught and worried, and wanted to speak out about what their loved ones had gone through.

Things got so toxic in the UK that the British prime minister at the time, David Cameron, asked people to boycott the Ask.fm site, calling it 'vile' and 'irresponsible'.[10] His comments came after a father named David Smith spoke to the press about his daughter Hannah (fourteen), who had died by suicide. He said that Hannah had been bullied online and offline. An inquest into her death revealed a complicated situation where the judge found that she likely posted some negative posts to her account herself.[11] After Cameron's public comments about Ask.fm, advertisers started to pull future ads from the site. Ask.fm's founders released a statement saying they did not condone bullying, and that they would be hiring more moderators.

Ask.fm was bought in 2014 by Ask.com, and its new owner told the BBC it even considered shutting the site down, given its legacy. Ask.fm's hold over teenagers has long since waned, but the site still exists. On its community guidelines, it says, 'At ASKfm we believe that questions and answers are the key to staying close to friends, exploring the world around us and learning something new about ourselves. Using anonymity makes it easier to ask questions and get to know others.'[12]

II

Who runs the internet? No one and everyone. Any rules that are there have been made on a site-by-site, space-by-space basis, at the whim of individuals or corporations, with the various laws of various countries there to fall back on. There's no one rule of law online, and there's also no cohesive pattern of how situations like cyberbullying tend to be dealt with. Instead, people are expected to monitor their own behaviour, with the platforms learning gradually how to deal with harm through moderation and easily ignorable community guidelines. The 2010 film *The Social Network*, directed by David Fincher, reminds us that the roots of Facebook lie in a young man making up his own rules. Jesse Eisenberg plays a cocky Mark Zuckerberg, who one drunken evening blogs about his ex-girlfriend. In the film, he posts tasteless misogynistic comments about her online. He then puts his programming skills to use to create the site Facemash, where Harvard students could rate each other's hotness. It was shut down and Zuckerberg faced expulsion (the charges against him were eventually dropped). His next website? The Facebook. While it was an online version of Harvard's 'face book' student directory, it was undoubtedly inspired by his discovery that people liked to connect with, and judge, others online. On the internet, he could make his own rules.

The nebulous nature of 'rules' online can mean it feels futile to think about change happening. What's one person in the face of the internet? This means it's hard to fight back against online bullying. You can mute, you can block, you can report. But that all happens after the fact. The bullying is done by the time Instagram or Twitter or anywhere else deigns to deal with the person who meted it out. We see that in the story of Nicole and Jackie Fox, which shows us the horrific impact of offline and online bullying. Dublin woman Jackie is Nicole's mother, and describes her daughter (who was nicknamed Coco) as a bright, funny and bubbly child. Like her mum, she was just five feet tall, but where Jackie is blonde, Coco had dark hair. Coco could be cheeky, always making sure she got the last word in during minor rows.

Coco was a happy young person, but when she turned eighteen, things changed in her world. A group of women, her mother says, launched a bullying campaign against her daughter that started offline, but soon migrated online. The bullying had its roots in a pretty ordinary occurrence: Jackie says it started when a woman tried to get close to a male friend of Coco's, but the pair didn't end up getting together. Coco and the man had a platonic relationship. In the fallout, Coco was targeted, says her mother.

It was the sort of thing that could happen so easily, being rejected and wanting to take it out on someone. But others became involved in the targeting of Coco. The abuse was physical at first. Jackie says her daughter was burned, pulled down the stairs, had her hip dislocated, and was beaten up. Then bullies started to use social media sites and WhatsApp to contact Coco, to bully and harass her. She was sent a YouTube video on how to kill yourself using a noose. A sexual video of a young woman (whose face was blurred out) with three men was 'put all over the internet', says Jackie, with the false claim that it featured her daughter. All of this pushed down on Coco, going 'deeper, and deeper, and deeper'. To try and cope with what was happening, Coco self-harmed.

Coco tried to take her own life in 2018, aged twenty-one, while the rest of her family were out of the house in Clondalkin. When they returned, an hour after they left her alone in the afternoon, Coco's mother and brother found her unconscious in the hallway. She died later in hospital. Jackie, who also has two sons, contemplated taking her own life so she could be with her daughter. 'Cole was somewhere where she shouldn't have been; she should have been here with her mam,' she tells me. The only way she could survive the situation was if she had a plan – something to encourage her to get out of bed, get dressed, and have a focus for the day. Without it, she stayed in bed, cried every night, and shut everyone out. Jackie thought about what had happened to Coco online: the messages, the videos, the fake Facebook accounts. No one had been held accountable. Online bullying seemed to be something people just had to put up with.

Coco had gone to mental health services for help, and she and her mother went to the Gardaí over the physical abuse. But they didn't tell the Gardaí about the online abuse. 'It wasn't a crime. No one did "anything wrong" if you like,' says Jackie of the posts and messages. 'No one could be held for anything.' She can't understand, though, how the people who cyberbullied her daughter were able to post the things they did. 'To leave up comments such as "Hang yourself", "Die", "Kill yourself", "Are you still here?", "Jump off a bridge". Anything like that should not be kept up for anyone to see,' she says. These comments weren't taken down, though Jackie says she tried to contact Facebook about them. Her experience taught her that you can put whatever you want online, and she maintains this is down to a case of 'profit over people's health'. But she also believes that even the social media companies themselves didn't realize how big the issue of online bullying would get, how far it could go. How it could become an offshoot of in-person bullying, another way of punishing someone. We might use the words 'trolling' and 'cyberbullying' to describe what can go on, but to Jackie the sort of behaviour her daughter experienced was more like torture and torment.

What drives this sort of behaviour in the first place, and how can it affect young people? Given that bullying exists already, and is seen as an unfortunate part of growing up, it follows that you would presume it could happen in 'cyberspace' too. Mark Smyth, a chartered clinical psychologist with a particular interest in social media, tells me he first became interested in this topic around the time of Ask.fm. He works in Dublin with young people, but he's not someone who believes that they should be banned from using the internet because of the potential for harm. The internet is an attractive, information-laden, entertaining place for young people. It's not easy for them to step away, once they've found their place online.

Smyth has learned that some young people who had vicious things said about them online still wanted to stay online, even when their parents tried to protect them. The parents would take the child's phone away out of concern, but the young person would use a friend's device to log in and see what people were saying about them. Even if they'd been told horrible things, like to go kill themselves, they'd still want to go back on and witness what else might be happening. It can feel better to know what's being said than to be in a state of ignorance. At least if you know, then you don't have to imagine even worse possibilities. But it means that if you're being cyberbullied, you can be cut by the sharp words again and again.

There's an identity element to this behaviour, says Smyth. Teenagers are trying to make sense of who they are, and that can mean taking cues from the world around them. How other people behave towards them, or what they say about them, can guide them towards their own identity. Smyth found that with adolescents in particular, even when the content posted about them is harmful or abusive, they might still want to know what is being said. 'If they're just getting feedback, even if that's really, really negative, they still incorporate that into figuring out who they are,' Smyth explains. He says that young people who are particularly vulnerable tend to already have massive self-doubt, or struggle with self-esteem, and so believe a lot of negative things about themselves. When critical words are shared on a website, you can return to them again and again. There's the worry that a person's negative opinion is the truth. 'We all engage in something called confirmation bias, where we're more likely to be biased towards information that confirms what we already believe,' says Smyth. 'But unfortunately, if we believe that we're not good enough, we will seek out information that confirms that – and then that reaffirms the pre-existing belief, which causes further harm.'

If an adult with a secure sense of self sees something posted online about them that's negative, it might not feel like proof of their worth. 'But if I was a vulnerable teenager who already doubted myself and whether I was worthy of life, that's going to have a much bigger impact,' says Smyth. 'And that reaffirms that thought, "Well look, it's not just me that thinks I'm not good enough to live – these other people do too." Even though it's a "@John123456", saying, "you're horrible, you should die".'

He's found too that a lot of the anxiety young people feel about threatening messages or targeted abuse is because they believe that nothing can be done about it. Their parents might threaten to go to the guards to get it taken down, but they might not be able to get the content removed. And so the young people can become resigned to the situation, and feel like there's no remedy for it. 'Your average fifteen- or sixteen-year-old is not going to initiate libel proceedings over something that was said about them on Instagram,' says Smyth. As we see in the story of Coco's Law, there isn't always a clear pathway for those who have been bullied or abused online, beyond going to the social media companies themselves and joining the many others vying for their attention.

Although Smyth acknowledges all of the harms that can happen, he still urges caution around the narrative of the internet only affecting young people's mental health negatively. There are echoes here of those old claims about televisions making our eyes square and killing our attention spans; the worries about what comic books would do to young people's brains. As new forms of entertainment and technology emerge that capture our attention, there will always be a backlash against the impact of this new way of spending time. Smyth points out that there are many researchers who see some of the alarm around young people and social media as a replay of those eras. 'If you reduce the narrative down for mental health issues to "you spend too much time on social media", you actually really invalidate the young people,' he warns. 'Cyberbullying, yes, has an impact. But young people also say, "I can turn off my phone, I can block them. But if I'm being bullied by someone in school, and I've got to go to school every single day . . . I can't block them in school".'

He's been interested in this long enough to know too that a site's popularity bubble can burst, and when it does, another site will pop up in its place. After Ask.fm's popularity waned, young people would tell Smyth about another site, Sarahah (an anonymous 'constructive feedback' social network, around which there were media reports about abusive messages). After that came the chatbot SimiSimi. On an app like Snapchat, the fact that messages are temporary means that cyberbullying and harassment is easy to take part in. The people who bullied Nicole Fox had a wide array of apps and sites to bully her through, and the knowledge that very little could be done about it at that time.

As to why people might be drawn to bullying behaviour online, Smyth puts some of it down to how behaviour is reinforced. On a very basic level, you can have what's called a positive reinforcer or a negative re-inforcer, he explains. A positive reinforcer can mean, for example, getting praise for doing a task, which makes you want to do that task again. But if a person wants to cause harm and get a reaction online, then when they get the reaction – even if it's negative – that could still be a positive reinforcer. That's not just the case for young people. Think of all the times you've seen someone troll or tease a person online, just to get a rise out of them. And this doesn't even have to mean extremely serious behaviour – it can be part of the craic of being on social media.

There can also be a compulsion in some people online to say something controversial just so that they can have abuse directed at them, in a sort of game. 'There are some who will sit back and go: "That's exactly what I wanted. I wanted to whip up a load of people who didn't like me and are talking about me, and it makes me feel powerful and strong and important,"' says Smyth. 'Not seeing the damage that it's caused.' He tells me that, generally, adults can self-regulate, but children haven't developed the ability to understand they're being trolled in the same way adults can. That's where digital literacy comes in, and why Smyth calls for a national curriculum around online activities, not just for children, but for adults too. After all, adults model their behaviour for children, and are sharing some of the same spaces online as young people. 'We have road safety plans, we have suicide reduction plans,' Smyth points out – but we don't have a consistent national approach to online safety. Instead, we have to try and learn from other people's experiences, and hope that the social media platforms are paying attention.

III

After Jackie Fox lost her daughter Coco to suicide, she found meaning and purpose in campaigning to bring in legislation to tackle cyberbullying.

She wanted the legislation to be called after her daughter: Coco's Law. 'I needed her legacy for her because she deserves it, she mattered,' she says. 'She still matters.' She started the process by approaching multiple politicians, telling them about Coco and asking what they could do for people like her. She says she 'didn't have a clue' how bringing in legislation worked when she first started, and learned along the way. The process to bring in new legislation is a considerable one, with a Bill needing to pass through the Dáil and the Seanad. Before it even gets to that stage, it would need a politician or a party willing to prepare the Bill itself.

But what Jackie did know was that in order to get some sort of push for new legislation, and to feel something would be done about cyberbullying, she would have to turn to social media. There, she could raise awareness about her daughter's story and her campaign for Coco's Law. The reaction to the Facebook page she set up showed how she was far from alone when it came to social media impacting on young people's lives. Soon she had people contacting her about what happened to their own daughter, son, aunt, uncle, cousin. As hundreds of thousands of Irish people joined sites like Facebook, personal stories and appeals could be shared easily, spreading from personal pages to groups and back again. Even now, though Facebook feels like less of a must-visit spot, posts shared on there have considerable reach.

What Jackie was able to tap into was the communal voice of people who also thought that enough was enough – that the harms being created online towards young people needed to be tackled. Online, voices could reach a critical mass. That in turn could show legislators and the platforms themselves that something needed to be done. But ironically, Jackie faced social media abuse during her campaign, and was called a 'Nazi lover' and a 'brownshirt'. 'I was called so many names that me and my friend had to Google them and find out whether they were being nice or horrible,' she says, laughing at the absurdity of it. 'I didn't even know half of the words.' She maintains that most people were lovely to her online, but adds, 'I got a lot of good people – and I got a lot of arseholes.'

The media knows that to get an impactful story, you need to hear what's really going on in people's lives. Facebook was for many years the ideal place to get a sense of what topics were occupying minds. So journalists picked up on Jackie's story, which helped the campaign for Coco's Law intensify. All her campaigning translated into real-life actions too: Jackie gathered a group to protest with her outside the Dáil one day; on another she marched with supporters through Dublin city, everyone holding a pink balloon for Nicole. Jackie and her supporters visited different counties across Ireland, sharing Coco's story on main streets as shoppers and locals passed by. She held regular meetings with TDs. But still, she didn't feel like she was getting anywhere with some politicians, and suspected a few were just trying to humour her.

Then she met Deputy Brendan Howlin, a Labour TD. She cried while speaking to him about Coco's story. Howlin is a longtime TD who was a minister in the 2011–2016 Labour–Fine Gael government, the period when Ireland was trying to recover from the recession. The time was a bad one for his party, which is reflected in his reply to my question about whether he looks at comments about himself online. He says he became 'very adverse' to it while in government. 'I was Minister of Public Expenditure when the economy was in freefall, and we were trying to rebuild it. And it was a very, very difficult time and I'm not sure I would have survived online commentary,' he says. Back then, social media was a way for some people of speaking truth to power. Unlikely to get face-to-face meetings with politicians, they could comment on their Facebook page or Twitter account about losing their job, or being in negative equity, or how they wanted a new government to be brought in. Politicians could bear witness to the unvarnished truths about what their constituents really felt.

What Jackie might not have known was that the area of online harassment was something Howlin had been keeping an eye on for years. She told him about her aims, but one snag was that Ireland had never called a law after someone before. If the eventual law was given the name Coco's Law, it would set a precedent. Howlin agreed to work with Jackie, but told her he wasn't sure about being able to determine the law's name. He describes Jackie to me as a 'doughty and stalwart campaigner'. He knew that her own personal story was important, as legislation in the abstract doesn't have the same emotional impact as people telling their personal stories. Without examples of the impact of cyberbullying, some people might not understand the urgency. Though he had been told many stories of cyberbullying and harassment, not everybody wanted to make a public statement. That was despite the fact that he found that for these people the impact of cyberbullying ranged from it being an annoyance to having life-altering consequences. Jackie's situation gave Howlin a moral imperative. 'I was aware there are lots and lots of Nicoles,' he told me.

Indeed, people had been speaking up about the impact of cyberbullying for years, but alongside their stories was the knowledge that very little could be done about it. Those early days of social media, the exciting and even lawless days where website founders could spot gaps online and fill them, directly led years later to a floundering around what to do about online harm. It was left up to individuals to go to the media and politicians to try and raise awareness. In the case of cyberbullying, parents typically went to the media because they desperately wanted to show the consequences of a place where you could literally say anything to anyone. The websites weren't listening, or if they were, their attempts to minimize harm were often inconsequential. But aggrieved and upset parents could try to force change by reaching out to the public, who use the sites and are the base upon which the companies can lure in advertisers. Jackie Fox went one step further by calling for specific action to be taken, and that happened to coincide with members of the Irish parliament also wanting something similar. Perhaps it was luck or coincidence, but in this case there was a result to Jackie's campaigning.

Howlin had already begun drafting his own Private Member's Bill on harmful behaviour online. He was bothered by what he saw people saying on the internet, in the knowledge that very little was able to be done about it. 'I don't know if there is a separation in people's minds, who wouldn't dream of assaulting somebody on the street, or saying the most vile of things in a public forum, but feel that with a keyboard in front of them they can say anything and cause incredible harm, and that there's no consequence,' he says. 'And I wanted to make sure that there was a consequence.' In 2019, his Bill broadened the offence of harassment to include communication that took place online. The offence would carry a jail term.

When Covid hit right after a new government was brought in, Jackie was afraid the Bill wouldn't proceed as planned. But her fears weren't borne out, and the law was set to become official on 28 December 2020. But when Jackie logged into Facebook with ten days to go, she saw that the justice minister had told the media that the new legislation was not going to be called Coco's Law. Feeling 'beyond shock', she sent a video over Facebook Messenger to Minister Helen McEntee. 'In the video I said if you do this, if you do this to Nicole, you are going to be the one that puts the final nails in my coffin,' she tells me. An in-person meeting was organized for the next day.

McEntee had recently announced she was pregnant. At the meeting, Jackie put four photographs on the table between her and the minister. The first was an image of a baby scan; the second was of Nicole's christening; the third, her communion. As she placed each photo on the table, Jackie told McEntee that she would soon be going through those very milestones with her own child (the minister later gave birth to a son). The fourth picture was of Nicole in her coffin, laid out in her grandmother's sitting room. Jackie pointed to the black-and-white pregnancy scan and the photo of Nicole after her death, and told McEntee of the latter image: 'Anyone can end up there.' There was silence in the room. McEntee nodded her head gently at Jackie, and in that moment, Jackie knew that the minister understood. Coco's Law became official on 10 February 2021.

Online, young people and teenagers can find a space for expression, places to experiment with their identity away from the family dynamic. It can be a creative space, a gossipy space, a fun space, an eye-opening space, a necessary space. To try and stop young people going online because of the threat of harm would be like not leaving the house in case you get into an accident. The online world isn't really a separate thing that young people step into anyway – they are always living with one foot in and one foot out of it as they and their friends go through their own rites of passage. But while Coco's Law is a tool for dealing with a harm like cyberbullying, it is not going to prevent the behaviour from happening in the first place.

A decade on from the spate of teen suicides linked to online bullying, parents are still having to go to the media about the loss of their loved ones, and fears about the role social media might have played in their death. Nine years after the Ask.fm controversy, in 2021, the family of teenager Eden Heaslip spoke to RTÉ *Prime Time* about his death by suicide, which followed a period of bullying, including online bullying. 'Eden was still getting horrible messages on Instagram when he died,' said his mother, Maggie Heaslip. 'People can set up an Instagram account under a false name, post their poison about him, and then close it straight away. And nobody can trace them.'[13]

Cyberbullying is just one example of harm online, but it shows how ill equipped social media platforms were – and are – to deal with the consequences. It demonstrates too how we as a society are still trying to deal with real-life harms making their way online. While the majority of young people might have a safe and enjoyable online life, the threat of cyberbullying highlights the gaps that are there in understanding why such behaviour happens, its impact on young people, and how that might affect their lives online in the future. In a way, today's young people are undergoing an experiment, and it might only be decades from now, when it's too late, that we understand the results.

Without Consent

For as long as humans have been able to take photographs, we've had an interest in taking nude photos. The invention of the camera in the nine-teenth century meant that an instant could be preserved forever; instead of just lingering in the mind, an image of a body could become permanent, tangible. While the sharing of physical, printed images of nudes without the person's consent undoubtedly happened, erotic images could never proliferate to the extent they can now. Put an illicit or private image online today and it can travel down unseen internet alleyways and into the hands of strangers. Imagine a photo tumbling into a dark void, like a scene from a Seventies sci-fi film, swirling around to be viewed by eyes unknown. A nude can end up on phones and iPads, hidden folders on family computers, saved to a hard drive half a world away.

The internet has allowed us to share our secrets and desires with others. As they've grown from teenagers into adults, it's allowed people to explore every little peccadillo they have. But it's also allowed us to share what others don't want us to share. You can get any kind of sexual content you want online, and people will have their own opinions and morals around such content. But when it comes to the sharing of non-consensual nudes, over the past number of years there's been a switch in how this is viewed. These images used to be referred to as 'revenge porn'. That term indicated these pictures and videos were there to titillate, and the person in them could be to blame for them being shared. In the past few years, the term has deliberately been taken out of use, with this behaviour more accurately referred to as image-based sexual abuse (IBSA). This puts the focus back on the impact the sharing has on the victim, and not on the photo's erotic potential. It also allows for the fact that the reason for posting the images might be nothing to do with 'revenge' – it could be to blackmail or bully, to coerce or to show off. It doesn't position the person in the photos as somehow deserving of it.

You've probably heard of some high-profile instances of what was then called revenge porn, like when the reality star Rob Kardashian (brother of Kim) shared intimate images of his ex-partner Blac Chyna on Instagram after their breakup. When it happens to celebrities, these sorts of examples can be laughed off by the public as if they mean nothing. But individuals sharing images in this way is often a confluence of the nastiest elements of toxic behaviour online: the male gaze, common-or-garden misogyny and coercive control. It removes power from the person in the photographs, leaving them at the whim of the internet. They know that once their image or video is out there, there might never be a way of reining in its sharing. Attitudes towards women and sexuality mean that there is an inbuilt shame in how survivors of IBSA might be treated, and how they can feel about what happened. And it wasn't until Coco's Law was brought in that the action was even criminalized in Ireland.

You might not have stumbled across any of this content yourself but it's part of the larger world of the internet. 'Almost as soon as smartphones became a thing, people used their phones to look at porn, to go on dating apps and to exchange nudes, because that's just who we are,' says sexuality educator Dr Caroline West. But she says that in the case of IBSA, culturally we didn't initially have the language to name what was happening, so it wasn't termed sexual violence. By calling these nudes or sexual images 'revenge porn', they were being put into a bracket saved for entertainment, which had the effect of silencing victims. 'It's not about porn and it's not about seeing naked people – it's about power and control,' says West. These images can lead to other disturbing behaviour, like what's called 'sextortion': blackmailing someone by using the images as a threat.

Even though the average social media user won't find themselves stumbling across revenge porn, the platforms know it exists. Meta recently partnered up with the UK Revenge Porn Helpline to launch StopNCII.org, a way of 'giving victims more control and security over their images'. NCII means 'non-consensual intimate images'. The fact that Meta says it doesn't allow this content on its apps, but is taking part in this initiative, shows that the threat still exists across its platforms (think of the fact that Facebook has closed groups, and how easy it is to share images on apps like Instagram and WhatsApp). How StopNCII works is that if you are concerned your intimate image has been used or shared online, you can use the site to create a 'hash value' or code for the image.[1] This is a secure digital footprint, as Meta terms it, so the image can be identified if it is used on a participating website, without the person having to circulate or share that image. Once the hash is created, the images can be found and removed.

On the internet as a whole, no one could pretend that IBSA was a new phenomenon. In 2009, the journalist Kashmir Hill warned in *Forbes* about 'angry' men who were posting photos of old girlfriends and ex-wives on the site Ex-Girlfriend Pictures, which had been around since 2005.[2] The men weren't always motivated by hate, she wrote. Some of them wanted other men to 'admire' their ex's body, and thought she might be flattered at the idea of thousands of strangers drooling over her. But as Hill pointed out, the site wasn't asking for consent either way.

The first criminal prosecution for someone running such a site in the US was in 2015, when Californian man Kevin Bollaert was convicted in relation to running UGotPosted.com, which was home to over 10,000 explicit photographs.[3] The court reports said he had a side business in extorting money via another website from the victims to remove their images. A recent Netflix documentary, *The Most Hated Man on the Internet*, was about a similar site, IsAnybodyUp.com, whose founder, Hunter Moore, bragged openly about the non-consensual nudes he posted and the fact it could ruin lives. It isn't just men who run these sorts of sites. Al Jazeera carried an article back in 2013 titled 'Meet the suburban mom who runs a revenge porn site', about the woman behind ShesAHomewrecker.com. She posted photos of women who had allegedly been having affairs with other people's husbands, sent to her by the rejected partner. The site is still online – as Alex Hearn wrote about 'revenge porn' for *The Guardian* in 2016: '[M]ost revenge porn sites operate in the same scattered fashion as the wider porn industry, defying easy categorisation and relying on a mixture of obscurity, legal loopholes, and anonymity to get around attempts to identify them and shut them down.'[4]

Beyond the usual social media sites whose names trip off the tongue easily – Facebook, Twitter, Instagram, TikTok – lies a wealth of other sites that can play a role (deliberately or not) in the non-consensual sharing of nudes. You might imagine that these places are on the dark web, or not easily accessible. But the disturbing thing is that they are often some of the most popular sites in the world. One site which frequently is mentioned in discussions about NCII and IBSA is the hugely popular Reddit.

Reddit is a dream of a site if you want to capture the feeling of the early 2000s online, but with all of the leaps the internet has made since then. It mines from the past, in that it is about providing niche forums where people can gather, but its users are fully immersed in contemporary online life, and the topics in the various Reddit communities reflect what's happening on the internet at any given time. Reddit has over 50 million daily active users and 100,000 active communities (called subreddits). It's a sprawling, fascinating place to visit, with its own social rules and language, ways to encourage and shut down conversation, and a specific approach to how people communicate. You can upvote or downvote posts, which the website founders believe helps the most interesting content rise to the top. If I ever start obsessing over a new TV or streaming series, I usually head to Reddit to find out what fans are saying about it, because I know the discussion there will be in-depth.

Reddit's approach to moderation is 'community-driven', and it compares it to a democracy because people can establish community rules and norms. There are 'principles-based rules' for the site as a whole, enforced by Reddit employees called admins, but each community's specific rules are enforced by volunteer moderators, or mods. In 2021, there were 187,258 instances of what Reddit calls 'involuntary pornography' removed from the site (there were also 117,093 instances of 'minor sexualisation'). The vast majority were removed after being spotted by automated moderation, and 17 per cent after being reported by users. Almost 16,000 accounts were sanctioned for involuntary pornography.[5]

Reddit specifically tells its members not to post any intimate or sexually explicit media of someone without their consent – including 'creepshots' or 'upskirt' photos, privately sexted pics, or offering stolen photos of someone. But often these pages hide in plain sight – there was a Reddit page called NSFW Revenge Porn, which was eventually banned 'due to being unmoderated'. A site that gathers stats on subreddits informs me who the top user of NSFW Revenge Porn was during its lifetime – I follow the link to their profile and see that they now post on an 18+ subreddit called Misogynistic Life, 'a safe place where the kinks, fetishes and ideas of misogyny can be shared and most importantly enjoyed without the hate and abuse'. There was a subreddit, r/rapingwomen, which was only banned in 2015 when the site brought in new moderation policies.[6] Reddit's free speech, anything goes approach was challenged when it brought in those moderation changes, around the same time other sites did too, like Google, Microsoft, Twitter, Medium and Facebook; it was also the same year the UK brought in a law against IBSA.

The move happened en masse because a tipping point had been reached. The fact that r/rapingwomen existed at all gave an insight into what 'free speech' on Reddit meant. But because of Reddit's lighter-touch community-led approach to moderation, you can still find plenty of NSFW content on there today, some of it vile and misogynistic, and you can also be sure there are non-consensual images on it as a result. On the subreddit r/wifepictrading, people are invited to share nude pics of their wives and partners. The community rules say 'no exes', and the images vary from nudes purportedly shared by the wives themselves to ones posted by partners. The page does ask for the couples to show images of both their faces during the verification process, but again there's no knowing the background to what's happening.

You'll also find posts from some members saying they'll do the actual pic trading on the app Telegram, away from prying eyes. The trading is part of what's known as 'collector culture', where women are objectified into images that are sold and traded. The men posting the pics on r/wifepictrading don't typically talk about the women as if they're trying to take some sort of revenge; they are proud, showing off the women and calling them 'milfs'. It's impossible to know what's consensual and what's not on pages like this.

Reddit is not the only site you'll find named in the IBSA discussion. I'd never heard of the site Discord until 2020 – not because it's hidden or nefarious, but just because I hadn't stumbled across it. Its name invites thoughts of disruption and unrest, but in reality it was getting known as a great place to join if you are part of a fandom, just like Reddit. But unlike Reddit, it's decentralized and made up of servers. Some of them are private, and you need an invitation to join, while the public servers aren't viewable unless you're a member. The servers are discrete – and discreet – spaces for people to hang out. Scrolling through the list of public servers that came up when I searched 'Ireland', I found ones aimed at teenagers, Xbox users, and a generic 'Gael Boogaloo'. In Gael Boogaloo, I scrolled through conversations happening in real time, threaded in and out of each other, without having a clue what was going on. As an outsider, I wasn't privy to their private language. Trying to negotiate how to use Discord, I felt exactly like I did browsing chat rooms in the Nineties, excited about what I might find but a bit confused about how to find it. I could see though that there were rules and norms within each server, and that Discord's public servers (you need an invite to join the private ones) catered for people across a multitude of topics.

Discord describes itself as 'interests-driven'. In 2020, it emerged that some of those interests included sharing non-consensual nude photos of women. Discord says that it doesn't monitor the servers, or conversations on them. It does offer some sense of control, as when it comes to bad actors, it says it 'makes it clear to them' that they're not welcome on the site – but it doesn't provide specific information on how it does this. The site is pseudonymous, so if you join you don't have to give your real name. There's a deep chasm when it comes to knowing what goes on on servers that enable pseudonymous accounts and self-policed behaviour. The trouble is, in amongst the light conversation and nerdiness, you can imagine terrible things occurring in hidden areas that you don't have the key to. And sometimes, your worst fear can come true.

In November 2020, my Twitter feed was taken over with the news that a now defunct online group calling itself the Victims Alliance was claiming that some servers on Discord were found to contain thousands of intimate images of Irish young women. Many of the photos appeared to come from the most popular places people spent time online, like Instagram and OnlyFans (where people pay for content, which is typically consensually shared intimate images or videos), as well as apps like Tinder and WhatsApp. The story exploded, ending up across all major Irish news outlets. There were many questions about what was going on, and that's the thing about online incidents like this – there can be questions that never get answered, like who was behind it, what the story was behind each image, and how it got found out.

The Victims Alliance, which raised the alarm, was newly formed. It was spearheaded by around ten people who spoke out about their own experiences with sexual harassment and abuse. Twitter was the perfect home for an online-based victim centred group, as it could take a fairly pseudonymous approach – if needed, as some of the women involved did do public media interviews – and was also following on from how the #MeToo movement gave women a platform to speak out about their experiences. #MeToo was started by activist Tarana Burke on MySpace in 2006, as she wanted to highlight the sexual abuse and violence that women – particularly black women – were suffering. Her advocacy was boosted after *The New York Times* published its article on Harvey Weinstein's sexual misconduct allegations in 2017, when people began using her phrase 'Me Too' as a hashtag on Twitter. Burke is based in the US, but Twitter helped the hashtag go viral globally. #MeToo turned social media into a platform for voices that weren't being heard, emboldening women in particular to speak out about being assaulted, harassed, stalked, and threatened with harm. It was powerful, though humbling and distressing, to see the streams of posts where women unburdened themselves online using #MeToo, many recounting what happened for the first time. Survivors were no longer gagged, and social media was proving its worth as a forum for human connection.

The Victims Alliance said it had been told about the servers on Discord, and went on to access them. The alliance's Twitter account is gone, so it's hard to get the exact information on what they said, but it was reported in the news at the time that the alliance passed the files to the Gardaí, after saying publicly that some folders contained from 5,000 to 11,000 images. The number of people involved in sharing the images was rumoured to be around 500. Screengrabs of some of the discussions on Discord about the images were shared online.

The fear on Twitter grew more heightened when the Victims Alliance claimed that some of the images were taken non-consensually, and were of women in changing rooms and other private spaces. It was nightmarish, with no concrete facts about exactly who those photos were taken of, by whom, and how they found themselves – in their thousands – on Discord.[7] There were also claims that some people in the photos were underage, though it wasn't clear how that could be verified, and Gardaí later said they didn't find evidence of child abuse. The situation led to a lot of fear and anger. Though the servers were closed, anyone who viewed and saved the images could effectively do what they wanted with them. A daisy chain of connection could be created with a few clicks.

The users were said to have shared social media handles with the photos in some cases, which made it easy to track down some of the victims –

but also opened them to abuse or doxxing (where private information like their real name and address is found and put online). Discord deleted the server and banned the hundreds of users involved, saying, 'No one should have to endure the pain of having private images posted online without their consent.'

No one has ever been taken to court over the Irish Discord leak, and there was some scepticism among people on sites including Reddit and Twitter about visibility over what had taken place. But the response to the allegations showed the fear and anger that existed over the very real sharing of private intimate images online. It was a heavy, almost paralysing moment, showing women that their private images were not safe, and could be traded and shared in a few careless clicks. That people were volunteering to comb through the images, in an act of apparent altruism, to identify victims, made me feel uncomfortable – it was hardly the ideal response to what was happening. Twitter can feel intimate at times like this, and the chatter about what was happening was constant on Irish Twitter over a period of a few days. This was because it was about more than just this one incident. 'This is a culture problem and a rape culture problem,' tweeted one woman about the leak, in a post that was liked 7.6 k times.[8] Though on the face of it the Discord incident could have appeared unusual – because of the volume of attention it got – it showed that out there on the internet things had barely evolved, and that women were as open to being objectified and digitally brutalized as ever.[9]

By 2020, there was no arguing over whether misogynistic behaviour was happening online, even though people still tried to do exactly that. Women were seeing it in their replies, or on their Twitter or Facebook feed. There were the questions about whether women could ever be funny, the sexually suggestive DMs, the gender-based assumptions. There was also the wider culture in Ireland and the history around how Irish women had been treated over the decades. Though the country is proud to have had two female presidents, this is still a place where the Constitution enshrines the importance of a woman's role in the home, as though to be a woman is always to be a mother and wife. Just a couple of decades before the internet as we know it emerged, in the Seventies Women's Liberation groups and the feminist movement began to force change in an Ireland that needed it.

The young women on Twitter watching the Discord story unfold knew that there were women who had travelled to the north to buy contraception, on the 'contraceptive train', to show the pitiful state of affairs when it came to reproductive rights and freedom. They knew of the Marriage Bar, which saw married women banned from working in the public sector until 1973. They knew Ireland was a place where shame meant that up until recent decades unmarried mothers-to-be were sent to mother and baby homes to give birth in secret; where some of those women were forced to work in Magdalene laundries. They saw the fight these women had to have their treatment acknowledged. They had lived through the campaign to repeal the eighth amendment of the Constitution, which saw women's reproductive rights debated on national TV and radio. They had the measure of what Ireland had thought of women across the years.

They could see on the 'public square' of social media that, despite all the changes for women, misogyny and sexism remained, and still there were young men who thought a woman's body was fair game. The Discord leak showed exactly how bad things could get, and how much of a fight was still on people's hands. There was anger at what happened, but also at what it represented: that no matter where they went, women could never really be safe. That anger turned to activism, with groups like End IBSA Ireland speaking out about the lack of punishment for IBSA in Ireland. A number of rallies were held calling for change and more education on consent, and victims of IBSA came forward to talk about what happened to them. On foot of all of that, Minister Helen McEntee, who had shared the emotional meeting with Jackie Fox, added IBSA into Coco's Law, finally making image-based sexual abuse illegal.

But in a disappointing coda, the Victims Alliance disbanded after controversial tweets from its founder, going back a number of years, were discovered. She apologized and then left Twitter. The group hasn't been active online since.

II

The fight against IBSA in Ireland isn't just a fight against the act of people sharing non-consensual content online. Take a look at the work of activists on their social media pages and you'll see their anti-IBSA work crosses into several areas. It sits in a Venn diagram that includes tackling misogynistic attitudes towards women and sexuality in Irish society, how sex workers such as adult content creators are treated, and education around consent. In raising awareness of the crime of IBSA, activists have to pick apart and highlight the attitudes that can lead to it, and those which make it difficult to punish.

The internet is a place of harm for IBSA victims, but it also provides a space for them to meet each other and speak out. Coming together, they could use collective activism to show the full impact of the crime – and call for legislation before IBSA was criminalized – as well as to support each other. Online activism is a way of becoming visible, of showing that IBSA won't be a tool used to shame victims into submission. The banding together of victims was, as Eboni Burke of End IBSA Ireland indicated in a Facebook livestream in 2020, a way of reclaiming their dignity.[10] The fact their dignity could be lost at all underscores how IBSA is a crime where the odds can be stacked against the victim from the outset, through no fault of their own, but instead due to societal attitudes rooted in misogyny and shame.

At that same livestream, several women detailed how IBSA had left them feeling violated and dehumanized. While watching, I was struck by how Burke gave multiple content warnings at the beginning of the event, urging those watching to 'stay safe'. The stories shared on the livestream were heavily dominated by a particular cohort of IBSA victims: women and non-binary people who create amateur adult content for subscription sites, chiefly OnlyFans. The site's popularity rocketed during the pandemic, as it became a new destination for sex workers who could no longer have a physical place of work outside of home, and also drew in amateurs who were looking for a new source of income. These days, OnlyFans has almost 187 million users: although it isn't just for adult content creators, it's what it's best known for. Post-pandemic, OnlyFans has tried to move past its pornographic reputation: on a recent visit to its Instagram profile, I saw that the posts were a mix of user-generated content by adult entertainers, comedians, chefs and reality stars. In 2021, the company attempted to ban sexually explicit content on its site, which it attributed to pressure from banks and payment processors; in just a handful of days, however, it reversed its decision.[11]

Making sexual content for an internet audience is obviously not a new phenomenon, and neither is making it in your own home – hence the long history of webcam adult entertainers, or cammers. Self-generated adult content can be, like everything put online, as niche or broad as you can imagine, and the creators are in control of how much or how little of themselves to show. Sites like OnlyFans enable creators to make erotic content more personal and niche, upping its value at a time when you can find any sort of pornographic content online for free. Media coverage of OnlyFans and virtual sex work sites tends to point out that creators can make thousands a month, though, as with any online work, building an audience is essential in making their subscription numbers grow.

As one of the End IBSA seminar participants pointed out, OnlyFans can be a great source of income, and it allows some women to take a form of ownership over their sexuality by consensually sharing photos of their body, posed as they desire. Creating this sort of consensual sexual content, however, is not going to be every person's idea of reclaiming their sexuality. Within the feminist movement, for example, there are those who are vehemently opposed to it and those who see it as a tool of independence. From reading OnlyFans creators' accounts about their experiences, it seems as though the majority feel that, for them, it was initially empowering. However, although they might have felt a sense of agency in posting their content, their lack of power over what happened once other people viewed it soon became apparent. The newer OnlyFans creators in Ireland quickly discovered that their images could be 'scraped' (stolen) and shared on. One online adult content creator said that she worked for two hours a night creating content during the pandemic, and distributed it a number of ways before making it available for download, "when it will inevitably get pirated."[12]

In 2020, Vice carried out an investigation which found 'an entire supply chain of people stealing sex workers' labor using scraping programs, without permission, in some cases by the hundreds of terabytes, and distributing it on other adult sites or selling scraping services through Discord."[13] Some content could end up on sites that hosted pirated porn content, but also on popular porn subscription sites. OnlyFans said it was aware of these issues and works to fight against it – but despite this, anyone can see that clearly it's not being effectively stamped out.

It doesn't take much to scrape and reshare content, and it was this which was making some new Irish OnlyFans creators - like those on the livestream – into IBSA activists. Being based in Ireland meant that they were part of smaller, tight-knit communities, so the fear around who could see their images without permission was heightened. The content creators speaking on the End IBSA Ireland stream spoke about how traumatic and violating it was to learn their content was downloaded and shared without their consent. Some felt it showed there wasn't any real protection of their images, despite the site's clear safeguarding regulations defining what users could do with the subscription content.

Once they were on OnlyFans, they realized some people – subscribers and non-subscribers – saw their images as fair game. They indicated the implicit message was that they were to blame for these thefts, which underscored deeper problems around the objectification of women in Irish society. One woman on the livestream said some of her OnlyFans nude photographs were taken and used to blackmail her, with threats that they would be sent to her family if she didn't send more photos to the perpetrator. This is something you'll find in many IBSA stories: the perpetrator will threaten to doxx or forward content on to the victim's family to punish them. This blackmail element has been linked with this sort of behaviour from the get-go, and capitalizes on the stigma around sex work and adult content. Fear around what could happen with the images can lead to a person capitulating, lest their private behaviour go public. As one young livestream participant explained, she had internalized the idea that if she displayed herself in a sexually confident manner, she deserved any behaviour that might come as a result. Since becoming a creator on OnlyFans, she had begun to expect IBSA, she said.

There is a fear among victims of IBSA of being dehumanized; when they are viewed as less than human because sexual images of them exist. This can make the person in the images or videos feel to blame for what happened, rather than those who re-shared the images. The blame comes from the question 'why did you let the photo/video be taken in the first place?' If the perpetrator dehumanizes a content creator and sees their images as 'nudes' rather than images of a person who can be affected, the victim can become nothing but a collection of pixels, absolving the perpetrator of guilt. Any residual guilt can be transferred onto the person at the centre of the image.

It was these sorts of attitudes that led to Deputy Holly Cairns of the Social Democrats – who campaigned for an IBSA law to be brought in before Coco's Law was introduced – to make a special appeal to alleged victims after the Discord leak. "I want to send a clear message to anyone whose images have been shared without their consent. It's not your fault. You didn't do anything wrong. You're not to blame. Unfortunately, the law isn't protecting you and it's not your fault, and that has to change," she said. Cairns went on to say that people in Ireland "need to have an incredibly serious and difficult national conversation on this and related issues", linking IBSA to other incidents on the spectrum of gender-based violence, like domestic abuse, sexual harassment and sexual assault.[14] Cairns was drawing attention to the fact that an online crime like IBSA isn't something that exists in a vacuum. It's linked to behaviour norms online, which in turn are linked to the beliefs and assumptions held by people in the wider world. The impact of IBSA is often disregarded: there's a tendency to lean into the assumption that because IBSA takes place in digital spaces, it doesn't do lasting 'real life' damage. This, coupled with an acceptance of the stigma around sexual content, means that policymakers and tech owners do not prioritize finding a solution to this behaviour.

In looking for the stories of alleged victims of IBSA, you can find many examples of people speaking out, either individually on social media or through activist groups. But in order to talk about what they went through, they have to go public, which requires sharing intimate details of their experience. This is complicated, too, by the fact that though Coco's Law is in place, alleged victims are just that - alleged - unless their case goes to court and someone is found guilty of a crime or a civil wrong. People now have a clearer path for taking action on IBSA, though before Coco's Law they could potentially have brought a case to court under different laws, like the Non-Fatal Offences Against the Person Act, or copyright laws. Yet regardless, by speaking out they run the risk of identifying an alleged perpetrator, and that person could attempt to sue them for defamation. This isn't unique to IBSA, but it's notable because the crime is an online one and the fight back against it happens heavily on social media, where people can identify an alleged perpetrator on a massive forum. And even aside from that, if they did pursue a court case, their intimate photos and details could be shared publicly, potentially traumatizing them.

Even though Ireland has introduced legislation to deal with IBSA, this has not, of course, put an end to the crime. It is a deterrent to some, but certainly not to all. Look for court reports on this sort of behaviour and you'll find recent examples. In June 2022, a Galway man was sentenced to nine months in prison for posting sexually explicit photos of his former girlfriend, along with links to her social media profiles, on a forum.[15] Just seven months later, in a Family Law Court elsewhere in Ireland, a woman was granted a Safety Order due in part to the fact her ex-husband admitted he was wrong to 'flash' an intimate image of her – which he took from her phone – to her and their teenage daughter. The judge said he suspected that the images were "malingering" in the cloud.[16]

In a recent report, Hotline.ie, where people can report non-consensually shared images and receive help with their removal, said that between September 2021 and September 2022, it received 773 reports of suspected intimate image abuse (IIA).[17] Of the people who contacted Hotline about IIA, 83% were female, 16% were male, and 1% didn't disclose their gender. The crime is certainly not limited to one gender, even if so far the bulk of those speaking out have been women. The majority of those reporting - 73% - were aged between 25 and 34, while 5% were aged 35-44, 16% were 18-24, 5% were under 18, and just 1% were over 44. In the breakdown of where the images were shared, just over half were posted on video streaming sites, just under a quarter on image-hosting sites, 19% on social media platforms, 1% on forums and 6% on other sites like blogs and general websites.

Even though the people who contacted Hotline wanted the images removed, just one in seven indicated they wanted to have the matter referred on to gardaí. This shows how people might want to keep IBSA or IIA private, for many of the reasons detailed above. Even though a specific law to help them exists, going through the legal process would be too much for some victims, and much of the blame for this, experts say, can be down to shame.

III

Ireland was relatively late bringing in the legislation on IBSA (Coco's Law), compared to our neighbours – sharing sexual images without consent has been illegal in the UK since 2015. Yet even with that in place, during the pandemic a British government-funded helpline reported a 22 per cent rise in calls about IBSA. The internet is littered with stories from people, particularly women, who didn't know their images were public until alerted by a friend.

Caroline West links the sharing of non-consensual images to the cultural impact of the celebrity sex tape, and the non-consensual leaking of celebrity nudes. They helped show there was an audience for this type of content, but also that the victims could be dehumanized, as if what happened to them meant nothing. In 2014, an iCloud hack saw personal images belonging to actors like Jennifer Lawrence taken and shared online on sites like Reddit and 4chan, where members gave the incident the moniker 'The Fappening'. Up until then, the cloud had been seen as almost faultless, a safe place to keep your images. The hack showed that it wasn't, but also showed the appetite for intimate photos of celebrities, and how willing people were to share them.

Meanwhile, the video which put 'sex tape' into the cultural lexicon was shot in 1995 by actress Pamela Anderson and her Mötley Crüe drummer husband Tommy Lee on their honeymoon. The pair seemed, back then, like cartoonish figures, or at least were depicted as such in the media. A disgruntled electrician named Rand Gauthier found the tape of the couple in 1995. He had been doing work on their house and, after being fired, concocted a plan to steal the contents of a safe – in which the tape was found – which was kept in their garage. By total coincidence, Gauthier also had connections in the porn industry. When he ran into trouble distributing the tape without the couple's consent, he turned to the internet to distribute it. The tape became a global symbol of the intersection of fame, sex, porn, celebrity, and the internet's ability to bring it all together. (A 2022 series about what happened, starring Lily James and Sebastian Stan as Pamela and Tommy, interrogated how the media failed Anderson in particular, slut-shaming and mocking her.)

Though the video made by the couple was consensual, its release was not. There wasn't a huge amount of public sympathy towards them. Instead, there was public fascination. When the Pam and Tommy tape went mainstream, it brought sex videos mainstream too, out of porn and into celebrity gossip. Two of the other most famous tapes are one of Paris Hilton and her then-boyfriend Rick Salomon (she later said in a YouTube Originals documentary, *This is Paris*, that it felt like she had been 'electronically raped') and Kim Kardashian and her then-boyfriend Ray J. 'It was just viewed as a laugh or a way to get famous, or to get attention,' says Caroline West of the Hilton and Kardashian videos. 'And it wasn't ever named as sexual violence.' She says the cultural response to these sex tapes minimized what happened, presenting it as harmless fun, and this had a knock-on effect on how the non-consensual sharing of sexual content online was treated.

In 2013, a viral Irish incident showed how vulnerable people were when it came to intimate images being shared on the internet, but also how those judgemental, shameful attitudes towards women can colour incidents when they are the victims. The rise of the smartphone from the mid-2000s has meant that good-quality footage or images can be taken of strangers and then shared online. If you have a social media account, you'll have seen tons of non-consensual but not sexual images and videos of strangers, but you might not have stopped to think about them due to the context. We often see videos of annoying shop assistants; would-be and actual thieves; nosy neighbours; cute couples. Last year, I watched a video on Twitter that was security footage from within an apartment complex, with a tweet accusing a clearly visible woman of dodgy behaviour. It didn't matter that it was filmed in another country, and without the subject's permission – it could rack up thousands of views in minutes.

In 2013 came the shocking case of 'Slane Girl', which showed public humiliation at its nadir. Photographs and video of a young woman – reported to have been seventeen years old – engaged in a sexual act with a young man at an Eminem concert at Slane Castle were shared on social media after the gig. There was something about that period of time on social media that made the conditions just right for sharing the photos: people were deep into using social media as a means to share images and connect with each other, and moderation wasn't anything like it is now; we hadn't yet experienced the full extent of the #MeToo movement; and there was a collective ignorance about the impact of shaming people online, not so much because people didn't know what could be the impact, but because they didn't want to think about it. Social media was still a playground where anything could happen, and people wanted to have fun – even if it was at the expense of someone else.

When the Slane Girl photos emerged, it was a grim day to be online, knowing that you could stumble across a retweet or share of the image, and that the girl in question was having her identity speculated on. She was exposed and vulnerable, with no protection from what people were saying about her, and no way of stopping the images from spreading. The images clearly showed the sex act, and both people were potentially identifiable. It happened in a very public way, but without the photos the incident could have been over and forgotten – except by those involved – quickly. In one photo, the man, who was topless and wearing a neon yellow hat and matching shorts, was raising his arms in the air triumphantly, while people stood around or passed by.

But there was no 'Slane Boy' – there was only 'Slane Girl'. The reaction underscored the double standards around female sexuality, and how easy it was to say the woman was at fault. On Twitter, women talked about how the photos made them feel angry and upset, and how the suffix 'girl' infantilized a young person on the cusp of adulthood. It reminded them, yet again, of the judgement facing a young woman when it came to sexuality, especially if she unwittingly found herself publicly humiliated. To be young is to have the freedom to make mistakes, but making a mistake in the social media era is to dice with shame. Social media sites moved to remove the image and footage after the young woman in the photo's age was revealed, but when I Google 'Slane Girl' now, there are still cropped and partially blurred photos of the incident available. It might never truly be erased. The viral image made its way abroad, onto sites like the *Daily Mail* and the *New York Daily News*. In a column in *The Guardian* after the incident, Eva Wiseman wrote, 'The damage didn't happen at Slane Castle; it happened later, on the internet.' It took seconds for the images of 'Slane Girl' to be taken and shared online, but the consequences could last for years. She was humiliated in the worst way possible.

This cultural shame around women and sex means that some victims of image-based sexual abuse find it hard to talk about what happened to them, Noeline Blackwell, CEO of the Dublin Rape Crisis Centre

(DRCC), tells me. She says that people who've suffered IBSA often blame themselves. This is unfortunately understandable when for years IBSA wasn't a crime. It's also because in Irish courts in the case of rape the survivor is treated as a witness. So women know that if they bring a person to court accused of rape, they can be questioned on their own behaviour: why they went with a certain person, what underwear they wore, how much they drank that night. I know I'm not the only woman who's discussed with friends what she'd do if she was raped or sexually assaulted – whether we would go to the Gardaí, given what we know about the court process and the low rate of conviction. If a rape survivor can find themselves questioned as though they are somehow to blame, then a victim of IBSA can find even more unjustified reasons to question their actions. They might not think justice is theirs to get.

Blackwell says that while with some crimes people are realizing that there's nothing that condones or excuses it – like, for example, a rape survivor drinking beforehand or being in a relationship with the perpetrator – people 'might not be there' with IBSA yet. There hasn't been a societal discussion around this shame, compared to rape. There can be victim-blaming, especially when an IBSA survivor consented to a photo being taken. They might feel judged for appearing nude, and embarrassed about drawing attention to what happened. They will have seen what people said about Pamela Anderson or Kim Kardashian. They'll have read the shaming commentary about Slane Girl, and seen the court reports on rape cases. They will be fully informed about the potential consequences of trying to bring someone to account.

Blackwell describes IBSA as 'one of the richest forms of sexual abuse right now, because there is so little consequence to it', even with the new law in place. There are positive things happening – from her work, Caroline West feels there's been a sense in recent years in Ireland that things are changing around sexual violence, and there's an appetite to have conversations about things like IBSA and consent. That is in large part due to movements like #MeToo and the platform social media gives survivors to speak out about topics like abuse, consent, and rape culture.

As a result, the Discord situation could be viewed as a setback, given all the work that's being done on consent education. But a setback isn't the death knell for equality online. Both West and Blackwell say it's important to educate people on these topics at an early age. 'We're never going to live in a society free of sexual violence and people who excuse it,' says West, 'but you can minimize a lot by working with young people around empathy and compassion, and educating them about what sexual violence is.'

But while this fighting back and speaking out is going on, still the leaks and the sharing of non-consensual nudes continues. In 2022, when I google 'Discord leaks', I find a site that details all of the servers dedicated to leaks on Discord. 'NSFW server with 300+ nude leaks' promises one; 'here you will find the best onlyfans leaks for comlpetely [sic] FREE!!' claims another.[18] The internet will always find a way to remind you of the worst it can do, if you dare to look.

Hate

I

It's a grim story I've been telling about life online so far in this book. But know this: we go online because of the good things. They're what reel us in: the connection, information, surprises, stimulation, *pleasure* we get from websites, apps, pages, groups, forums, servers, videos. Our time is precious to the tech companies who run the platforms because we are good and eager consumers. We willingly sacrifice every spare second of our time to using their products. We hold our smartphones as if they are the hand of a friend; we tenderly tuck devices under our pillows despite the risk of fire. We use our bathroom breaks as time to catch up on the apps we've just looked at.

While we admit to knowing companies need to keep us hooked in so they can make money from our attention, we can feel like we've fooled them as we also get so much from their products. Most of all, we don't want to miss out. When I've had days or sometimes just hours away from being online, I've come back into familiar spaces only to feel like the new student in class, clueless and unable to keep up, missing the reference points and obsessions of the day. And so I reach out my thumb and do the 'refresh feed' dance until I feel like a regular again. I have a hunger to know everything that's happening in the online spaces where I hang out. I don't like the ache of being an outsider.

The act of spending time on these sites and apps isn't always enjoyable or pleasant. But even though I've had to angrily block and mute people over the years, or rolled my eyes at a sexist comment aimed at me, I'm insulated from some of the worst abuse because I am white. My skin colour and ethnicity do not make me a target the way they do others. As offline, racism online can be overt or latent, sewn into comments that people deny have prejudice behind them. But no need to strain yourself looking for racist comments or viewpoints online, as they aren't hidden very well. Just look at the comments below any post or video where people speak out about race. Witness how people respond to a plea against racism by expressing the exact prejudice the original poster is calling out.

The social media platforms took their time before properly introducing moderation and ways to deal with racism, from blocking or muting to closing replies on posts. But once you spend enough time online you realize that there can be all the rules, standards and guidelines in the world, but not everyone will pay attention to them. There are people whose entire online presence is built on sending hateful messages. Often they are shielded by anonymity, by a name and avatar that hides who they are, but it feels like just as often they wear their identities proudly. It might be easy for some people to skim through social apps without being faced with much abuse or hate, but for others all it takes is a quick glance at their replies or comments to see it. Innocuous words can become weapons of hate when knitted together in a certain pattern, with stitches made of colloquialisms and twists on everyday phrases. Sometimes moderators need extra context to pick up how deeply these harmless-appearing weapons can cut, and that context can vary from country to country, or even county to county. Colloquialisms and vernacular can be deliberately used to enable the hate to continue to spread. It's hard to predict which posts will be removed, because the sites or apps can use both human moderators (which I also discuss in this book) and machine learning or AI. Often, AI is used to pick things up proactively – Facebook, for example, said that 97 per cent of hate speech taken down in the final three months of 2020 was spotted by AI before it was flagged by humans.[1] But regardless, the removal happens after the fact.

The Ryan family's story shows exactly how far hateful messages can travel online in Ireland, and how people can be targets just because of their race. It shows too how you don't even need to do anything online to be subjected to internet-based abuse. I first heard about the Ryans on Twitter in 2019, when people started asking Twitter's support account to tackle abuse aimed at the Ryans. It turned out the family – the mum, Fiona Ryan, is Irish and white, her partner, Jonathan Mathis, is British and was born in Brazil, and they have a baby boy, Jonah – were starring in a series of TV and billboard ads for Lidl. The ads told a sweet tale: Ryan and Mathis had moved in with her parents so they could save up for their own home, and began shopping at the discount retailer to save money. Ryan and her mum featured in one ad, browsing the fruit and veg aisle while baby Jonah slept, cosy under a striped blanket in his buggy. Another ad showed Jonah eating spaghetti with his parents, his face smeared with tomato sauce.

These Lidl ads followed a similar pattern to the other campaigns that the German retailer ran in the late 2010s. Instead of being about misery and frugality, the ads were relaxed and fresh-looking, making budgeting attractive. It could be presumed the participants were paid for their appearance, and watching the ads you couldn't help but feel a little inspired by their savviness. But in the case of the ads starring the Ryan family, the internet reaction showed how racism and hate speech can be found online not just in the dark corners, but right in the most mainstream of spaces. There were some people who felt so put out by and suspicious of these ads, based purely on the race of the family, that they took to social media to post their conspiracies. Some were aggrieved at the representation of a multicultural family on the TV, and what they perceived it 'said' about Ireland. When I watch the ads on YouTube now (the comments have been disabled), I see a loving family shopping in a supermarket. But to others, their existence was a threat, and social media provided a forum for them to connect with people who felt the same. Once published online, anyone – including the Ryans – could read their disturbing bile.

I'm nervous when I approach Fiona Ryan to ask her to speak about what happened, as I've seen more conversations lately about people being retraumatized by having to speak out about something that was done to them, particularly in the case of racism. It's an understandable point – that victims of hate speech have to talk about the abuse in order to draw attention to the harm, and that in itself can have a further impact. That's even more so the case when there's no guarantee that when they do speak out people will actually believe them. But Ryan is willing to talk because of the difficulties she had in getting her case dealt with by authorities. She wants to tell her story because not only does it highlight how bad racism can get online, it also shows how difficult it is to get anyone to do anything about it.

The first she heard about the reaction to the Lidl ads was when a member of the video production company which made them called her. They said that a tweet had been posted about her family by the Irish journalist Gemma O'Doherty, and Lidl wanted the family to hear it from them first and know that it was behind them. Ryan went online and found the tweet. It had a photo of a billboard ad starring her smiling family, and a comment which read: 'German dump @lidl_ireland gaslighting the Irish people with their multicultural version of "The Ryans". Kidding no-one! Resist the Great Replacement wherever you can by giving this kip a wide berth. #ShopIrish #BuyIrish.' The 'great replacement' is a conspiracy theory that alleges white indigenous Europeans are being deliberately 'replaced' by non-Europeans due to immigration and a drop in the birth rate in Europe.[2] Even if you didn't know that when reading the tweet, the subtext was clear: this family was seen by those who wanted Ireland to be 'white' as a negative sign of demographics changing. O'Doherty is an award-winning journalist who reported on major news stories like Garda whistleblowers. In recent years, after leaving the mainstream media, she has pivoted her career towards covering issues about what she sees as corruption in Ireland,

and was involved in establishing the group Anti-Corruption Ireland. This organization believes the pandemic was a scamdemic, that water fluoridation should be ended, and that 'uncontrolled' immigration should also be ceased.[3] A recent post on her website was headlined 'Historic Moore Street Now an African Ghetto Courtesy of the Government Who Loves You So Much'.[4] She unsuccessfully ran for the presidency the year before the tweet about the Lidl ad.

Lidl tweeted to say it had blocked O'Doherty's account and reported her tweet to Twitter. 'We are proud of our multicultural & diverse team and our customers. We are proud to work with, and serve, each and every one of them. Everyone is welcome in our store,' Lidl said.[5] While there were tweets in reaction to O'Doherty's initial one decrying what she said, other users agreed with her. Soon the reaction had spread beyond her initial tweet, with the image shared by other people against the ad, and more jumping in to reiterate O'Doherty's point. Within the subgroups on social media sites that follow the same topics, there's a cohort that want to share their prejudiced thoughts on multiculturalism in Ireland, and so an ad like this was a magnet for that sort of commentary. Once someone had criticized it, other people could see it as fair game. It was like trying to stop the flow of rain; the stream of negative and offensive comments just kept coming, and could not be cut off.

Fiona Ryan knew that her son, being mixed race, would inevitably be subjected to racism during his life, just as his father had been. But she didn't expect it so soon and in such a public way. Seeing her family written about online made her feel sick. She asked her mother to mind the baby, unsure of whether she should even tell her what had happened, and read through the comments to grasp the full scale of what was being said. 'I felt terrified about how individuals could have such hate towards a person, and a child at that, and then terrified that the hatred could actually make them do something,' she says. She felt isolated and intimidated, reading the 'threatening, aggressive language' in some of the posts online. It didn't matter that they were written by people she didn't know, and in a digital space; they felt very real.

133

In the days afterwards she was afraid while walking down the street with her son that she would bump into someone who had posted about them. The family cancelled some trips and nights out. They were even unsure whether to bring Jonah swimming. As Mathis had experienced racism, Ryan says he was equipped to deal with it all in some way, but she wasn't. 'I didn't realize that Ireland was like that in a way, so I felt naive,' she says. She was devastated that she had encouraged her partner to move to Ireland, where they could stay with her parents and save up for their own house. 'I felt like I let my family down by bringing them there,' she tells me. She had thought Ireland was a safe place. 'But now I'm thinking – I was so sheltered because I'm white.'

That first evening, Ryan told her family what had happened. They were 'shocked, appalled, disgusted'. She felt that the waves of online racism and abuse must be against the law, so she rang the Gardaí the next day. They told her it was a civil matter and to get a solicitor, as they couldn't deal with it. She didn't believe that could be correct, so she did some research and spoke to people about what had happened. She was told about the Prohibition to Incitement of Hatred Act 1989, which covers actions, broadcasts, and preparation and possession of material that is 'likely to stir up hatred'.[6] When she went to a Garda station to report the case under that act, 'the Garda on the desk didn't know the legislation,' she tells me. They went into a private room where she gave the Garda a leaflet about the legislation, and said she wanted to make a report under it. The Garda took a report, but as Ryan was leaving she didn't have full confidence in how her situation was being dealt with.

The first time a case was brought under the Incitement to Hatred Act over online content was in 2011, after a man created a Facebook page called 'Promote the use of knacker babies as shark bait'. The man told Killarney District Court he set up the page after an incident where he refused to serve members of the Traveller community drinks, claiming they became abusive as a result, the *Irish Examiner* reported.[7] He said that he set up the Facebook page when he got home, as he felt 'angry and powerless'. He asked three friends to join it, but the membership grew to 644 people.

He had forgotten about the page until Facebook emailed him asking him to remove it. He told the court he was 'sickened by my own behaviour' and apologized. The judge said that 'the once-off insertion of material, while revolting and insulting, could not be deemed to be an incitement to hatred', and that apart from his initial comments, the man hadn't added to or commented on the page until it was removed. The man was cleared of the charges. Afterwards, Siobhan Cummiskey, the Irish Traveller Movement Law Centre's managing solicitor, said, 'The Prohibition of Incitement to Hatred Act is an under-utilised piece of legislation riddled with major weaknesses – many of which have been borne out in this failed prosecution.'[8]

II

When you are a victim of online abuse on the scale Fiona Ryan was, you have to decide whether to go public about it or not. It can be easier to try and deal with the situation alone, to not share what happened, to leave it in its own corner. For some people, the desire to go public is strong because it shows others what is going on: that the internet is not a safe place, and that individuals need to be held to account. Over the years, I've wrestled with what to do if I've gotten an abusive response to something. I know the sense of 'triumph' when you feel like you've held someone to account publicly. It's like you've outsmarted them. But it also means you must acknowledge what happened. Hauling yourself over the digital parapet to talk about how you have been abused can also make you even more of a target. People who agreed with the first antagonist now have another platform to tell you what they think.

The backlash over speaking out can force people to stay silent. One woman I spoke to told me about an incident where she felt unnerved by a stranger's actions while she was walking home. It was the sort of incident that the perpetrator could have attempted to explain away as 'but I just wanted to talk to you', but to her was creepy and loaded. It spooked her so much that she tweeted about it, as a way of sharing her unease. While people supported her, she also had people reply to ask why she hadn't confronted the person, or to tell her that actually what happened was a *compliment*. Her initial story ended up being retweeted hundreds of times, and soon she had hundreds of people responding to it. It was too much, too fast.

'I realized: this is out of my control now,' she says. 'And I felt it was actually traumatizing me more than the actual event.' She regretted sharing her story, even though she'd done it in good faith. That in itself bothered her. 'Why did I regret speaking? There was nothing about it to warrant that much attention, and I just felt like it had gone out of control.' Sharing an incident like this can help you feel supported, while also being a way of sending a message to anyone who might think such behaviour is normal. But it can make you even more vulnerable, and it can be hard to get back to square one – even if you end up deleting what you've said, you can't erase the feelings the reaction dredged up.

Fiona Ryan decided to go public. She spoke to Shane O'Curry from INAR, the Irish Network Against Racism, and told him, 'If I have a voice, I'm going to use it. Can you help me get my story out there?' He put her in touch with *The Irish Times* and the family did an interview with the newspaper.[9] After the article came out, Ryan got back in touch with the Gardaí about her case. They asked her to gather evidence of what had been happening, and pass it on to them. 'I thought that was really cruel, because I had to go through the tweets and posts,' she says. She suggested that they contact the social media sites themselves, but was told that it could take years to get the information needed about the people running the accounts, due to international laws.

So Ryan trawled through Twitter and Facebook, reading comment threads and screenshotting all of the racist, threatening and aggressive statements about her family. The evidence was sent to the Gardaí and a file was prepared for the office of the Director of Public Prosecutions, which would make the decision on whether to take a prosecution.

The Gardaí managed Ryan's expectations about whether the case would be able to be prosecuted. At that time, only five cases had been successfully prosecuted under that act for incitement to hatred. Just because the law was in place, it didn't mean that anything could be done legally – and yet that felt like the only recourse she had to deal with what had been going on, the only way to exert any control.

Seven months later, the DPP contacted Ryan to tell her that charges would not be brought over what happened. She wasn't able to appeal the decision. It didn't matter how much she had been hurt, how many awful words she'd seen written online about her and her family. No one was going to be punished for it.

III

We already know from Coco's Law that dealing with harm online can be difficult, and that the law can take ages to catch up with what's actually happening to people on the internet. Ireland doesn't have any specific hate crime legislation, but there is some on the way. When the government decides to bring in a new law, it usually opens a public consultation on it. It did that in 2019 over proposed new hate crime legislation. The public submissions are available online, and I wanted to see what people sent in. Even though the legislation wasn't specifically to do with dealing with online hate crimes, it was set to be the law under which posts like the ones about the Ryans could be dealt with in the future. So I thought that the submissions would give a sense of what people thought about this, and about dealing with hate crimes in general, which might feed into their own behaviour online. It could be a litmus test for public attitudes, albeit an unscientific one.

The submissions page had a warning on it: 'The reader may find some views expressed in these submissions distasteful and objectionable and in some cases, disturbing, insulting, offensive and deeply upsetting.' There were 104 submissions. As I read through them I was reminded of the myopia of our own existence. We can presume everyone thinks exactly how we do, but we're always wrong about that. I had presumed that the majority of the submissions would welcome this law. But they were overwhelmingly opposed to any change in hate speech laws in Ireland. Here's a flavour of what I saw on there:

I know the hate speech submission has closed but we do not need any more (((hate speech laws))) it gives people licences to be offended by everything, it only allows the indigenous Irish to be censored of which this will actually CAUSE more hate speech

Hate has different meanings for different groups of people / cultures at different times in history. What one culture finds something funny, other groups might find it offensive or hateful.

Hate speech is not a thing . . . it's a soviet/nazi style censorship!! Most crime is motivated by hate . . . I have the God-given right to hate anything I want. I hate hate speech laws!![10]

Those submissions don't represent the overall public opinion on hate crimes in Ireland, but they do show there's a significant contingent of people who believe these laws would be censorious and would affect their free speech. Many of the conversations about racism online these days end up snagging on that question of free speech: who has the right to say what and to whom. Some believe that if they're troubled by an ad starring a multicultural family, they have the right to say whatever they like about it, and if they're stopped then that's censorship. Others believe those thoughts should be silenced as soon as – or before, if that was possible – they are aired. In the middle are the people whose existence is being kicked around as if it's a football.

There's a fear among some people that if social media sites want to prevent users from airing racist views, this could trickle down into people being unable to express any thought at all about race. Reading those submissions, I saw how some people believe tackling hate is akin to silencing people, that proactively tackling racism is really to shut people's mouths. But from what I was seeing myself online, and through experiences like the Ryan and Mathis families', if anything social media was the perfect place to air racist and prejudiced views, because very little was happening to the people who did it.

Fiona Ryan reported all of the social media posts about her family to the sites they were on, but that didn't give her a sense of control. 'I didn't feel like there was a very clear line to actually talk to anybody with any kind of clout on the social media sites,' she says. 'Pretty much everything came back saying it's not against our policy, and if you don't like it, block the user. That's it.' But if you are not a Twitter user and there are comments being made about you, that's not an option for you. She says Lidl requested a meeting with Twitter over the tweets. The tweet from Gemma O'Doherty was removed, but related posts were not removed from Facebook, says Ryan. O'Doherty's Twitter account was permanently suspended a year later, in July 2020, for repeated violations of Twitter rules.[11] Her YouTube account had been suspended the year before for violating policies on hate speech and harassment. She subsequently picketed outside Google's Dublin office, accusing them of breaching her right to free speech, and livestreamed the picket on her social channels.[12]

The online abuse from strangers continued as Ryan and Mathis did more interviews with the media. Ryan is an actress, and her career choice was used to falsely allege she had been hired by Lidl to pretend to be part of a multicultural family. There was a belief among some people that a multicultural family couldn't be Irish, ignoring the many such families that have been in Ireland for generations. There were people out there who believed the family were fictional, trying to hijack the idea of Irishness – as if 'Irish' was synonymous with 'white' – so Ryan's IMDB page with her acting roles was shared as a 'gotcha!'. People were talking about her family, trying to take her character away and discredit her, she tells me. 'It just spiralled out of control after that.' People started sending her links to right-wing websites where her family was discussed and 'disgusting racist stuff said'. She gave those links to the Gardaí too, but nothing was able to be done.

The most high-profile moment for Jonathan Mathis and Fiona Ryan in telling their story was when they went on *The Late Late Show*. But while it brought a new wave of support, their interview ignited the online hatred again. On the show, Fiona told the presenter Ryan Tubridy that they'd received death threats. The couple had been on the fence about doing such a high-profile Friday night show, afraid in particular that people would know they were in the RTÉ television studios. (They ended up pre-recording the clip.) Afterwards, there were social media posts saying, 'Who does she think she is?' and 'Look at this white snowflake', Ryan says.

Because of the abuse, she removed her Facebook account, even though she'd had it since she was young. She stayed on Instagram and kept the page private, as the abuse hadn't carried over there. Online abuse shrinks the ability of the victim to have a safe space online. 'I lost my freedom to be able to contact my friends based on how people view me,' Ryan says. 'So [the racists'] freedom of speech means people not having their own freedoms.' Nearly three years after the incident, she made her Instagram account public. Though she hadn't been acting for a few years due to having her children and the pandemic, she thought it would be good to make her profile public again. The very next day, she got a racist and threatening direct message. 'And comments underneath my family photo saying I should educate my children on the "white Irish",' she says. 'Disgusting racist comments under my photos.'

By the time we talk, Ryan is in a better place, and able to rationalize that she can't be a public figure on social media. She doesn't want to become a martyr to the abuse, or have her life revolve around it. But she can't make decisions about her internet presence with any sense of freedom.

IV

On one of Dublin's northside Georgian streets is the base of the non-governmental organization (NGO) Irish Network Against Racism (INAR), who Ryan had turned to for advice on the racist posts. Just around the corner from the INAR office is Parnell Street, which could be seen as a symbol of modern Ireland, with its Chinese, Indian and Vietnamese restaurants, local grocery stores that sell bitcoin alongside chocolate bars, and hip pub that holds vinyl-only DJ sets. The network has around 100 members (like the Immigrant Council of Ireland, the Roma Integration Association and the Irish Traveller Movement), and calls itself the 'voice of anti-racism in Ireland'. It has an iReport system online where people can report racism and hate speech, which is how it can gauge the level of racism people are facing in Ireland year to year, including online.

INAR says there's a gap between the social media platforms' aspirations of maintaining a safe environment, and the everyday reality for minorities. A look at its 2021 report shows there were 65 reports of online hate speech, the majority of which (23) were on Facebook.[13] One of the incidents reported involved a security guard who was filmed at work by a group, which shared the video on TikTok to incite racist abuse against him. The 2020 report has higher figures, showing 282 reports about racist hate speech online – 119 were on Facebook and 42 on Twitter.[14] In INAR's 2021 report, Una-Minh Kavanagh, an Irish journalist and author who has written about how she was adopted by an Irish mother from Vietnam, said: 'When online racism rears its ugly head, it's easy for people to dismiss it because they see it often as faceless attacks and therefore should not be taken seriously but the reality is, it's no different to offline racism.'

The 2020 INAR report also highlighted the role the internet can have in spreading race-based disinformation, like the false stories that were spread online about George Nkencho, a twenty-seven-year-old black man who was fatally shot by the Garda Armed Support Unit in Dublin in December that year. The disinformation disseminated online about Nkencho, who was experiencing serious mental health difficulties, included false claims that he had previous convictions.[15] The spurious rumours were spread across social media and WhatsApp and Telegram groups, anywhere there were suspicions about him not being an 'innocent' victim. There was a real-life impact to these false rumours, said INAR: it undermined wider community sympathy for Nkencho and his family, and stoked community tension. Made-up 'facts' about a person who had been killed could be shared easily, and with encrypted apps like WhatsApp and Telegram, it was impossible to tell who those false claims had reached.

But at the same time, social media helped people to rally and show their support for George Nkencho's family, and express their upset and anger over his killing. A shooting like that involving the Gardaí is incredibly unusual, and that it involved a man of colour who had mental health difficulties added to the distress caused by what happened. Online, people were able to arrange and share information on vigils for Nkencho. So while the online space was where bad actors could try and make false information go viral, it also functioned as a forum for grief. A mass mourning can take place online when people meet untimely deaths, though that doesn't cancel out any related disinformation. After George Nkencho died a number of protests took place, with some of the protesters holding up signs saying 'I can't breathe' and 'Black Lives Matter'.[16] An online social justice movement started in America had helped them to find a shorthand for expressing the hurt, anger and questions that his death brought up.

'Fuckfuck fuck'. The tweet, sent on 9 August 2014, was short and sharp.[17] Attached was a photograph showing the body of a man laid out in the middle of a road. The man, his face turned away from the camera, was wearing a cream top and trousers. Above him stood a police officer. Michael Brown was just nineteen. His death was one of the catalysts that pushed an online anti-racism movement global, making three words stand for both a whole world of hate and anger, and for the hope for change. The ripple effects of that movement meant that after incidents like the killing of George Nkencho, people in Ireland had a vocabulary and discourse to take from when talking about black lives in Ireland: that black lives matter.

Brown's death on a residential street in Ferguson broke something for people in Missouri and the rest of the US. It showed that police brutality in the country would keep continuing. The photos of Brown's body were shared across social media. By the next day, there were protests in the city, with the police responding with tear gas and curfews. Buildings were set on fire. The world was watching as children and parents protested, as photos of burning gas stations were shared online, as the hashtag #BlackLivesMatter joined #Ferguson on Twitter and Facebook, a stream of angry, confused and sad tweets accompanying them.[18] The protests around Brown's death built on the Black Lives Matter (BLM) protests and outcry that occurred after neighbourhood watch volunteer George Zimmerman was acquitted of the killing of Trayvon Martin (seventeen) in Florida in 2012. The acquittal kicked off the kind of protests we now associate with BLM, taking fears about systemic racism, prejudice and police violence to the streets in a call for justice. Tragically, #BlackLivesMatter got a boost in usage each time another killing of a black person by police or a white person got publicity – and there were many examples to come over the following years.[19]

The phrase 'hashtag activism' might appear to be – and could certainly be intended to be – reductive or dismissive, but the Twitter hashtag has been a powerful part of social movements. 'Black Lives Matter' as a phrase was used for the first time on Facebook by a woman named Alicia Garza, and turned into a hashtag by her friend Patrice Cullors. Those three words, whether tied together in a hashtag or standing separately, told the story of racism and police brutality in the so-called 'land of the free' while also projecting a vision of a future where the worthiness of people's lives was not dependent on their race. The hashtag was soon used way beyond the US.[20]

Here in Ireland, we don't have the US's permissive and damaging gun laws, and we don't have the exact same shameful history of race relations. But we do have our own embedded issues with racism, be it how, while forcing mothers into mother and baby homes, parents and babies of colour were treated appalling; the prejudice against the indigenous Irish ethnic group, the Traveller community; the treatment of people of colour who were born or brought up here. Moving BLM into new contexts meant new meaning was put on its aims, and new aims were created. It served as a way for people in Ireland to speak about racism online. Just like MeToo enabled women to talk about the issues of sexism that are layered throughout society in Ireland, BLM gave people a new platform, a new voice, a new space.[21]

Celebrations of multiculturalism were happening online too, like the articles written in Ireland and abroad about the latest wave of black and Irish musicians, like JyellowL, Tolü Makay, Erica Cody (who wrote the song 'Where U Really From'), God Knows, and Soulé, who were, as the blogger Nialler9 put it, 'absolutely running the Irish music scene'.[22] People shared tweets and playlists online of their favourite black and Irish artists. But to be more visible could also mean becoming more of a target for abuse online. The Zambian Irish singer and rapper Denise Chaila became one of the biggest musicians in the country in 2020, her music a salve for many during the pandemic. But by early 2021 she had to ask the media not to tag her in social media posts – because of the racist replies that would automatically follow a mention of her name.[23]

This became a time where black and Irish people saw the lens turned on their individual experiences. Instead of being told who they were and what their identity should be, the mic was passed to them. Black and Irish emerged during this period, a social media movement set up by Femi Bankole, Leon Diop and Boni Odoemene. Black and Irish is significant in its simplicity. Each post has a photo and a short piece written by a person who is black and Irish about their life story. Sometimes people use the space to write about the racism they have experienced. Some barely touch on the topic. Some celebrate their achievements; some focus on their parents' story and what they went through. It's a history of Ireland, a history of Irish racism, and a sign of hope for the future, all in one.

Eric Ehigie joined Black and Irish about a year after it was founded, and once featured on it himself. Today, he's Black and Irish's political co-ordinator. He's a lot younger than me, and was twelve when he first went online in the early 2010s. Growing up in a Nigerian family in Longford, his mother encouraged him to watch Malcolm X videos after school, while around the dinner table they would have discussions about racism, empowerment and Pan Africanism. But in school, it wasn't easy to be black and Irish. Ehigie describes himself as a big extrovert, good at reaching out to people. I can see too that he's great at observing people, able to step back and place their actions into a cultural and societal context. And so he knew from a young age that behaviour can be amplified on social media, or 'put on steroids', as he describes it.

Seeing fights break out on Facebook comment sections showed him the hostile side of human nature. 'I grew to learn how social media is. It's such a useful, convenient mask for many people to offload a lot of the negative feelings and views they might have – discriminatory views, hateful views – knowing what little repercussions they will meet as a result of it, simply because of the nature of social media,' he tells me. When you are not at risk of abuse online because of your identity, you can be more fully yourself. But Ehigie tells me that he and others who come from ethnic minority homes, but are born and/or raised in Ireland, can end up facing an identity crisis, and that can take place online too. 'At home you are open with associating with your African roots. But out in the world, you have to disassociate in order to fit in,' he explains. 'So when racist jokes are made, when derogatory things are said about Africa, you simply have to keep quiet unless you are called a snowflake, or someone who can't take a joke.'

He knew from his offline life to keep quiet when words were being thrown at him. He expected to encounter racism on social media when he was young. He'd see jokes that he knew the joker thought were subtle, but which were aggressive in his eyes, but also knew he couldn't respond in a particular way. Instead, he might write 'haha' or 'lol', when inside he was burning from the embarrassment and shame. One year, a comedian's song about Ebola went viral. 'He was joking about Africa and talking about how everybody in Africa has Ebola, every "crappy village" is riddled with Ebola,' says Ehigie. He saw it on Facebook and heard people in his town singing it. If you complained about it and were of African descent, you'd be told you couldn't take a joke. 'And then you lose brownie points in the cultural hierarchy that everybody cares to be part of at school – and nobody wants to be the outcast in school,' continues Ehigie.

While he wasn't complicit in this behaviour online, he says he conformed by being silent out of fear and insecurity. His mother raised him to be a proud African, but it's not easy to be outwardly proud when those around you are making your identity the butt of a joke. Ehigie refers to his behaviour back then as 'suicidal conformity'. Sometimes he and his friends of African descent in Longford would take the stereotypes and embrace them to fit in or make people laugh. When a new stereotype emerged on social media, he says, like black people liking chicken, or all Nigerian people being poor, he and his friends would make snaps about it on Snapchat, or post about it on Facebook, so their native Irish friends would comment and laugh. 'It was an act of self-hatred, nearly,' he says. When he thinks of this time, he thinks of the story of Malcolm X, and how when X – born Malcolm Little – was in his teens, at one stage he would 'try and straighten his hair, he'd try and do the most white American thing he could to fit in within school, to be liked by everybody, even if it meant humiliating himself'. Ehigie understood where that compulsion came from, that it was the case for him and many other black Irish people he grew up around, and that it manifested itself on Facebook in a strong way. Online, they would have to conform to get by.

It wasn't until he was sixteen or seventeen that he started pushing back on this conformity. He got involved in the Irish Second Level Students' Union (ISSU). 'When I was there, the manacles were off, shackles were off, mask was down, I was able to fully be me, and engage in conversations that I had never engaged in with anyone back home in Longford, apart from my mom,' he explains. He posted photos of the first ISSU event on his social media accounts with pride, without caring about any potential reaction. From there, his true self began to manifest incrementally, and it expressed itself online. He set up his own YouTube channel and talked about different social issues, like England's knife crime epidemic, and his vision for Ireland in 2029. The conformity had been 'like a civil war within me, it killed me every time I did it', he says. But after the ISSU event, he could fracture that part of him off and turn it into splinters to be reabsorbed as the real him emerged. It wasn't long before racist comments were posted under some of his YouTube videos. 'People were saying "provide a vision for Africa, you don't belong here'" on his video about a vision for Ireland's future, he says. But if you scroll through the comments on this video now, you also see messages telling him well done, 'keep grinding, bro'.

After George Floyd was killed in 2020, which pushed the Black Lives Matter into an even bigger wave of protest online and off, Ehigie began to question his Irish identity again due to what he saw online. He was among a group that organized a Longford Black Lives Matter protest over Floyd's death. But when he looked at comments about the event on social media, some were 'really aggressively unsupportive'. And to make it worse, there were familiar names in the comment sections. 'Reading that really, really bogged me down, because I didn't expect that from some of the people who commented, so it called me to question my place in Longford, and whether people are really willing to embrace its diversity,' he says. A comment written by someone without a second thought could have infinite power to injure.

Pressure has been growing on social media sites over racist behaviour on their platforms for years. Even aside from the many individual examples, there were flashpoints that showed how real life events can intersect with far right and racist behaviour online, that what is happening on the internet, even in small or private spaces, can impact on real life. Fires set at mooted direct provision accommodation in Rooskey (on the Leitrim/Roscommon border) in 2019 and Moville in Donegal in 2018 showed that the nexus between online hatred and organizing by the far right and real-life hate crimes was undeniable, says Shane O'Curry from INAR. Word had spread about the accommodation plans on social media, and the fact that in Moville the locals only found out about it online upset some people.[24] The controversy was then jumped on by far right groups and figureheads online, as it was in the case of mooted accommodation in Oughterard too. It was very easy to see the messages that these figureheads were spreading. For example, far-right figurehead Rowan Croft, who built a following of thousands on his YouTube channel, travelled to towns allegedly earmarked for direct provision centres to do live broadcasts.

In the 2020 general election, there was an attempt by the right-wing National Party to get into government. It failed dismally, which showed there wasn't a broad appetite to vote such people into power here. But online, there's no need to be an elected official to have power in the right-wing or far right space. You can bring your views to big audiences through social media, and you can amass a huge following as you do so. There can be no geographic borders when it comes to how these beliefs spread too – what happens in Ireland can be of interest to people abroad. When Noteworthy (a sister site to The Journal) looked at mentions of Oughterard's direct provision centre on Twitter, it found people like the UK's Katie Hopkins (who was later barred from Twitter) saying 'Ireland is about to take on a new wave of African migrants in converted hotels across Ireland' and Gemma O'Doherty saying 'The Irish will be a minority in #Ireland by 2050 if the government has its way.'[25]

Both women were later kicked off Twitter, but only after years of tweets like this. The fact that people like O'Doherty and Hopkins – as well as other high-profile people of similar ilks, like Stefan Molyneaux and Rowan Croft – no longer have public profiles on sites like Twitter and those run by Meta shows that the companies have been able to successfully crack down on them, but it took an incredibly long time. They're not even gone from the internet: they've just moved onto new, less mainstream pastures, which could be even more of an echo chamber. At least when they were in mainstream spaces, their intentions and thoughts were easy to view. But their removal took a long time to happen, not because these platforms approved of what was being said, but because in large part of the fear of being seen as censoring people, of cracking down on their free speech.

In their book about Facebook, *The Ugly Truth*, Sheera Frenkel and Cecilia Kang write, 'Facebook was designed to throw gas on the fire of any speech that invoked an emotion, even if it was hateful speech – its algorithms favoured sensationalism.'[26] In the mid-2010s, that meant that no matter what emotion spurred on the clicking, the algorithm picked up the fact a post was being widely read, which meant it could then be promoted more across Facebook. Even when Facebook made changes to how its news feed served up information, to pull people away from the more toxic material (after being warned by some of its own engineers about the issues this was causing, write Frenkel and Kang), that didn't stop people from continuing to be drawn to clickbait and bad quality content on the site. Twitter, meanwhile, started cracking down on hate a little earlier than Facebook. The biggest sign of change was when, due to violating its rules about 'glorifying violence', it hid President Donald Trump's comment 'when the looting starts, the shooting starts', posted after BLM protests took place following George Floyd's killing. Facebook didn't do anything of the sort – and Trump even called Mark Zuckerberg, write Frenkel and Kang, to ask that action not be taken over what he said on its platform.

All of us who are members of these sites have been powerless to do anything other than take the most minor of individual actions while racist and far right figureheads and groups have used the same platforms as us to spread hate. It was frustrating, to say the least, to be able to easily view videos of these hate figures on the sites and wonder why the platforms were sitting on their hands. What's interesting, though, is comparing my experience on the sites now to back between 2016 and 2020. I do feel the impact of the most well-known figures being booted off the platforms, because I remember what it was like to see people regularly discussing and criticizing what they were saying by sharing (and amplifying) their work. I didn't have to follow them or even search for them to see their content. I notice that if I go on Facebook now and try to search for some of these figureheads and related topics, it's hard to get to the info – but I also know there are closed pages and areas which are unsearchable. But by 2023, things had changed again, when Elon Musk reinstated previously suspended Twitter accounts.

Overall, though, things haven't actually changed that much. A UN report in March 2021 from the Special Rapporteur on minority issues, Dr Fernand de Varennes, said that online hate speech was increasing against minorities.[27] When the UK youth charity Ditch the Label commissioned a study on online hate speech in the US and UK, it found 50.1 million discussions or examples of hate speech, and that they tended to spike during major news events, like the pandemic and Black Lives Matter protests.[28] Shane O'Curry says the success of the Brexit and Trump campaigns 'gave courage' to ultra conservative and far right actors in Ireland. 'While not all racist trolls belong to the far right, I think that the far right presence and activism online has created an enabling atmosphere for anybody,' he says.

Now that Fiona Ryan has come out the other side of her own experience, she's been able to see how it was part of a larger moment in Irish society in recognizing harm caused by racism or hate speech online. She's also aware that her own ethnic background could have helped some people to truly understand what she, Jonathan and Jonah experienced. 'Unfortunately, because I was the white counterpart of my "multicultural" family, people in Ireland could see themselves in me. They realized, "Oh, it actually could happen to anybody", she says. 'And that woke a lot of people up, and if I'm honest, me included – which needed to happen.' Ryan and Mathis ended up moving to the UK, where they feel they will have more protection for their children. But the fact nothing was done about what happened to them lingers. 'I just feel really, really sad for the people that have to go through this abuse every day because of who they are, and have absolutely no power whatsoever to say, "this is wrong"', says Ryan now. When I check to see if there are any tweets about the Lidl campaign still online, I find a few accusing Ryan of being an actress who made a fake ad. Though time has passed, it's almost impossible to escape those sorts of messages about her family. They are targets simply because they exist.

But while social media continues to provide a fertile landscape for racist and prejudiced viewpoints to sprout, the same ground is being used to allow people to push back. An initiative like Black and Irish is a positive and powerful way of crowding out the racist voices, allowing people to take up space on social media and show new viewpoints, new experiences. Black and Irish is about expansion – expanding the concept of Irishness, and giving individuals their own place in a greater movement. For Eric Ehigie, it's about 'how we can't limit the definition of borders of Irishness, we have to allow it to encompass all people who are willing to be a part of it'. He believes doing that in itself is an Irish act. For him, an online movement like Black and Irish is a mirror that had been hidden. Having the cloth pulled off gave him a sense of 'long overdue relief'. Thanks to its social media presence, he could get a new view of things. 'I could finally see myself in the broader mirror, not just my explicit Irishness,' he says. 'To me it was a signal, a herald of positive change.'

WHO'S WATCHING WHO?

You're a backslapping and inbreeding white feminist
with a Twitter account. Not a snowflake.

*

I have told you multiple times to stop contacting me.

*

It's perfect for a bigot like you.

*

It's funny when people like you talk about diversity
you backslapping and inbreeding fool.

*

This is really freaking me out now.

BOD

When harassment online is abstract or hypothetical to you, you can envisage all the things you would do if it happened. But when it does happen to you, any of your plans and presumptions shatter, because the situation feels so unreal and out of your control. In 2019, I was one of six women involved in a landmark court case which saw a man jailed for harassing us online. Even now, writing about it for the first time, it feels odd, and slightly shameful, to be sharing what happened. My initial urge is to minimize what occurred, to say it wasn't that bad, to emphasize that I'm fine, that it hasn't had long-lasting effects. And though I am fine, it would be a lie to say that what occurred didn't affect how I behave online, or that I've forgotten the experience.

It was strange to watch myself and two of my colleagues on the *Six One* news on RTÉ the day the sentence was handed down to our harasser. I didn't need the footage to remind myself of what it was like to walk, in our winter coats and scarves, up the road beside the Circuit Criminal Court as the reporter detailed how an 'internet troll' had harassed us and three other women for years online. That day was the culmination of a period of seven years which showed me that I had to act, at all times, like someone I didn't know was watching with interest what I was saying or doing online.

It had started off, as these things tend to do, in a relatively uneventful way. I started working for a digital newsroom, and around the same time I joined Twitter. Those two things led the troll to me, but my presence on Twitter became a particularly big part of the harassment. For a few years, I really loved Twitter – even with all the drama around it, I still have fond feelings about it – and I used it a lot. I had joined after a friend told me that it was like Facebook, but for status updates. Twitter had its roots in conversations and hackathons by the employees at the now defunct podcast start-up Odeo. After Apple announced iTunes would have a podcast platform, Odeo pivoted. An engineer at the company called Jack Dorsey was interested in the 'status' – as on Facebook – and came up with an idea around being able to send the one message to all your friends.[1]

So Twitter started off as an SMS service, before moving online. In its early days you could only send a message that had up to 140 characters, but you could fit a lot into that confined space, and it was a satisfying challenge to get across your message in a limited amount of words. Unlike Facebook, Twitter was stripped of extras. There was no need to add photos of your nights out, or go through the rigmarole of sending a friend request. It was public by default, unless you put your profile on private; you could follow whoever you wanted, and anyone could follow you. You didn't have to use your real name or image. A few years ago I looked back at my earliest tweets and they were mostly embarrassing complaints about how busy I was, or my thoughts on an album I was reviewing. They weren't really bids for attention. If someone did reply, it was a bit of a thrill. I didn't think, back then, too much about who might be reading what I was writing.

From the early days of the site, a small community was formed that began to call itself 'Irish Twitter'. Just like on forums or Facebook groups, Irish Twitter's members all had a common interest, but in this case it was, well, being an Irish person on Twitter. While Twitter is commonplace now, at the time it felt special and intimate. The content and conversations shared among us were varied – from film to music, politics to policy, parenting to work, it was all there. There were many cliques on the site;

subgroups of the greater Irish Twittersphere. I got to know a fair few people in 'real life' thanks to Twitter meetups, or recognized others from their avatars out in public. (Meetups were important for Twitter, and Instagram too – in Instagram's early days the owners saw them as a way of cultivating a connected and almost curated membership).[2] For a few years, Irish Twitter felt like a small, neat group of people who generally were happy to be connected, and the site proved the internet still had interesting things to surprise us with. The stream of information on Twitter never felt like the torrent it is today. Almost a decade and a half on, Irish Twitter has a much larger and more varied membership, and it's not a distinct grouping like it used to be – some people have understandably rebelled against the idea of there being an 'Irish Twitter' at all. Cliques can be great until they feel claustrophobic.

It was probably because of those early Irish Twitter days that I continued to tweet over the years as if my following was as small as it was initially, just a few hundred people paying some level of attention to what I was saying instead of thousands. Early on, tweets had been arranged chronologically, and retweeting wasn't as strong as it is now, so it did seem like a tweet today could be tomorrow's digital chip paper. But then I started getting emails from a person I didn't know about my tweets, and this seemed to coincide with a slow dawning that what made Twitter great also made it an uncomfortable place to be. Gathering together people from across the world onto one website to share their thoughts means that you are not going to have a place that's always full of pleasant conversations and light banter. Just like offline, there will be people who deliberately want to harass others, or target them, or just be a nuisance.

Because of this, Twitter has had to firefight when it comes to dealing with reports of abuse. There was never any real deterrent to bad behaviour or trolling, though the site's moderation policies and guidelines tightened up as time went on. By the time it got to 2021, Twitter users could be forgiven for thinking almost anything was allowed on Twitter. We'd spent years watching the president of the United States saying polls were rigged, Covid-19 was a 'China virus', and that he was going to build a wall in

Mexico to keep immigrants out. We'd witnessed Twitter make controversial right-leaning commentators into stars. Like Stefan Molyneaux, who espoused anti-feminist beliefs, or alt-right activists like Tim Gionet, aka 'Baked Alaska', who pleaded guilty to taking part in the US Capitol riots.[3] Both gathered huge followings of fans and people who hated their content, and both were banned (after a membership of years) for their tweets. Twitter might not have overtly encouraged these sorts of people to join its site, but it let them stay, and this showed people in Ireland, too, what sort of behaviour was acceptable online. Twitter only banned Donald Trump in 2021, which didn't send a message that it knew how to deal with powerful people who post controversial things.

By 2016, I was growing weary of seeing overblown, racist, sexist or offensive tweets, and feeling like nothing was being done about them. There was a marked difference in the pre- and post-2016 Twitter. All of the harmful behaviour I was seeing on the site was making me wonder if a dam had been breached and more and more badness was seeping online. It felt like some people were shoving back against the malevolence they were seeing by hauling others over the coals for minor infractions, piling into people's replies if they were accused of anything at all. Celebrities were finding themselves criticized over minor remarks that were shared without context. Tweets were widely retweeted that seemed to pathologize normal behaviour, or lacked nuance. The fun memes and in-jokes of early Twitter were getting lost in the mud.

It wasn't until years later, during Elon Musk's takeover, when it felt as though the site was under actual threat of collapse, that it really became clear both what a unique website Twitter was, and how heavily all the toxic behaviour on it weighed on people's psyches. Though on paper it was a site that seemed to struggle to make as much money as its rivals like Facebook, it had massive power. Being absorbed in its world also meant that, like the proverbial lobster in boiling water, as toxic behaviour increased, we adjusted to the temperature. The fact that Twitter couldn't seem to curb the racism, sexism, and toxicity, but also provided us users with a platform unlike any other, which had reach into parliaments, boardrooms, and behind locked doors, meant many of us were willing to put up with the bad sides because of all the good we got. In doing so, we might have made fools of ourselves.

And it felt like no coincidence that this was happening in the late 2010s while I was still getting emails from a stranger who had first contacted me in 2012, letting me know they were watching what I was saying on there.

At first, the connection between my tweets and the emails wasn't clear. The initial email was a plea from a person with the initials 'BOD' for some help. He emailed me in 2012 at my work email address and I became concerned about his mental health, so I sent him the contact details of the Samaritans. The email lingered with me. I was worried about whoever had sent it, wondering why they chose to reach out to a stranger. It was sad to think that I might be their only way to try and get help. Then I got another email from BOD. And then another. His emails never again mentioned that first troubling message. Instead, he sent me, and some of my colleagues, two of whom were also involved in the eventual court case, his thoughts on articles on *The Journal*. Instead of posting them publicly, he wanted us to read his words ourselves. People tend to be feeling very strong emotions when they email journalists – sometimes you've annoyed them because of what you have or haven't written about. Getting emails from readers (or people who haven't read the article, but still have a strong opinion) is just part of my job. Often it's how I get leads on stories. But BOD stood out because his comments got more personal as the years went on, and it was clear that he really didn't like me.

It was also clear that, despite this dislike, he was following what I was saying online. I was still tweeting throughout the day, and checking the site regularly. I wanted to write funny tweets, little observations about my day, and I wanted to share the sort of 'well, actually' tweets that undoubtedly riled people up. Twitter and my work coalesced, as I spotted potential stories on there and people could get in touch with me. I liked that I could make people laugh, and get likes for what I'd written.

One day, BOD emailed my personal email account. He had Googled me and found that address. This new move felt violating, as he had gone beyond the tacit boundary that separated my work life from my personal life. He'd also figured out I had been involved in different radio stations, and mentioned this in an email. That brought with it a fear of what the remnants of my earlier days online could provide him. Of how easy it was to follow my journey around the space of the internet for almost two decades, when I hadn't ever thought anyone would follow me around. I thought of the hours I had blithely posted personal thoughts on forums, and was glad that I'd never said anything too revealing which might pop up in a Google search. But I didn't know how careful I'd been. I was sure that somewhere on Twitter I had let slip where my apartment was. I was always going on about being from Cork, and figured it wasn't too hard to guess where I grew up.

In my late teens and early twenties, giving out personal information online was part of the relationship code, a way of forging connections with strangers. If I hadn't given out titbits about myself, and made sure I shared my thoughts and opinions, I wouldn't have moved so easily and intimately through social media. Posting online gives a sense of who you are, even if you are writing under a pseudonym. I was writing under my own name, so I knew each tweet and post helped contribute to an overall impression of me as a person. But if I gave such information out, I wondered if I deserved to be in this situation. Put yourself out there, and you're available for anyone to hook onto. All of the breadcrumbs that I'd innocently and ignorantly trailed behind me made me wonder if I'd accidentally led BOD to my door, or at the very least, the door of my office.

Though there were often months between BOD's emails, when he did message me he'd send a clump together, as if to reinforce the fact that he had never really gone away. He started sending me screengrabs of my tweets with comments written below them. I'd picture him scrolling through my feed, deciding which ones to target. I tweeted once in a fit of body shame about whether there was a German word for trying on lots of dresses and none of them fitting. Even though it could be seen as sarcastic and throwaway, it was a deeply felt moment, and it felt vulnerable to share it. He emailed a screengrab of it to me, along with a message: 'faat kunt' [sic]. In 2017, he sent a strange email that just said *'There are no records for Aoife. *Due to confidentiality reasons, only names with 3 or more instances in the relevant year are included.'* I knew this meant he was searching for my name on a website, but had no idea why, or what website, or what he wanted me to do with that information. I emailed him back to tell him to leave me alone. Sometimes he sent links to YouTube videos, or attached strange images, like one of the Joker from *Batman*, his elastic smile looking even more menacing in that context. By sending me the messages, he was telling me, I'm thinking about you. I did not want him thinking about me. I did not want to know what hidden messages lay beneath the sarcastic emails and images, what he was trying to tell me. I just wanted him to leave me alone.

One July evening in 2016, I went to see the *Ghostbusters* movie reboot with a group of women, most of whom were on Twitter, for a night out that was organized via social media. The movie was – ironically – at the centre of an online argument about the fact it had an all-female cast, and some of the cast members were trolled and abused on Twitter. I posted a photo afterwards of the group of young women who attended the screening with me smiling in the lobby of the Cineworld cinema, in front of a big poster for the film. The next day, BOD emailed me a link. When I clicked on it I saw it was the same photo. He had saved the original image and uploaded it to an image-hosting site. I made my Instagram page private and contacted the site where he'd uploaded the photo to ask them to remove it, which they did. I stopped saying in advance on social media if I was going to an event. Even a night out could be spoiled by his need to let me know he was following me around online. When I did have to say I was doing an event, because I was a guest or interviewer, I wondered if he would be in the crowd. I had no idea what he looked like, but I knew he lived in Dublin because of things he'd said in the emails.

In his correspondence, BOD wanted me to know he thought I was stupid. A phrase he used regularly in his emails, and in comments he left on my personal blog, was that I was as deep as a bucket of water. But he'd also call me 'a backslapping and inbreeding white feminist' and a 'wannabe'. The mention of feminism highlighted how being an outspoken woman online could foster a particular type of gender-based criticism. Not only might someone disapprove of your belief in gender equality, but they can imagine you and your fellow feminists are part of a shadowy, interconnected anti-man cabal (sorry to disappoint on that front). They can imagine that you hate them, based on their gender, or that you're trying to steal their power. Your voice becomes a threat to their existence, and they want to use their own voice to tell you that. Feminism found a foothold online, with groups and individuals able to espouse their beliefs and raise consciousness there. Initiatives like Everyday Sexism were set up where women could catalogue sexist incidents.[4] But feminism being so visible on the internet, not hidden away in dusty academic books or in private messages, can lead to pushback and immediate putdowns from men opposed to it. I got involved in 'debates' with men about sexist behaviour and misogyny on forums so many times over the years that a few years into the 'new era' of social media I decided to curb that as much as possible. I learned from personal experience that when it comes to arguing about feminism online, you will generally come away from it feeling like a loser, no matter how right you are.

It's also mortifying to realize that someone thinks you are a bit stupid, because even though I was fairly sure that I could ignore BOD's comments about me being dim, they sparked off the less secure side of my self-esteem. Being online gives us ways to boost ourselves up, and every like and retweet can bolster our flagging opinion of ourselves, even if momentarily. Finding out through emails that at least one person thought I was an idiot crushed me a little. When I hosted an event on imposter syndrome, he wrote: 'This is so perfect for you.'

His messages seemed to highlight any flaws I thought I might have: maybe I *was* stupid, maybe I *was* a bigot but hadn't realized, maybe I *was* a 'white feminist', a term that was being used at that time to describe insular and ignorant white women who didn't speak out about other forms of oppression. Maybe, I sometimes thought, I should just *shut up and stop posting*. It was my own words, after all, that were getting me into this trouble. The bait to hook him in was me. Social media had given me a platform, but by following its rules I was making myself visible, and visibility meant that people like BOD could target me. But I wanted (and still want) to take part in social media. I didn't want to silence myself. Yet when I'd post something, I'd wonder how long it would be before he'd contact me about it.

The more BOD emailed, the more I wanted to ignore him. I filtered his emails into the trash section of my inbox, but checked every once in a while and found emails. Deleting what he had written didn't erase his words; sending his messages into cyberspace didn't make me feel any better. You can block someone, or mute them, but that only gives you an illusion of control. Not being able to see them might be a reason to worry even more, because if you can't see them, how do you know if they have escalated their behaviour? The emails were like little rocks in my inbox, thrown in there to hurt.

What I didn't know while my colleagues and I were getting emails from BOD was that other women online were too, and his behaviour was even more egregious against them. He must have spent a considerable amount of time contacting us all, based on the volume of contacts we received from him. The odd thing about the harassment was that BOD didn't interact with us on Twitter – that we knew of – but read our accounts, and paid attention to what we wrote on there. The harassment occurred in one of the many in-between places online. He was emailing us, but it's not within Google's remit to read emails and flag what could be harassment. The case involved our social media accounts, as well as sites like Goodreads, but it felt like there was no one specifically to complain to, beyond BOD himself, and we had no idea how to track him down. The only way to deal with what was happening was to go to the Gardaí.

But I asked myself if BOD needed to do something like threaten me or a loved one to have 'really' committed a crime. I worried that the bar for online harassment was a lot higher than I was able to reach, and that it wasn't fair to bring a stranger to the attention of Gardaí when I had no idea who they were or what their intentions were. When the group of us harassed by BOD connected after realizing we were all being contacted by the same man, I heard their stories and realized that the situation went beyond me. It was not just about what I experienced: it was about the collective experience. I learned that some of the other women were enduring things far, far worse than I had, and I wanted that to stop. The emails felt like they were in an odd, liminal space, not real, yet very real.

When abuse happens online, or through online channels, it suffers from this tension between being real and unreal. It can be a little – though not always – easier to explain when someone's behaviour in real life is threatening. If you have physical evidence of their actions, that's tangible in a way an email landing in your inbox isn't. I didn't know BOD, what he looked like, where he lived, what he intended. I only knew how I felt when I received his emails, which was uncomfortable, harassed, on edge, weirded out. His emails made me realize that I was being watched, and that even if I told him to stop, he would be able to contact me. He used multiple email addresses, so if I blocked one then he'd just use another one to pop up in my inbox. I'd Google the addresses and try to find him somewhere online, but he wasn't like the people he emailed: he was invisible. Because it was happening in a digital space, that real–unreal tension was threaded through the tapestry of the whole thing like a neat line of embroidery. It was hard to explain to others how palpable his actions were, and it was hard to acknowledge it to myself also.

I did, though, find a strange sense of solace in realizing that in going through this, we weren't alone. I don't even mean the fact that there were six of us involved, because that of course brought a sense of solidarity that carried us all through. I mean the fact that if I look for statistics on the online harassment of women and girls, I find numbers that show there are many, many others who have experienced something similar. The solace comes from knowing that others will understand how it feels: the sensation of being watched, the anxiety when opening a new email from an unknown person. The strangeness comes in feeling like the solace is wrong, because it's only there due to the prevalence of online harassment.

There's a Plan Ireland survey where they spoke to 14,000 girls across multiple continents, and found that 58 per cent of them experienced some form of online harassment on social media. It didn't even matter what part of the world they lived in: 63 per cent of girls in Europe; 60 per cent in Latin America; 58 per cent in the Asia-Pacific region; 54 per cent in Africa; and 52 per cent of girls in North America reported it happening.[5] The harassment could take different forms, from racist abuse to stalking. The report said that girls 'are harassed just for being girls' online. The helplessness that you can feel when you're being targeted – in any small or large way – online was highlighted by how the report said that the abuse got worse if the girls spoke up about issues they cared about. Though it was good to know we weren't alone, it was a shocker to know definitively that so many younger women were having their experiences online tainted by the behaviour of others. I thought back to my early days in chat rooms, and recognized that although I knew back then I was exploring somewhere new, I soon figured out it was actually worse than the real world in some ways. It usually wasn't long before some guys would try cybersex – they'd just jump right in with it once a private conversation was started. At that time, I was a teenager in a school uniform who was lucky enough to have had a safe experience growing up. Teen me had to figure out how to defend against sexual behaviour online too. Nothing had really changed by the time I was an adult, only the younger generations now had more ways of being targeted. According to the Plan Ireland survey, the abuse was making them leave social networks, or change how they expressed themselves.

Our harassment from BOD seemed to have been aimed at us because we didn't silence ourselves on social media. None of the six of us were public figures, but five had what you could call public-facing jobs, being writers or journalists. But I think there is more to our visibility than that: we were also women who had prominent voices on 'Irish Twitter'. Our personal profiles were helped by our professional ones, and vice versa. I wanted my voice to be heard, but having my voice heard and my work read meant a level of visibility beyond what I realized. Sending a tweet or posting to an app can feel like an intimate thing, but with thousands of followers, anything I said online could be carried on invisible threads to many, many strangers. Of course, there was part of me who was there for that very reason, who felt she had things to say that should be retweeted and commented on. I had no idea who was reading what I was writing, which was part of the appeal – who wouldn't want an imaginary audience? And yet it required some ignorance on my part, as in naivety I only wanted nice, respectful people to be reading my tweets.

And yet, I had countless examples of where people said sexist things to high-profile social media users – go into the replies or comments on anything a famous woman posts and you'll find toxic words. I'd received my own share of sexist replies. I'd seen famous women targeted too – from Hillary Clinton to Irish female politicians. There's always been something particularly egregious for me in seeing female politicians targeted, because here in Ireland we are struggling to get anywhere near gender parity in our parliament. A University of Galway study in 2020 found that online abuse of female politicians was on the increase, and I could see how social media abuse could turn women – and minorities – off being public figures, depriving us of a more balanced government.[5] Seeing a women piled on online (by men and women) doesn't make you think that the harassers hate that specific woman. You can instead feel the oily misogyny in what they're posting, and know that it could be any female they're aiming their bile at – and in turn, any minority, because sexism crosses over with so many other prejudiced viewpoints online. Woe betide if, as is the case with many people, you find yourself at the cross-section of a few of the characteristics that draw most harassment online.

After the group of us receiving emails from BOD got in touch with each other and started sharing our experiences, the scale of what had been going on emerged. We had run out of options – BOD was not listening to our requests for him to stop contacting us, and still the emails continued. On the day we first met at the Garda headquarters on Harcourt Street, part of me felt we might be told there was nothing that could be done.

What happened showed me the lengths to which victims have to go to achieve justice – but also that the idea of 'justice' for online harassment is more knotty than people might want to acknowledge.

The Gardaí asked us to gather together all of the contacts we had received. So I learned that to keep myself safe I needed to have evidence of abuse, which meant seeing the abuse happen. In order to put a stop to it, I needed to witness it. In the end, our keeping his emails for years was how the Gardaí figured out who BOD was. An email address he used to contact me was linked to a comment he made online. It turned out that while I was worried about all the breadcrumbs I'd dropped over the decades on the internet, it was the digital detritus he'd left behind him that helped move the case forward.

Feeling Watched

The BOD harassment was both an individual and group experience. Each of us involved in the case was affected in a different way, and each of us was treated differently by BOD, even though the modus operandi was similar. We were all part of Irish Twitter, but differed in terms of our careers and what we used the site for. As much as I write about my experience, I can't speak for any of the others. But talking to two of the other women involved showed me the extent to which what happened had not only affected them at the time, but led to them changing how they behaved online. As I reflected on what they told me, I saw how I too had been changed by what I experienced, and I wondered about my reticence at times to even acknowledge that I had been harassed.

When I speak to Sarah Maria Griffin, a Dublin author who was first contacted by BOD in 2010, I'm struck by how deeply the harassment cut into her life, carving out parts of the inherent trust she had in people online. It was Griffin who started unpicking the harassment, and who reached out to a few of us who had been contacted by BOD. As we talk about what went on and how it affected us, her black and white cat Mo, who has a wildly expressive face, wanders around the table. When I listen back to the recording, I can hear an occasional 'mew' from him punctuating our conversation, as though he was offering emotional support.

Griffin, who has the gift of an author's turn of phrase in everyday conversation, collected information on BOD for years. But by the time another of the women involved in the subsequent case, Kate McEvoy, contacted her she was jaded and beaten down by what had been happening. Sometimes we need someone outside of us to make us recognize the depth of an experience, and it was McEvoy who helped Griffin realize that something needed to be done about the emails. As a result, the pair have bonded. McEvoy gave Griffin the courage and the conviction to take the case to the Gardaí, she tells me. 'She was so clear that it was unacceptable,' she explains.

By then, the messages had become a dull background noise in Griffin's life, just as they had to an extent in mine. They began after she was interviewed on the RTÉ Radio One arts show *Arena* about 'Scarleh Fer Yer Ma Fer Havin' Ye', an event she'd set up with a college friend, where people would read out their old diary entries and mortify themselves in front of an audience. She was in her very early twenties then, doing a master's degree in creative writing and trying to figure out what direction she was going in. In a word, she was trying. 'BOD would always manage to remind me that it was obvious that I was *trying*, and that trying is somehow shameful,' she says of the emails. A part of his approach worked on her. It made her feel bad for trying – made her think that her journey to writing and a creative life looked in some way desperate. (Since it all happened, she has published several novels and has a blossoming career as an author.) Intentionally or not, he had honed in on a way to make her feel bad about doing what she wanted to do.

Things spread beyond Griffin as an individual. For a while, it felt like anyone she communicated with on Twitter would subsequently get a message from BOD, as though he was a third, invisible participant in their conversation. Sometimes he would go quiet for patches, but then his behaviour would change. Her boyfriend (now husband) started to get emails from BOD in 2016. Things moved up another level when BOD contacted book bloggers pretending to be Griffin. He set up email addresses pretending to be her. He also compiled negative Goodreads (a book review site) reviews of her books and sent them around to editors. She wouldn't know until they reached out to her. 'It was adding insult to injury,' she explained to me. Not only was it humiliating, it could also be professionally damaging. 'And when you're starting out, you don't have anyone to help you. You don't have anyone to protect you,' she says. Any time she had a 'win' in any public capacity, BOD would be there in her inbox to bring her back down to earth.

She wanted to find out who this person emailing her was. With her 'little Nancy Drew hat on', she started gathering information about the email addresses he was using. During this period, Griffin and her boyfriend moved to San Francisco, and during one moment of sleuthing she discovered that the IP address for some of BOD's emails was in that very city. It turned out to be an email deferral service, but briefly she was worried he had journeyed across the Atlantic too. In the absence of information, whatever you fear most can be possible.

In the summer of 2017, Kate McEvoy, a senior producer from Dublin, also started getting emails from BOD. Unlike the rest of us, she didn't have a job that required her to have a public profile. But by dint of being a woman active on Irish Twitter, she'd drawn his attention. Like the rest of the six, McEvoy is a feminist who shares her opinions online. A film and rugby nut, McEvoy posts passionate tweets about both topics, and it's chilling to think all it takes is just that – tweeting about what you like – to draw the attention of someone who wants to tell you they dislike you. We'd come across each other on Irish Twitter, but never met until that first day outside the Garda station to report the emails.

In the months running up to our chat, social media had become a forum for a lot of discussions about women's safety in Ireland, following high-profile incidents such as the deaths of Ashling Murphy and Urantsetseg Tserendorj in Offaly and Dublin respectively. The discussions that occurred on social media after these and other women were killed were in part triggered by the #MeToo movement. Women in Ireland saw how MeToo could be used to make public the vast spectrum of violence against women, and how they could use sites like Twitter to organize rallies, to express their grief, to rail against a society where they felt unprotected based on their gender. MeToo gave people a way to use their voice online to speak up and to try to force others to change. If nothing else, even just having a space to speak out on your own terms is powerful. There is power in seeing hundreds of tweets expressing anger about the same thing. It shows you're not alone, which is hugely meaningful when we're used to these conversations happening in private, and that privacy being rooted in shame. Seeing all of this encouraged McEvoy to speak out about her own experience, particularly as she had – away from the BOD case – experienced violence from a stranger offline herself.

McEvoy was the last one of the six of us to start getting the emails. The messages tended to reference her Twitter account, so after getting three emails from BOD in one day she sent a tweet asking whoever was sending them to stop. I'd been in a similar situation, posting a tweet in an attempt to send a message to BOD, knowing he would most likely see it. It felt a little like begging, and made me feel grubby. After she tweeted about it, McEvoy was messaged by people who asked for more details, and subsequently they told her that they'd also got similar messages. As he had done with Griffin, BOD moved beyond emailing her – he started emailing her workplace and some friends, pretending to be her. She didn't know until they asked about the messages from 'her'. She also didn't know how many emails were sent under her name, or what was in them, or how many people had been fooled by the imposter. 'Anyone who says, "oh, it's just online", I don't think that boundary really exists,' McEvoy tells me of BOD's behaviour. 'It very obviously didn't exist for us.'

Meanwhile, Griffin and her husband created a master document of all the emails and contacts from BOD. She'd type the contents of the emails into Google, to see if she could find the same sentences elsewhere (comments were left on my old music blog with a similar wording to the emails I got from BOD). Every so often she would tweet to ask if people had got any weird emails from anyone pretending to be her. She heard back from others who had experienced similar behaviour, and eventually was put in touch with the Garda National Cyber Crime Bureau. The Garda she contacted in the bureau suggested there might be a case, and to collate contacts and emails. But it wasn't until a year later that McEvoy got in touch with Griffin, and they decided to speak to the Gardaí officially, bringing in the rest of us. 'In a way, the time can seem very short. But that's whole years of your life,' says Griffin. Compiling emails, going to the Gardaí – no one wants to have all this in the back of your mind for years.

The email that went around to the group of us from McEvoy and Griffin was a galvanizing message. Griffin had noticed that BOD's approach towards every individual was somewhat personalized. She found that daunting, but also found it 'deeply comforting' to know she wasn't alone. What strikes me when I'm talking to Griffin about her experience is how she felt it was humiliating. Even now, she doesn't bring the case up socially a lot. 'I feel like it makes me look like there's something wrong with me' is the reason why.

I know exactly what she means, I tell her, 'I feel like I look like I'm causing a fuss about something I shouldn't be causing a fuss about.'

'Or there's something so profoundly wrong with me that I attract these people,' she replies. 'That I made him do it.'

This is something that people who haven't been harassed online might not understand – how deep the emotions around it go. How much it can tap into any self-consciousness you have, any niggling feelings about your worth. If a stranger is persistently emailing you to tell you what an unworthy and flawed person you are, and they ignore you when you tell them to stop, that can do a number on your self-esteem. Not to mention the frustration and powerlessness of not being listened to. When you get emails telling you to shut up when all you've been doing is tweeting about random parts of your life or your opinion on something, it makes you second-guess everything you post. Which post is the one that will draw someone on you? And when online harassment isn't a crime that you typically see being dealt with, or even talked about as something that *can* be dealt with, it's easy to double down on the feelings of low self-worth.

Griffin is a novelist whose work crosses into the worlds of sci-fi and magic realism, with themes of dystopia and body horror, and so her tweets, Instagram posts and TikTok videos don't tend to be aimed at fitting in with online trends. Her tweets – like one about awkwardly posed mannequins in a clothing store – often go viral, racking up hundreds of thousands of likes and retweets. Her TikToks have a sense of the absurd and existential about them, but can be deeply moving. She tells me that since the harassment case she has changed how she posts online. 'I post nothing about myself. I used to be a bit more human,' she says. 'It's funny because people respond very well to the nothing.' Even though she tweets about elements of her life – like her love of visiting supermarkets on holidays, and the unusual snacks she picks up – she says her approach is deeply impersonal, because she doesn't feel safe, and feels like any day she could go through harassment again. Depersonalizing her internet persona helps create a safety barrier against that happening.

But Griffin loves the internet. She doesn't just know her way around its cultures and corners, she sees the wonder in it. 'This is the Hitchhiker's Guide to the Galaxy!' she says at one point to me, holding up her phone like it's a precious gem. By this she means it's full of possibility: tap a button and you can get a lift or a flight to wherever you want, or have food arrive on your doorstep. 'It's so weird and fascinating. What a utopia – what we could have done. It's science fiction made real,' she says. 'The second we stop treating it as a marvel, we're fucked.' She pauses. 'I do love the internet. But I'm also a person outside of it.' She doesn't want to become a martyr, to tolerate the abuse so it becomes part of her personality online. She has to find her own way to deal with it.

It put a dent in Griffin to know that while she was swimming in the warm waters of the internet that she loved, someone was hiding in the metaphorical bushes watching her. She frequently refers to her behaviour online now as 'pottering along'. She'd like to participate in the internet more humanely, she says, because she believes it can be a place for real magic. 'If you go in with good intention, and soundness, and light humour, there's a lot of joy to be had in an otherwise very terrible place,' she says.

There are quirky little wormholes online where you can find others who collect baked bean memes, or weird photographs of Furbys, or share dashcam videos. There are pockets of the internet full of strange joy, and pockets full of strangeness. Griffin doesn't have it in her to log off forever. She loves her job, which entails having an online presence. But for Griffin and McEvoy, the dents the harassment created in their online behaviour can't be manipulated back.

You can love the internet, but it doesn't have to love you back. The internet wasn't created as a place of infinite support and positivity, or even somewhere where you should go to find people who like you. It was created as a place for discussion, for discovery, for connection beyond the places we're offered in this sometimes humdrum 'real life' of ours. The contrast between the internet that I chose to visit in the Nineties and the internet that's enmeshed with my life in 2023 is huge, but back in the Nineties I didn't have to visit it every day for work; I didn't depend on it for the latest news, or to let my friends know how my life was going, or to find out the latest pop culture obsession, or just to prove that I existed. It was enough to exist as you were, in those days before the internet took over, when long phone calls and hanging around coffee shops were how I proved who I was and learned what I was interested in. For many of us, certainly for me and most of my peers, we now have no choice but to maintain a presence online, but not being loved back can feel like a slap in the face. Or more like a pie in the face, because the joke is on us – we've become dependent on somewhere we know we could encounter trolling and abuse at any turn.

Some days, a probing comment on Instagram, or an offhand TikTok comment, can be ignored if you're feeling emotionally secure. But on those days when you're wobbly, where you might actually turn to the infinite scroll of your beloved social media apps to distract and soothe your fizzing brain, a nasty comment can feel like a punch. How to try and balance these competing impulses, of being online and yet being offline, and needing to be both at the same time, is a modern-day riddle.

It's a constant push and pull, of trying to feel in control of what you do and where you go online, without removing yourself from it totally. And if what you experience goes beyond light trolling or negativity, the question of what to do next makes the situation feel even worse. Blocking someone on Twitter or unfriending someone on Facebook doesn't feel like putting an end to the behaviour – it just means you can't see what they're saying.

In McEvoy's case, it was hard not to take the insults in the BOD emails personally. They might sound fairly mild to read, but receiving them in a torrent was disturbing. 'You find yourself wondering, *am* I a terrible racist, shiny white feminist? And then you're like, wait – *what*? There were times where it was overwhelming,' she says. 'Especially when he started being obsessed with where I lived.' BOD let her know at one point that he knew the area she lived in, after she had featured in an article online that mentioned the locality where she had bought a house. He messaged her telling her it was good she was alone, and that he'd be there soon – and they'd 'see how polite she was then'. After she got that message from him, she went to her parents' house 'and cried, and cried, and cried'. She felt extremely vulnerable. He didn't turn up at her house, but just the thought of it was horrifying.

BOD knew a lot about us, but there was a void of information about him, which made any threats – empty or not – feel very real. McEvoy diverted his emails to one folder in her inbox, so she could choose when and whether to look at them. Her social accounts were made private while the harassment was going on. But she still resisted posting some things, like a Christmas wreath she'd been gifted, for fear it would identify her house. Similarly, when Griffin was doing a residency in Dún Laoghaire, she had to tweet about the events she was hosting as part of her job. She feared that BOD might turn up at one of them. Towards the end, BOD's messages made her and her husband feel like things were closing in on them. She knew from her years online that harassment campaigns don't begin and end with one person, and can become teams of individuals. She didn't know if her details were somewhere like the anonymous troll site 4Chan, or if it was many people bombarding her. Literally anything could be possible.

We all take steps in the real world every day to stay safe. I wear a seatbelt. I look both ways before I cross the road. Online, I take steps towards safety too, but it's hard to keep yourself safe on the internet. You can do the practical things like not give out personal information, or not use your own name, though ironically that might make you look like a troll. Every day across the apps and sites I use I see photos of strangers' homes, children, pets; details about their jobs, holidays, and health conditions. I've recognized countless people just from what they posted online – and I've had people recognize me because of the photos I've put up. The line of safety is different for every individual. You might say that to be fully safe online, you have to stay offline – but a video or photo of you can be shared online regardless. You can be discussed online, your name can be used without you knowing.

'I think it gets into victim blaming, the idea of what counts as "risky" online behaviour,' cautions McEvoy. To blame someone for being harassed when all they did is join a popular social network and do what's asked of them is to dive into some very murky waters. And to opt out of social media would be opting out of a massive part of your social and professional life for many people, McEvoy points out. If people feel like being online doesn't serve them, that's a different thing. 'But not being driven off it,' she says. 'We're having a discussion in Ireland at the moment around acceptable behaviour towards women. That applies online as well.' It's not enough just to say 'remove yourself from the internet' if you could be a target. That's a lot of people who would be forced offline. That's a lot of voices silenced, and only being silenced because of the actions of someone else.

You can, of course, choose to leave the internet of your own volition. In her 2019 book *How to Do Nothing*, the writer and artist Jenny Odell sets out a tantalizing idea of not taking part in the 'attention economy' online, which she argues is deeply connected to a greater capitalist message.[1] Social media apps and sites are part of this attention economy, using our precious attention to track our behaviour and then sell the data on to advertisers. As users, we don't always analyse how – if at all – we benefit from them doing this. That's because we get something from these sites, and we get it 'for free'. We can feel like we're the ones benefiting overall, but social media will never stop sucking up the time you offer to give it. It will always provide new, entertaining ways for you to give up hours of your life to it.

I loved *How To Do Nothing*, the punchy way that Odell doesn't advocate switching off from life online, but instead presents a vision of a world where we actively choose when to go online, and where when we're not online we interact in a better, deeper way with the world around us. We do things like watching birds; we learn about the history of the places we live and spend time in. We keep our chins up and our eyes open. It's a grounding perspective. I read the introduction to her book while on the Luas, as it slid through Dublin city centre. It felt like reading a ground-breaking, life-changing manifesto. My body felt full of possibility and promise. But it wasn't long before I was rooting in my bag for my phone. Still, I felt hopeful because I share her belief that life is better, and more enriched, if we pay more attention to the natural world. A blade of grass or a bubbling stream is a nourishing thing to witness. I share, too, her cynicism about us being encouraged to live a more online life for the benefit of others. But people choosing to step away from having a voice on social media is entirely different from being silenced because of the treatment you get online.

Part of the reason why people return to the internet again and again and again, ad infinitum, is the sense of community. When you find 'your people' online, that can be powerful and validating. That's especially the case if you don't have a community offline, or if, like in 2020, you literally can't leave the house due to an unforeseen global pandemic. Kate McEvoy says she felt the massive sense of community online during times like Covid: the friendship that's offered when you are lonely, or when you bond with people over watching *Derry Girls* or nurturing house plants.

As it has for me, social media has informed McEvoy's feminism and broadened her understanding of other people's experiences. This in turn has made her think about the fact there were six white women involved in our case. 'Did that help us navigate the system better? Did that make us more sympathetic? Probably,' she concludes. She believes that while we must be aware of that, it doesn't mean that what happened was acceptable. But it's something we can't ignore. In the greater discussion around how online harassment is dealt with, there are factors to consider beyond the harassment itself, and whether the victim or victims have the ability to bring the case to the Gardaí, and through the court system. As we know from the experiences of people like Aoife Martin, some of the most vulnerable people in society do not feel like they will be listened to if they try to speak to the Gardaí about abuse online. Even if that is not always the case, there are concrete reasons behind their fear.

When it came to BOD, we felt bolstered by having a group of people to approach the Gardaí with. It meant that it wasn't just one person asking for help. 'I can't imagine rocking into my local Garda station and saying, "someone's sending me mean emails"', says McEvoy. Being part of a group gave a greater sense of validity to what had happened, even though it would have been just as valid if it was us alone. But I've spoken to people who approached Gardaí in stations about harmful behaviour and online harassment and were told it was a 'civil matter' (meaning the Gardaí couldn't deal with it), or to contact the social media sites, which didn't bring any resolution.

I ask an ex-Garda source about this, and they tell me they're concerned about it too, and about resourcing for the area. Because there's a bind here: if the harassment cases aren't reported, they might as well not exist as far as the people who are allocating the resources are concerned, the source tells me. So if people aren't able to report their case to their local Gardaí, it's not possible for them to build up a picture of how widespread online harassment is, and the resources subsequently aren't allocated at the scale needed. There's a dependence on people reporting incidents, but there's also the need for training so the individual Gardaí know the law.

If people are continually turned away, then this can make online harassment or bullying look like far less of a problem than it is.

But of course, they might only be approaching the Gardaí because the sites themselves haven't done anything to stop the behaviour, or, like us, they are trapped in an in-between space where no one website can be deemed responsible. In our case, the main person responsible for what was going on was BOD, and the only way we could really stop his behaviour was to get the Gardaí involved, because our appeals to him personally had not worked.

BOD was described in court as being a loner who hadn't left the house in seventeen years. The image of a single white male who spends his time trolling online in his bedroom has become an internet cliché, which made it even stranger when it played out in our case. But it showed that clichés are, of course, grounded in truth. BOD's lawyers told the court that he had depression and social anxiety. He spent his time at home, often on his computer, and this was how he was able to spend the time reading our Twitter pages and contacting us and people connected to us. For me, beyond the clichés, this showed the need for mental health supports for people, and the potential consequences when some individuals don't get that support. It also showed how easy it is to target someone when you've set your mind to it. I didn't know if he realized what he was doing felt very real to us; that we were not caricatures, we were people.

I also didn't know his personal situation beyond what I heard in court, but I felt empathy towards him if he had suffered with his mental health. At the same time, as McEvoy (who has similar concerns about the availability of mental health supports) says, 'Mental health is a reason, it's not an excuse, and he still made conscious choices to do what he did. And again, the internet enabled those choices.' The internet didn't cause him to behave that way, but it did give scope, scale, and means, as she puts it. Griffin wrestled with all of this too. 'A lot of people are mentally ill, and a lot of people have depression, and a lot of people are at a deep social disadvantage, and don't do that,' she says of the harassment. Just as BOD

179

didn't know what went on in our lives beyond what he saw online, or how deep his insults could cut, we couldn't imagine the circumstances of his life. All we could see were his actions towards us, and the impact they had. I didn't want to cast him in the role of a 'bad' person who 'had' to go to jail. I'd rather have seen him get the support he needed, and that he stopped the harassment. But the court system was the only route we could take – and even at that, Coco's Law wasn't in place at the time, so we had to take the case under the existing harassment legislation.

On a broader level, the internet lets us connect with many varied and niche communities, some of which can be troubling and dangerous. A few years ago I read the book *Men Who Hate Women*, by the British author Laura Bates, which gave me a pretty frightening insight into aggressive misogynistic spaces online, and the reasons why some men join them. Bates had herself been the victim of online harassment, after she launched Everyday Sexism, a project where women could share their experiences of sexism. First, people shared their examples on Twitter, and then on a website; Bates wrote a book about it too. Bates wanted to catalogue all of these instances online because if they were gathered together, she knew people couldn't say that sexism doesn't exist. But she suffered because she did this, receiving rape and murder threats, which spiked after she wrote *Men Who Hate Women*.[2] She spent two years researching the book, using the name 'Alex' while visiting the darkest recesses of misogynistic spaces online. In raising awareness about harassment online, she became an example of what she was writing about.

While there's no suggestion BOD was involved with any such groups, away from our case Bates's book tells you all you want – or don't want – to know about why women are targeted by certain men online. I knew these groups existed. But Bates describes a 'manosphere' populated by pick-up artists, 'men going their own way', incels (involuntary celibates who blame women for their arid sex lives), and men's rights activists, all groups who believe that a feminist conspiracy has dumped males at the bottom of the societal food chain. Some of them worship men like Elliot Rodger, an incel who killed six people in 2014. He wrote a 141-page document detailing his life story and how he came to believe women are evil and manipulative, which I find in a quick Google search. To men like Rodger and his ilk, a woman like me – like any of the six of us – is a symbol of the thumb they feel is being pressed down on them. Bates's book shows that there are lone people harassing others online, but there are also vast networks of men connecting due to their hatred of women.

Even though in the BOD case it was one man contacting a group of women, Bates's book showed that our case was linked to wider societal problems around the treatment of women. Online misogyny doesn't just happen in a vacuum. 'I think if we divorce online harassment from a societal issue, then that's not solving the problem – that's finding something else to blame,' says McEvoy. 'It's symptomatic of attitudes that exist in the real world. And also, the internet *is* the real world. It's not like we enter some sort of virtual simulation.' I didn't know what spurred BOD on, and I would never know, but I wondered about any thoughts he might have had about feeling less than us women who had a profile online. What we had was normal to us – and it certainly wasn't uncomplicated – but to an outsider who felt sapped of power, we were a symbol of all they didn't have.

To the misogynists who populate the spheres in Bates's book, we would be more than that – our gender would mark us out as worthy of silencing, because of the threat they see us as representing against the power they hold in society. As gender balance has started to right itself, and as people are beginning more and more to explode the idea of a gender binary at all, the gender that held most of the power is having to cede its role in society. Some do that willingly; others use the internet to fight back against it in the most awful of ways.

Being in court for the case, and taking to the stand to describe my experience, was strange. I didn't relish seeing BOD sitting in handcuffs with Gardaí on either side of him in the courtroom, or describing in front of him how his behaviour had made me feel. I didn't like knowing that this appeared to be the only way to make someone stop harassing people online, that there was not yet a middle ground between *nothing* and *jail*. In other online disputes, like domain disputes, people can turn to an arbitration process for resolution, rather than having to go to the High Court. There must surely be ways of solving online harassment that don't have to involve going to court, both in terms of the impact on the alleged victim and the alleged offender.

In the end, the judge granted an order which meant BOD could not contact any of the six of us women again for the rest of his life. This was all that we wanted. However, he also sentenced him to five years in prison, with two years suspended. Judge Martin Nolan said during the sentencing that 'undoubtedly the internet has wonderful advantages', but our case showed 'the dark side which allows a man sitting in his house to inflict huge amounts of trauma on six women'. As a group, we released a statement after the verdict, in which we said:

> *We hope this case shows other men and women in this situation that what they say will be taken seriously if they come forward, and that online harassment is harassment and will be treated as such.*

We also said we hoped BOD received the help and rehabilitation he needs.

In court, he apologized for his behaviour. He was released after serving his sentence in late 2021. The six of us women have all moved on, but for some it's left a mark in terms of our relationships with the internet. We can't hold a presumption of being safe online, whether we let what happened affect how we behave or not. But something Griffin says about this stuck with me: 'It becomes a colour in the marble of your life that you don't want there. It's not the story of my life, mercifully.'

TRUTH AND LIES ONLINE

They changed the definition of what a 'pandemic' is. They changed
the definition of what a 'vaccination' is. I, guess, they must have
changed the definition of what 'safe' is, because something
they regard as 'safe' is killing and injuring people.

*

A completely bogus claim about Boris Johnson
with 10,000 retweets and 48,000 likes.

*

You won't see the MSM reporting this!!

*

Don Jr. didn't tweet to urge Trump supporters not to walk
on the lawn at Mar-a'Lago. It's a fake and created
by a satirical Twitter account.

Fool Me Once

One of the appealing things about living a life online is how I get to carve out a tunnel in it just for me, where I go where I want and explore whatever it is I want to explore. If I was just slightly different – if my tastes were a bit more esoteric, or baroque, or darker, or dirtier – that other version of me could tunnel into a radically different version of the internet. I picture these tunnels not like those dug underground by sharp-nailed animals, but like the floaty, gaseous portals in the film *Donnie Darko*, bright and shimmering. My life online could be a little seedier, or a little grittier, or it could be lighter, less hellscapeish. I could spend time mooning over images of silky-haired popstars if I wanted to, or I could become obsessed with a right-leaning conservative who posts three-hour-long podcasts on YouTube (perish the thought). Just a tiny shift in personality or curiosity can make your internet experience a little more unusual.

Sometimes I think maybe I'm too much of a creature of habit online, especially when I stumble across a particular wormhole, an obsession shared by many people but which is something I've never thought about or noticed before. It reminds me that my own small worldview is just that: my own small worldview. As much as I read and watch and absorb and discuss, I am limited by my own tastes and inclinations, as well as hours of the day. I barely have enough time to consume what I want to consume as it is. Choosing a lane and staying in it helps me cling to an illusion of climbing over that content hill. But for all of its individuality, social media is also a communal thing – it's rare the person who goes online assuming they won't collide with someone else. We sniff each other out, we feel the presence of someone just as they round a digital corner. The energy of other people is imprinted everywhere online, on every site we visit, on every line we read. And that means we rub up against other people's opinions and viewpoints too, even within our own 'special' spaces, and sometimes our personally curated online worlds end up being intruded on by – or intruding on – other people's.

I felt like I knew the measure of the internet I was part of – able to assess and balance its good and bad sides – until the pandemic, when it was proved that online conspiracy theories and flagrant spreading of misinformation were not strange or unusual things. To an increasing number of people, they had become acceptable and important means of connection. I saw on some websites, posts, and tweets that the truth I held as infallible was a lie to someone else, and that the distrust in those who govern the structures that hold society together – for ill or for good – could be heightened to a literally unbelievable level. I was like an alien landing on a new planet, one where behaviours I thought were unusual were now normal. And as I watched it all unfold, I found the vista to be odd, garish, and compelling.

It was an interesting period too because it wasn't just the usual social media sites that were involved. What played an initial role in this new moment was WhatsApp. It was a messaging app that I'd been using to chat with friends on, solo or in groups, and which felt like a more sophisticated and personalized version of the text messages we'd been swapping for years. In my world, nothing unusual happened on WhatsApp. I shared videos and funny posts with friends, poked fun at strangers saying ridiculous things on websites, made plans, sent loving messages.

WhatsApp is owned by Meta, because nothing popular in the social space online seems to remain Facebook-free for long. It was acquired for $19 billion in 2014, after Facebook's trawl through the latest data on user behaviour, via a VPN called Onavo, showed that WhatsApp was becoming a juggernaut heading straight for Facebook HQ.[1] Facebook bought Onavo. Then it bought WhatsApp, as reported by Buzzfeed News in December 2018. No matter what Meta does, WhatsApp, with its bright green branding, remains far more popular in some countries than Facebook Messenger, Meta's messaging app. In India, among the very top countries when it comes to WhatsApp use, the government even partnered with Meta to make official documents available through it.[2][3]

But India was also where WhatsApp was used to incite people to take part in lynch mobs in 2018, which led to the deaths of innocent people rumoured to be involved in child kidnappings. The Indian government put pressure on Facebook to do something after three people were killed by mobs. WhatsApp wasn't the cause of these killings, but it gave a platform for rumours to spread, and the fact you could 'forward' messages on and on and on – with no sign of where they originally came from, because of the app's built-in encryption – meant that lies and rumours could crawl into people's hands incredibly easily. Here in Ireland, we probably smugly presumed we were past any stage of WhatsApp manipulation; that in a smaller country these sorts of mobs couldn't take off, that they were more for the social media sites than messaging apps. By 2020, we were proved wrong.

Part of the issues stemmed from one of the main things that makes WhatsApp popular. Unlike other forms of social media, the app is very much a closed loop for users, as the messages are end-to-end encrypted. If messages are flagged to WhatsApp as being abusive, then the last five messages sent by the reported person (or group) can be viewed – otherwise, they're unseen. If a person forwards you a message on the app, it's next to impossible for you to discover the true source of it or how many times it's been forwarded. This in turn makes it impossible to know the message's true impact. The encryption and privacy makes it a good place to share personal and private things, but it also makes it a great space for misinformation to sprout and grow, and given how easy it is to take info from WhatsApp to more public social channels, the misinformation can wind its way onto Facebook, Twitter, YouTube et al. quickly and easily, fed by the fertile soils of curiosity, fear, and conspiracy. That all came to a head during the pandemic.

The first mention of 'coronavirus' in my WhatsApp messages is a jokey one I sent to friends at the end of January 2020. 'Hey! Gonna skip the cinema cos I'm feeling shite – better not be the coronavirus,' I wrote, adding an emoji rolling its eyes and sticking its tongue out. Until early March of that year, most of the messages I traded with friends about coronavirus were about what we were reading online, or how we were fatigued about reading about coronavirus online. But alongside those were the messages, typically sent to WhatsApp groups I was a member of, that had been '*Forwarded many times*', as a little italic line warned at the beginning. They always claimed to hold important information, and often kicked off with an encouraging opening salvo, like 'Useful message I received from a friend', which wasn't written by the actual person sending the message, but was put there to fool you into thinking that was the case. The next line was sometimes an official-sounding quote, such as, 'Recommended by the Stanford hospital board . . .' followed by a long message about how to check for the virus using tips from nameless 'Taiwan experts' and 'Japanese doctors'.

After so long in the online journalism world, I've an inbuilt cynicism about messages like this. I've seen too many doctored photos, videos and screengrabs to trust a lot of what I see online, which is quite annoying. Who wants to be the pedant when your pals are sharing a forwarded message that claims to help people? This was heightened during Covid, when people I'd never normally see sharing viral messages were all of a sudden sharing them. Before (and during) the pandemic was a misinformation wave focused on false claims about 5G, but I knew none of my friends would have shared something about that. So it was immediately obvious this latest wave was moving more into the mainstream. At first, I wanted to ask if they had done this by mistake. But after my initially bristly reaction, I could see why it was happening: people didn't know what the truth was. They were scared. We all were living in a new reality.

*

In the newsroom, we had been seeing reports on the wires about a new SARS-like virus in China in late 2019, but at that stage it didn't seem to warrant much coverage. By January, that would change. In an ironic way, the spread of these viral messages helped us report on what would come to be known as Covid-19 because it showed exactly what most concerned people. We knew by the popularity level of specific messages what people were really worried about: how they could contract the virus, what to do when they had it, who was most at risk, if there would be a lockdown, and what the impact of lockdown would be. There can be some truths in these sorts of misinformation-led messages, because they often come from exploiting a genuine fear that people have.

Thinking back on the messages, I can see exactly why they hooked people in. One particularly eerie video I recall being shared (another strange feature of all of this is how unless things were reported on or screengrabbed they've disappeared into the digital ether) was of a person entering a building on Pearse Street in Dublin's city centre. It was daytime. There were no signs on the building describing what it was, but the accompanying message claimed it was a hotel. The person was wearing a white, full-body protective outfit, what we'd come to call personal protective equipment (PPE), and which was recommended to be worn in cases of suspected Covid-19. An ambulance, its neon yellow shell glowing like a warning, was parked nearby. The message claimed that there was a case of coronavirus in the building, the subtext being that this was why an anonymous figure was going in, dressed head to foot in protective white plastic.[4]

This video no doubt contained elements of truth: if there was a suspicion of a Covid-19 case in a hotel, you could presume that medical staff would be told to wear PPE. But these were the early days of the pandemic, and the image looked stark, not in any way comforting. It forced you to imagine the occupants of the building, locked away in their rooms as the virus particles floated in the air, invisible. The video didn't so much hum with ambient anxiety as slam the reality of coronavirus fear in your face. To see it shared in your WhatsApp account, unprompted, was to be left a little shaken. But it emerged that this video falsely claimed to show a hotel in Dublin being locked down. The building wasn't even a hotel. And yet, all of the parts that could be true were enough to encourage sending it on.

Often the missives sent on WhatsApp felt like old-school chain letters containing a not-so-subtle pressure to pass them on or else. Sometimes they were audio messages – the voice of a stranger telling you something urgent but secret. There was a sense of prophecy about the viral messages in the early months. They sometimes warned about lockdowns to come, and it turned out that they were right. Lockdowns did come, only later than those messages warned. I could understand why people sent some of the messages on, when many claimed to come from members of the Defence Forces, Gardaí, or relations of workers in those sectors. They were presented as being sent by real people with real links to those in power, but far enough away that they didn't hold power themselves and so were trustworthy. They had a sheen of authenticity. Maybe a Garda or soldier *had* decided to break ranks and share information to make sure people were fully informed. Why not trust a whistleblower, someone who is kicking back against the official line? The first three months of the year were full of questions with few answers.

Anything new could spike fear. Public concern, for example, reached a new height after the first confirmed case of Covid-19 turned out to be a young schoolboy who had returned from a trip to Italy. Parents wanted to know what was to happen next, and how safe their children were in school. But at that stage, nothing was certain. It made some sort of sense to imagine that those on the inside were making plans that the ordinary citizens didn't know about, given the frustration some people were feeling about what was going on. There could be a sense of comfort in knowing that members of those powerful groups, further down the ladder, were willing to speak out so that people out of the loop didn't feel lost and confused. But those messages could also sow more confusion.

Even members of government were getting them – the then Health Minister Simon Harris told *Today with Sean O'Rourke* on RTÉ Radio 1 in

February 2020: 'I get texts on a regular basis saying "X hospital is in lockdown. The coronavirus is here." Not true.' A message in early March claimed that the Health Service Executive (HSE) was suggesting 'stocking up for 3–4 weeks at least. Groceries/medicine, etc', and that the government was planning to deploy the army for a lockdown. The tone of the message was curious. It even said, 'I don't want create [sic] hysteria or drama for you' but that things were 'worse than the news is making out'. Another pre-lockdown message read: 'Just got from Guarda [sic] friend. Hotel in Dublin just gone on lockdown. Cases in Mater, Vincent's, Beaumont . . . current media blackout . . . gonna break soon . . . From my brother'. The mention of a 'media blackout' in many of the messages intrigued me. The only times in my reporting career that I've experienced genuine media blackouts are during incidents like hostage situations or where a person is armed and the Gardaí are trying to engage with them. They're unusual but do happen, and the Gardaí even call them 'media blackouts' in their press releases. I'm not naive enough to think that reporters know everything that goes on politically, but I honestly didn't believe there was any sort of blackout in action over the spread of Covid-19.

At the same time, I knew that the government wouldn't be releasing the minutes of its undoubtedly frantic and urgent meetings to the public. I knew from reporting experience that there would likely be a small gap between, for example, the first coronavirus case being discovered and the official word coming out. In the end, the media were told about all of these things swiftly, and there were nightly briefings on the Covid-19 numbers. But early on, there was major fear that the government knew a lot that people didn't. In *Pandemonium*, a book about the pandemic in Ireland by political journalists Hugh O'Connell and Jack Horgan-Jones, I read about what I couldn't be privy to at the time – how the then Taoiseach, Leo Varadkar, and his colleagues were trying to balance what their public health experts were telling them with the emails and texts arriving from concerned experts in other areas.[5] Putting further pressure on were the daily news reports on Northern Italy's overwhelming experience with Covid-19 – replete with chilling camera pans across lines of hospital beds where all the patients were on ventilators – and the fears that Ireland could follow suit.

Some of the most worrying messages said that people should stockpile baby food, because soon it wouldn't be possible to leave the house. Those were the ones that made me the most angry, because they manipulated parents and caregivers into believing that children, already so vulnerable, were at risk from food shortages. How dare they? I thought. How dare they manipulate people like that? And yet I didn't know, really, how unfounded the rumours were, or how useful the advice was. I hadn't lived through a pandemic, the last one occurring six decades before I was born. But I knew from extreme weather events in recent years that the first things to go from shop shelves in Ireland were the essentials: the squashy loaves of bread, the plastic-wrapped packets of toilet paper with gurning animals on them. During those events, we also saw how social media posts created and reflected panic.

Twitter and Facebook posts in February 2018 during the Beast from the East and Storm Emma about empty shelves led more shoppers to stock up out of fear of future empty shelves, creating extra pressure on supplies. One tweet from a reporter said that a bright yellow Brennan's Bread van – picture attached – had received a Garda escort into Ballyfermot.[6] Bread suppliers told the media that they had increased production after the first warnings about the storms. A year later, Storm Freya hit and again we saw those gleaming, empty shelves being photographed and shared, their emptiness a sign of danger.

Behind each viral message, no matter how untrue it was, was a hint that this sharing of information was a way for people to hold onto control, to wrest back some power from the government. Ireland had never been a country with a huge amount of misinformation floating around in very public spaces. We'd read the stories from abroad, about the fake news farms in North Macedonia, the senseless deaths in Myanmar encouraged by Facebook posts, the hate speech in India, the 2016 US election and how it played out online. We knew that messaging apps like WhatsApp, as well as Facebook itself, could be used by bad actors as forums to spread mistruths and whip up hysteria. But what the Covid-19 period did was show that Ireland was ripe for its own moment of misinformation, and we weren't prepared for it.

One of the ways to tackle the spread of misinformation online is fact-checking, and that became the internet's first call for fighting back against the Covid misinformation waves on WhatsApp and as it spread to social media. Fact-checkers are given an important and specific task: to sort the lies from the truth. It's easier than we might think to accidentally share an image or post that is misinformation, because of how well they tend to be packaged up, and how they play on our fear. Fact-checkers know how to confirm what's true, what's not, and what's a mixture of falsity and facts. The internet is a natural home for fact-checkers, as it's a place where you can go deep, tear things apart, analyse queries and claims. One of the longest-running fact-checking websites is Snopes, which was initially set up in 1994 to catalogue urban legends, while FactCheck.org was set up in 2003. At *The Journal*, we had been running our FactCheck initiative for four years by the time the pandemic rolled around. But when the WhatsApp messages kept on pinging, we had to roll out something new: a new form of FactCheck, called the Debunk. The majority of the claims were very easy to debunk, which made it even more troubling that they had taken such a hold of people. It was their popularity which alerted us to the fact they needed to be debunked, so that recipients could go on to share the verified information to the pal or relation they'd got the original message from. It was hoped that debunking and fact-checking worldwide could become a new wave, fighting back against the forceful wave of misinformation. Whenever I was able to send on a Debunk or factual nugget of information to a worried friend, I felt relief.

The wave of misinformation was a strong one. 'It happened quite slowly, and then very suddenly it grew from a very small thing to become a huge thing,' my colleague Christine Bohan, who leads *The Journal's* FactCheck initiative, says of those early pandemic days. Previously, misinformation would have been seen as mainly occurring on Facebook, and a bit on Twitter, but not really happening on a wide basis in Ireland. 'So to start seeing this in our WhatsApp inbox was a really big deal,' she says. At the very end of February 2020, the misinformation had clearly become the news story. Bohan set up a WhatsApp account so people could send on concerning messages they had received to be fact-checked. The account was set up on a Friday. By Sunday there were 800 messages waiting on the phone. 'I remember realizing: this is in Ireland now. This is here, we need to be concerned,' says Bohan. 'I don't know if there's anybody in the country who didn't get a viral coronavirus message on WhatsApp during that first month.'

While fact-checkers were digging for the truth, there were researchers taking stock of who and what was helping to spread misinformation across social media. Aoife Gallagher is an analyst at the Institute for Strategic Dialogue (ISD), an independent London-based think tank. She works for its Digital Analysis Unit, focusing on the intersection between far right extremism, disinformation and conspiracy theories. Where disinformation and misinformation differ is that while both centre on the spread of false information, disinformation is deliberately spread. It was typically seen as being connected to government activities or propaganda, but the term's meaning has slightly broadened over the years.

Gallagher and her colleagues dig into the back end of sites and use open source technology to find publicly available data that tells us what people are doing and sharing in extremist spaces on the internet (and that doesn't mean the dark web – it means the social media sites anyone could be a member of). She wasn't surprised to see people jumping into the Covid misinformation space, because of all she had witnessed by early 2020. Yet at the same time, she was 'still probably slightly naive' about how bad it was going to get. Those early WhatsApp messages were all about fear and uncertainty, she says: misinformation exploits people's lack of knowledge about certain topics. It was easy to fill the vacuum around Covid-19 information with rumours and speculation. 'A lot of it wasn't nefarious. It wasn't coming from a really bad place,' she says of people sharing false messages and posts. 'It was coming from people just trying to figure out what the hell was going on.'

Up to early 2020, Christine Bohan had thought that Ireland had buttresses against false news. She says our media and politics aren't hugely partisan, and we don't have major figures like the UK's Katie Hopkins or Nigel Farage, though we do have niche leaders in conspiracy and far right circles. Some have attempted to enter politics, with varying degrees of success, but none have come near entering government, and none of the parties or organizations have garnered significant support. But this didn't do anything to stop the spread of the misinformation. Bohan was surprised at first that WhatsApp was the initial source. 'If you're going to set up a place to share misinformation, Facebook would be perfect – you can have closed groups, you can just say things to your friends and family, or you can also say it to larger groups, and anybody with common interests,' she says. 'But WhatsApp is so personal.' The messages on WhatsApp showed that misinformation was now creeping like a silent cat into the bedroom. It was in the private spaces people use to talk to loved ones. In 2020, misinformation had an intimate edge. But it didn't stay on WhatsApp. Soon the wave crashed, and as the water receded a new wave headed to another location: the sunny beach of social media.

Soon I wasn't getting any forwarded messages, and the queries from readers about fact-checks began to reference what they were seeing online more and more. This phase moved away from what we'd seen before, where there were attempts to try and share some sort of 'helpful' information, even if it was completely wrong. The conspiracy side of the messaging went from the government withholding information on how bad things were to the ultimate conspiracy: that the pandemic wasn't real, or not as bad as what was being reported. Some people took screenshots of scientific journals or news reports and shared them on Twitter, TikTok, and Facebook, claiming they said or meant something different to what they did mean. Some manipulated headlines, doing bad photoshop work to push a false message from a real source. The torrent of claims was like a collection of B-movie plots: criminals were putting chemicals on face-masks; a 'coronavirus vaccine' was created in 2001 (the photo was actually of a canine coronavirus vaccine); the coronavirus was invented in 2015.[7]

A doctored tweet which claimed to be from Leo Varadkar said that everyone returning from the Cheltenham racing festival – which had a significant Irish contingent – to Ireland would have to go into isolation for fourteen days at the Maldron Dublin Airport Hotel.[8] It was false, but there was a real fear that Cheltenham returnees could spread the virus, as more than 65,000 people attended the event. The messages online could be shared because the people sharing them believed them, or alternatively because they wanted them to be true. By September 2021, the HSE had reported more than 1,000 social media posts for misinformation about the Covid-19 pandemic, as well as the country's vaccination programme, journalist Ken Foxe discovered through a Freedom of Information request. The vast majority of the posts – 739 of them – were posted on Twitter.

Next, the viral tweets, Facebook posts and YouTube videos claimed the pandemic was a 'scamdemic' or 'plandemic', organized and faked by the elites of the world. Irish people shared videos made by Irish people, British people, American people. The claims were similar no matter what part of the world they came from, all serving up the same toxic stew. There were claims about Bill Gates being potentially charged with crimes against humanity in Italy, and that he, his then wife Melinda, Anthony Fauci (the medical advisor to the US President, a particular figure of distrust in Covid-sceptic spaces), and the World Health Organisation were being charged with genocide. The pandemic was fake, it was a sham, it was a global plan to keep people docile and powerless. Once the vaccines came, they were branded dangerous, life-threatening, pre-planned. It was easy to laugh at these wild claims at first, but such laughs turn hollow when you see the amount of shares these posts get.

I could see how the previous actions of governments and powerful people could turn individuals into fearful, distrustful misinformation-sharers of a variety of degrees. It wasn't pure ignorance behind the sharing of some of these messages. In some cases it did stem from a fear about how Covid-19 vaccines hadn't existed months earlier, and what that meant for people's health. But the leap between curiosity and conspiracy could be extremely quick in some online spaces.

No matter how disturbing the claim, it could be shared incredibly easily online. I suspected some knew what they were sharing was false, but it was the 'kicking against the pricks' element that they wanted to showcase: that they were not nodding dogs who believed everything powerful billionaires said. One element of the virality comes down to trust, cyber security expert Brian Honan tells me. 'People trust their connections on a personal basis more than they trust what they see as commercial organizations,' he says. He believes that the misinformation on these major platforms turned a large swathe of the population away from reliable, trusted sources of news. People might lean further into trusting their friend or relative's posts online more than a radio presenter or TV news anchor 'because they're just large media companies – forgetting that the platform they're posting on is a large corporate platform, looking to make money out of people and their interactions,' he says. Added to that, if people were liking, posting, and sharing this sort of content on the bigger social media sites, then this could lead to them seeing more of this sort of content, the algorithm trapping them in an echo chamber of false claims, and exaggerating how many like-minded people there are. 'How you interact with Facebook, and within their platform, will influence the algorithm as to how ads are served to you,' says Honan. This information can be sold on to companies who then target people based on that.

As humans, we thrive on interaction, but Honan says we thrive on bad news too, and on knowing something somebody else doesn't know. 'That creates this environment where I think people willingly take in all the crap and fake news that social media promotes,' he says, because this new nugget of news or info can be easily shared. If it's novel, and just being shared with friends, then some people might not feel the need to check out its veracity. They're not publishing it – they're just passing it on. And maybe in some cases it's a bit of a laugh. But it's one thing to whisper a rumour to a friend over a pint in the pub. It's another thing to share it on WhatsApp where it can be forwarded on for infinity. This goes beyond misinformation – most Irish people will have heard the WhatsApp voice note allegedly made by Aoife McGregor, sister of MMA star Conor McGregor, which inspired some glorious memes. But it was a private message, never intended to be heard by anyone but the recipient. And all it took was for it to be forwarded once, outside of its original recipient's phone, for it to go viral.

Honan says that the social media companies are not there for the good of society, and we can't forget they're commercial companies who have commitments to shareholders and other stakeholders to make a profit. In order to make a profit, they will generate as much revenue as possible, and keep their costs down. He believes that's why with the major social media sites 'we see this lack of proactive activity' in cutting down on or stamping out false information and disinformation. When someone posts something on a social media site, it can be amplified and rebroadcast over and over again. But the social media companies by then have their inter-action, their likes and their retweets, all of which they can monetize. 'So they don't then tend to invest in good ways to practically manage that and stop [misinformation] from happening,' says Honan. 'Because if they stop it from happening, people lose interest in the platforms, and then will probably move on.' But he cautions that we need to be 'very careful' about censorship of online interactions.

As misinformation in 2020 moved deeper online, and onto apps that were popular with younger people, it was harder and harder to ignore that what started on WhatsApp, with anonymous people behind false but sometimes mild messages, was becoming a movement with figureheads, some of whom were based here in Ireland. The pandemic was bringing misinformation online to a head, and one of the ways it was being spread was through an app that people were also using to distract themselves during the Covid-19 lockdowns.

The Infodemic

While misinformation was spreading online like pixelated wildfire during the pandemic, people were also turning to the very apps it featured on for some respite. One in particular, the Chinese-owned video app TikTok, became a diverting, family-friendly way of having a bit of craic during a tough time. The fast-growing app is one of the biggest in the world, with 1 billion users.[1] Its rocketing success has aggravated Mark Zuckerberg and Meta, which has been trying to turn Instagram into a TikTok rival through prioritizing 'reels', which are almost exactly like TikTok videos. Unlike Twitter or Facebook, TikTok's main appeal is that it's all about video, and users can make and share short edited clips using music and other audio. It's a noisy app, being less about calm and more about joyful chaos. While it's common to find Twitter users calling the site they spend hours on every day a 'hellsite', TikTok tends to garner a different form of criticism. When people talk about their use, they usually tell me they just can't stay off it – it's so entertaining, even if they don't always like the content they're served. Even if they actually hate the content they're served. It's hard to step away as TikTok seamlessly serves you up new videos – you, the user, barely need to do a thing.

Almost half of TikTok users are aged between eighteen and twenty-four.[2] But on there you can also find weightlifting grandmothers, older gay couples sharing experiences, school-going teens doing dances and middle-aged dads into polyamory. Extremely niche fandoms and subgroups blossom on there, and trends swell up rapidly, bursting as quickly. I've watched videos on 'slugging' skincare products (following your routine with a final layer of vaseline); how an American mother of ten makes food for her brood (using industrial-sized quantities of ingredients); and how to prepare a 'goddess' salad (which I wouldn't eat as I loathe cucumber). TikTok videos are snappy, with quick edits and fast-paced voiceovers. This speed is exploited by some users to make you watch the videos repeatedly, by making their final reveal short or unclear. The app encourages repeated viewings as the videos are looped, even though the way it works is that its 'home page' is where you are served up a never-ending roll of videos. For influencers or creators, it's such a powerful app now that you can become as popular as a YouTuber there without having to upload an hour-long video. For the users, you can sit slack-jawed on your couch and forget about life as you flick through, your over-worked thumb doing ballet on the screen as you're served up clip after clip without noticing the time passing.

ByteDance, the Chinese-owned company behind TikTok (whose motto is 'Inspire Creativity, Enrich Life'), has faced constant scrutiny over the past few years about what it does with user data, and whether that data makes its way into the hands of the Chinese government.[3] It denies the claims. But speculation about this hasn't turned off its millions of users. Part of this is because it's an app primed for virality – you can go viral on the strength of one video, if the algorithm works in its favour, and if enough users show interest in it. Its algorithm – more on that in a moment – is also what makes it more absorbing than the likes of Twitter. As you'll see later on, it is heavily personalized, drilling down closer and closer to each individual user's specific tastes and desires. In contrast, Twitter's ads and cluttered landscape can make it more of a clunky visit. And anyone who's visited Facebook knows how awkward and ugly it is these days.

TikTok users can be self-aware – the most popular person on the app at the time of writing is Khaby Lame, who made his name mocking the very antics that brought fame to its previous biggest stars. Just below him is a more traditional TikToker, seventeen-year-old Charli D'Amelio, who reached 100 million followers in 2020 thanks to her dance videos, make-up tips and life updates. TikTok videos don't require much set-up, but if you're popular you need to get your content from somewhere. Hence the setting up of 'collab houses' where influencers live and create content together. When I watched the Netflix series *Hype House*, which follows one particular group of TikTokers (the eldest of whom is barely into their twenties) living in a collab house, I felt a pang of sadness for these youths. Their every action, emotion or reaction was used as visual fodder for their followers to gnaw on. I wondered how much of their 'real' life they actually got to live. The episodes made it seem like very little of it was lived without the awareness of an audience.

Online, things can never be all fun and games. So while TikTok was becoming known as an entertaining, escapist app during the pandemic, it was also becoming a new space to spread misinformation. Once WhatsApp was in the rear-view mirror, conspiracy theorists and manipulators could turn to the latest apps to exploit their beliefs, and TikTok was soon jumped on. Ciarán O'Connor works with Aoife Gallagher in ISD, and his speciality is combing through TikTok looking for right-wing and extremist content. He's been doing that since 2019. 'From the beginning of the pandemic, TikTok was as prominent for people spreading mis- and disinformation or conspiracy content around Covid as other platforms,' he tells me. Part of how misinformation found a comfy home on TikTok was driven by how different it was from the favoured sites and apps of old. 'Facebook is the place where you organize, you set up a group, you communicate, you mobilize,' explains O'Connor. But TikTok is different. While it doesn't have the group chat features that other apps have, it can make things go viral in a way other platforms don't. The first sign O'Connor got of its potential for spreading misinformation was when he saw a TikTok video of an old clip of Bill Gates talking about the overpopulation of planet Earth. An added caption claimed the billionaire was referring to Covid, and thus that the pandemic was a pre-planned 'plandemic'.

On TikTok, people could promote and amplify sceptic and conspiracy movements in various ways. They could recycle old clips like the one of Bill Gates, make new ones, or do straight-to-camera videos, for starters. You can make a really impressive or persuasive piece of video on it without possessing any formal editing skills. It has a green screen feature, which allows you to appear in front of a news article or image and comment on it or reference it, giving an air of authenticity as you point to the text. You can look smart, even if you're talking absolute rubbish. You can also add what are called 'sounds' to your videos, which can be any audio or music. '"Sounds" is one way in which misinformation and conspiracy theories on TikTok, especially around Covid, have spread,' says O'Connor. That's because, crucially, the video and sound are created separately, so someone can share the sound without the visuals, and add their own visuals in a new video. 'TikTok may have removed the original video because it got so many complaints. But when people shared these videos with the audio of someone saying something like "vaccines are deadly", the audio lives on and can still be shared and used in new videos. And that's something that's not on any other platform,' O'Connor explained to me. Without intending or endorsing it, TikTok had provided a unique way for people to produce and promote misinformation and conspiracy theories.

And so we get to the power of the TikTok algorithm. All apps are driven by an algorithm, with hidden levers directing what is shown to us users based on factors we do know about – like what we've already clicked on or who we follow – and we don't, like what the company that owns the app wants us to see. As anyone who's used a Meta product for business knows, the algorithm can also change on a whim, leading people to scramble to keep up. That's why Instagram's prioritization of 'reels' as a way to push back against TikTok angered people – overnight, they had to start making videos, or else their content wouldn't get enough eyes on it. TikTok's algorithm means that relationships between users don't play as big a role as they do with other apps, O'Connor says. It's not like Facebook, where I might be served farming content because my friend is really into tractors. 'On TikTok, it's completely turned on its head,' he says. I'm an infrequent TikTok user, so I am always interested to see what the app serves me. After a gap of a few months, it once started showing dance videos made by school-age teenagers, which was a bit disturbing. The videos flow in a never-ending stream and you flick through them, so you don't know what you're going to watch in advance. It can be a case of *Surprise! Here's a cute baby*, or *Surprise! Here's a bareknuckle fight in a field*. 'There are different factors like your location, the time you spend on content you watched so far, whether or not you interact, and to what degree – it's all these different black box things,' says Ciarán of what influences what we're shown on the app. By 'black box', he means that the information isn't in the public domain.

On TikTok, you don't scroll through profiles as much as you scroll through videos that the app itself serves you. It's similar in a way to a Twitter stream, only you don't have to be following anyone. What I noticed was that the longer I lingered over a video, the more I would be served similar content, and that this would happen almost instantly. Spend two seconds more on a 'what I ate in a day' video and soon I would be served more of them, plus additional weight loss content. As I heard from friends who use the app daily, TikTok gets to know your tastes very well, gradually honing and honing down to what you want it to show you. That's both useful (why would you stay on an app that only serves you what you don't want?) and disturbing (what is the impact on a teenager of watching multiple videos about calorie counting?). It raises questions about the rabbit holes it can lead users into, where their feed is only focused on one thing. If you linger over a conspiracy or misinformation video out of curiosity, even if you don't believe in what it's telling you, you could then be served more of that content. The app doesn't know why you stayed viewing something – only that you viewed it. You have to take deliberate steps to add new content, like telling the app you're 'not interested' in certain videos, or searching for fresh topics. As the app encourages passivity, that approach could be unnatural for some users.

It's via the mysterious algorithm that the app's 'for you page', or FYP, comes into play. It's a hugely coveted place for your video to appear, as it's essentially the 'front page', with the potential of millions and millions of eyes viewing it. For people trying to create an audience, it gives them more opportunities to go viral. Its algorithm is what makes TikTok such an interesting and dynamic app, but it's also what can create 'influencers' out of conspiracy theorists or anti-vaccine activists, says O'Connor. On his visits, he saw the FYP promoting not just ordinary people and TikTok celebrities, but also users with conspiracy-fuelled beliefs and anti-vaccine conspiracy beliefs. He saw a lot of importation of content from abroad, not necessarily because people were trying to target an Irish audience, but because the world of Covid conspiracy and misinformation is a flat and far-reaching one, with content in English understood by English-speaking communities everywhere.

What O'Connor discovered while doing research was that on TikTok, the communities who typically engage in harmful or misleading content are aware of how to get around moderation. Some will rejoin after being removed, with a new username that has 'v2' at the end, signifying 'version two'. 'There seems to be a real awareness of: you will get taken down, it's a matter of time, but you can just as quickly come back and pick up where you left off, and it's almost a badge of honour,' he says. TikTok is a very visual app, and O'Connor explains that visual content is being used to circumnavigate the platform's efforts to curb the spread of false content. Some users put emojis on their profiles as a symbol of their beliefs, like a raised right hand to indicate a Nazi salute, or syringe emoji to indicate they post about vaccines. This can help people to get around blocked hashtags and find like-minded followers.

It's not like these apps say, 'Come on in, conspiracy theorists – the water's fine.' TikTok's community guidelines prohibit misinformation related to Covid-19 and anti-vaccine disinformation (as well as false or misleading content generally). Users can report misinformation, and from April to June 2021, TikTok removed 81,518,334 videos globally for violating its community guidelines or terms of service – which it said was less than 1 per cent of all videos uploaded. The vast majority – 93.0 per cent – were identified and removed within twenty-four hours of being posted, and 94.1 per cent before a user reported them. In the breakdown of why the videos were removed, TikTok said that 0.8 per cent were taken down for 'integrity and authenticity' reasons, which includes but is not exclusive to misinformation (it also includes impersonation, for example).[4]

It's easy enough to think that you'd have to be some class of eejit to fall for misinformation on TikTok or other social media apps, but that's to disregard the many reasons why people are drawn to that sort of content, and how the purveyors of this content attract followers. Some of the content might look blatant, but to those who aren't familiar with how misinformation presents itself, or who have a low level of media or internet literacy, misinformation can seem just like any other form of information. They can fall victim to the trap of confirmation bias, where a statement backs up a suspicion or opinion they already have. There are also powerful figureheads within the misinformation movements who exploit how people look to experts to guide them. Aoife Gallagher examined how certain individuals became well known in Ireland and abroad for their anti-vaccination or Covid-sceptic opinions. Some used their own personal social media profiles to share information that was misleading; others set up groups; some used their social feeds as a way to funnel misinformation written by someone else to their audience. Individuals could also re-share the figureheads' misleading information themselves on their private pages, potentially attracting new followers. While an app like TikTok shared individual videos, it didn't allow private and public groups. That's where Facebook could play a particularly important role in spreading opinions and enabling figureheads to increase their audience.

In Ireland, some people became well-known names due to their Covid opinions and the following they gathered. Professor Dolores Cahill became a public name and face thanks to her views on Covid. A lecturer at University College Dublin's school of medicine – though she's now a former staff member – she was a well-respected immunologist when she started making social media appearances to talk about Covid-19. With her knowledgeable tone and persuasive demeanour, she seemed to be a voice of reason. After all, she was an expert on immunology and it was presumed she could inform people about how Covid-19 might affect them. But Cahill and a group she was part of, World Doctors Alliance, were accused of spreading misinformation about Covid-19 and vaccinations on social media. In May 2020, Dolores Cahill did an interview with the vlogger Dave Cullen, who goes by the name Computing Forever, about the pandemic. The hour-long video was a defining moment of the pandemic for Aoife Gallagher. In it, the pair discussed Covid-19, masks, social distancing and lockdowns. Dolores Cahill said in that interview there was no need for the original Covid lockdown, or for people without symptoms of Covid-19 to wear masks. The video was removed from YouTube due to its content. Within a few months of the Computing Forever video, Dolores Cahill was speaking at anti-lockdown rallies in Dublin. She became a prominent figure in the media as articles were written about her controversial comments on masks and how to treat the virus. Her Facebook page was removed in December 2021 as part of Facebook's efforts at fighting Covid-19 misinformation.[5] Cahill ceased working at UCD in early 2021.

The ISD researchers who'd been monitoring Covid-19 misinformation communities online had already seen how veteran health misinformation influencers were increasing their visibility, but so too were new and emerging players who used the pandemic to 'elevate themselves to fame' within the Covid-19 sceptic movement. It was always shocking to stumble across misinformation and see it was written by a doctor or medical professional – I could understand why some people believed what they were saying. The World Doctors Alliance, of which Dolores Cahill was a member, also had eleven other doctors and scientists from seven different countries among its membership. A number of them spoke at anti-lockdown protests across Europe throughout 2020 and 2021. The popularity of the Alliance during the pandemic shows how quickly groups can attract followers, even if what they're saying is controversial or being debunked.

The ISD found in November 2021 that the Alliance's Facebook following increased over a hundredfold since the start of the pandemic, to more than 550,000.[6] This was despite the fact that members of the Alliance had been fact-checked multiple times by fact-checkers working with Facebook. The company doesn't fact-check internally. Instead, it partners with fact-checkers to examine flagged posts and then applies warnings and information to material that has been found to be false. Once a piece of content is rated false, Facebook reduces its distribution and puts warning labels on it. But you can still read the content after you've read the warning.[7] It's a way of balancing claims of censorship, but I found myself often just clicking through to look at the misinformation, in an attempt to understand what people were reading and believing. I could see that people would just ignore these warnings if they believed the social media giant was itself not worthy of trust. When users saw those warning labels, 95 per cent of the time they didn't go on to view the original content, Facebook said. But with people producing and sharing misinformation in high quantities, it was like trying to stem a tide with your hand. Christine Bohan says that some people spreading misinformation were able to build up significant audiences on Facebook. 'Facebook did take a lot of [the controversial pages] down in the end. And I think that they've learned a huge amount from it, but they could have done more, I think is the message,' she says. 'I think they would acknowledge that too.'

It's not as though the major social media platforms didn't know early on that misinformation was bubbling up on their sites. On 16 March 2020, mere days after Ireland had gone into its first lockdown, a joint statement from Facebook, Google, LinkedIn, Microsoft, Reddit, Twitter, and YouTube said they were working together, 'jointly combating fraud and misinformation about the virus, elevating authoritative content on our platforms, and sharing critical updates in coordination with government healthcare agencies around the world.'[8] In Ireland, they shared an external link to the HSE website whenever users searched 'coronavirus'. Soon, they were putting up automatic banners on some social media posts. Bohan says that in some ways Facebook did more than any of the other platforms, 'But at the same time, the problem was in their house and they had to get their house in order.' Since 2016, Facebook has used a strategy called 'remove, reduce, inform'.[9] It removes harmful content that goes against its policies, reduces the distribution of problematic content that doesn't violate its policies, and informs people with additional context. In April 2020, warning labels were put on about 50 million pieces of content related to Covid-19 on Facebook, based on around 7,500 articles by its fact-checking partners.[10]

Despite all of its initiatives, in the US Facebook found itself in a face-off against President Joe Biden in the summer of 2021, when he criticized social media platforms over Covid-19 disinformation. Even the White House had flagged posts containing disinformation to Facebook. By early 2021, more than 12 million pieces of content were removed from Facebook and Instagram for containing misinformation that could lead to 'imminent physical harm'.[11] Here in Ireland, a report called CovidCheck was commissioned by the Broadcasting Authority of Ireland (BAI) in 2021 and looked into how good social media companies were at monitoring online disinformation. Overall, it found that they needed to improve their monitoring procedures. The companies had adopted the EU's self-regulatory Code of Practice on Disinformation in 2018, but the BAI report found 'critical shortcomings' in implementing it.[12]

If you kept an eye on misinformation online during the pandemic in particular, you'd notice that different topics would emerge as a priority at different times. After the initial flurries of misinformation on targeted lockdowns, government activities and the Covid-19 virus itself, the next major challenge facing fact-checkers and social media sites was misinformation about vaccines. Some of the worst offenders in this area became known as misinformation 'super spreaders'. A report from the Centre for Countering Digital Hate (CCDH) – a UK/US non-profit and non-governmental organization – said that anti-vaccine activists on Facebook, YouTube, Instagram and Twitter reached more than 59 million followers.[13] The CCDH focused on twelve online personalities who it called the 'disinformation dozen'. This grouping showed how anti-vaccine content was spread across different social media platforms, but also how the platforms treated similar content differently. After analysing content shared more than 812,000 times on social media platforms over just two months, the CCDH found more than two-thirds of the content came from this dozen. There were inconsistencies in how these people were treated – one of the dozen, Robert F. Kennedy Jr, was banned from Instagram but remained active on Facebook. Another, Rizza Islam, was removed from Facebook but was still active on Twitter and Instagram.

Another thing that became apparent to fact-checkers and researchers was that pandemic misinformation wasn't siloed off into its own category. 'If you think of Covid-19, one thing we say a lot is that what were once more disparate communities are in a Venn diagram, they all criss-cross now,' says Ciarán O'Connor. 'The common thing being this belief that Covid was manufactured or planned; or perhaps it was a natural thing that happened, but is being used as an anti-democratic power grab by corrupt elites against the pure people.' A typical anti-vaccine account might be expressing support for other conspiracies. There's almost a 'conspiracy pipeline', says O'Connor. Christine Bohan says the groups don't all have just one belief or ideology. 'They have lots of them. And it appeals to this sense of "the country is in a bad place; the people in charge don't know what they're doing: here are your people, stick with us and we will show you the path".'

In the early months of the pandemic, Covid misinformation crossed paths with the belief that 5G technology is damaging for humans. Some conspiracy theorists alleged that 5G made people more susceptible to Covid-19, or that the masts gave people the virus. Some claimed that 5G weakened the blood-brain barrier and let pathogens in, and that the tactic had already been used effectively in Wuhan. These online claims had real-life consequences, showing that even the most out-there claims can be taken as fact. Two 5G towers were set on fire in Donegal in April 2020, and Gardaí believed the blazes were connected to the spread of 5G coronavirus misinformation online.[14] Tens of similar incidents were reported in the UK, with videos and images circulating of flaming masts and burnt-out sites. One hoax video shared online claimed that 'COV 19' was found inscribed on a circuit board found in a 5G mast. The man making the claims wore hi-vis and a hard hat, and even said that he wasn't a conspiracy theorist. The circuit board was found to have come from an old TV box.[15] At a Downing Street press conference in April 2020, 5G claims were rubbished by the then Minister Michael Gove, who wore the exasperated look of someone absolutely sick of being asked about the topic. But eventually the claims died down in popularity, replaced by new theories. Maybe that's because 5G gives us higher data speeds, making being online that bit smoother and easier. For some theorists, the benefits might eventually have outweighed their fantastical claims about the negatives.

The social media sites are caught between dealing with the content and not overstepping a line – a line which hasn't even been defined online as it is. With no agreement on what defines 'free speech' online, the platforms have all had to take their own approach to pandemic misinformation, and how quickly to clamp down on individuals or groups. And even though the content might be removed, it might not curb popularity, or prevent people from sharing their opinions. A person or group could have a Facebook page, Facebook group, TikTok page, Twitter account, and multiple other social media pages if they wished. Aoife Gallagher tells me that the content of the Dolores Cahill and Computing Forever video was worrying – but so was the fact that the video was removed. Like cyber-security expert Brian Honan, she says that the issue of removing content and the idea of what is censorship and what isn't is a knotty one for the social media sites. She describes platforms removing content from their sites as a double-edged sword. On one hand, it means removing misleading information. On the other, 'it really gives credence to people who say they're being silenced, because they kind of are', she says. 'So for anyone who doesn't trust the media or had doubts about what was going on, I'm sure they were thinking: well, Dolores Cahill is qualified. She is a professor in UCD. She has a PhD in immunology. And she has been silenced for saying these things.'

When we talk about free speech online, we must talk about Donald Trump. Many of the people I spoke to described a pre-Trump and post-Trump internet. Trump's election saw him become one of the loudest voices on Twitter – *The New York Times* referred to him as using social media 'as a megaphone'. As the 'leader of the free world', he denounced other leaders, announced policy decisions, and made all-caps proclamations on Twitter in particular, but was also a heavy presence on Facebook. He was obsessed with 'fake news', but often the news he decried as 'fake' was real, or an opinion he disagreed with. Social media was now where even presidents could say whatever they wanted. This encouraged other individuals, publications and politicians to take a similar tack, as for many years Trumpish behaviour was consequence-free. A new bar had been set online.

By the time Trump's term was coming to an end, it was reported that Facebook was preparing for what to do if he disputed the election, because he had spent months undermining the integrity of the vote.[16] The violent US Capitol insurrection in January 2021 capped off his ignominious reign on social media, and was a watershed moment for showing how online activity could turn into vicious livestreamed riots. But despite all of the many controversial comments he made online, and the brutal consequences of the Capitol incident, it wasn't until June 2021 that Donald Trump was permanently kicked off Facebook and Instagram.[17] He had already been suspended in January after the insurrection, while Twitter had permanently suspended him that same month, 'due to the risk of further incitement of violence'.[18]

For Christine Bohan, you have to draw a line from Trump to the current misinformation climate online because of the way the platforms dealt with the situation. 'They had the opportunity when they could see what was happening to be proactive. And they chose not to,' she says. She believes that if Trump hadn't been elected, we wouldn't be seeing so much 'homegrown' misinformation online – or the spread of US-specific misinformation on social media. The disappearing gap between US-centric beliefs and the rest of the world was captured when the journalist Mark Tighe shared a photo on Twitter in 2021 that he'd taken of two women at a protest in Dublin wearing sweatshirts with the slogan 'RTÉ sold there [sic] souls'.[19] It was a reference to QAnon, a formerly niche American conspiracy movement which fomented online and embraces many truly out-there beliefs, like that within the US government there are paedophiles who worship Satan. QAnon supporters were seen at the Capitol riots – they are fervent supporters of Trump. Tighe interviewed some of the Irish conspiracy theorists and commented on Twitter afterwards: 'Fairly wild and scary what people believe.'

It's probably no surprise that these beliefs made their way to Ireland. As Aoife Gallagher puts it, 'the internet has no borders and you can't control the narratives that are coming in and out of the country'. It's extremely hard to get the numbers on how many Irish people actually believe in, for example, Covid conspiracies due to what they've read online, but if we look at Ireland's high vaccine uptake rate, that could be an indication that the number is small. But Gallagher warns that there isn't room for complacency. 'You just don't know what's going to happen in the future,' she says.

Most of the biggest social media platforms are run by American companies (except TikTok, or a new app like BeReal, which is French). Free speech is a major part of American democracy, as it's effectively protected by the First Amendment of its Constitution. And so this mindset of protecting that right of free expression is part of the social media platforms' DNA. Christine Bohan says this can make it hard for sites to do things pre-emptively, as the values of free speech are prioritized above the impact of free speech. She suggests that if Facebook or Twitter had been set up in Europe, where there is not the same culture around free speech, the focus could have been switched. 'I think the impact of the things that are said is so much more important than a theoretical right to free speech,' she says. 'For me, these have real world impacts.'

Those real world impacts were broadcast online. In 2021, a video taken in a Donegal hospital and shared on social media showed a man named Joe McCarron being encouraged to leave hospital by an anti-Covid vaccine campaigner. McCarron had Covid-19, but the man in the video tells him being in the hospital would 'fucking kill' him. McCarron tells doctors in the video that he wants to leave. 'I'm very worried about you,' a doctor replies. 'I want you to stay.' He tells him that he is at risk of dying if he leaves, though it is his choice. What stood out when I watched the clip was that it wasn't covertly filmed. The man trying to convince McCarron to leave was filming and talking to the camera, wanting it to have an audience. McCarron left the hospital, and died a few weeks afterwards. The man in the viral video with him, Antonio Mureddu, was an anti-vaccine and anti-mask campaigner. He was investigated by Gardaí over the incident, but not charged with any crime.[20] Had the video not been broadcast online, it is arguable it would not have come to the attention of the Gardaí. McCarron's wife later told the *Irish Independent* that her husband had been 'brainwashed' to believe that Covid was a hoax.[21]

Spending time online during the pandemic was a time of extreme highs and lows. Sometimes I went there to escape the news cycle, to watch something mindless and to disconnect. Other times I went online because it was the only place I could find reams of information and data on Covid-19. I could gorge on it like junk food, taking in so much of it that I would feel nauseous. I hoped that eventually the Covid misinformation would start to wash away, that the wave would crest and fall and the beach would remain dry. But even though the volume of misinformation felt like it was reducing as the pandemic moved into 2021 and 2022, in reality it was just shifting in shape. Both Ciarán O'Connor and Aoife Gallagher agree that Covid misinformation purveyors are now pivoting into climate change denial and other topics (which already had audiences online). Some people have already started sharing the idea that the Covid lockdowns were a test case for climate lockdowns, says Gallagher. They see the pressure on governments to reduce emissions, the climate protests and dire predictions for rising global temperatures as a means to gain more control over citizens. Gallagher didn't believe that people settled in these misinformation communities were going to leave them as the pandemic waned. Having ready-made newer communities to join, which also shared similar sentiments, gave them a familiar home once they had moved on from Covid.

At the same time, there's no definitive 'leader' of these scenes in Ireland, something which everyone I spoke to pointed out, though figureheads have emerged. This could be a positive thing in terms of how the overall misinformation scene develops, as without a leader, it might lose focus. And yet Christine Bohan thinks it's likely some of the conspiracy figureheads will move into political issues, and even run for election. She says the popularity of the Covid-sceptic and conspiracy pages is concerning, because it shows how many people don't trust the media, or don't trust what authorities say to them. 'The only thing that is really clear is that these communities will not go away,' says Ciarán O'Connor. 'But we have to remember, these conspiracies are such a small pocket, but they're very loud. And they can be potentially harmful for people if they are spreading wilfully wrong things.' If you see conspiracy content – no matter how subtle – on an app like TikTok or Facebook nestled next to videos about make-up, fashion, or books, it can normalize it, but can also make it seem like it's a widely held opinion. You just don't know, because each of us has our own personalized internet world that we visit.

The WHO called the pandemic misinformation period an 'infodemic'. During major news events these days, I scroll through social media apps wondering how long it will be before I'm confronted with some form of misinformation – a fake video or image, or maybe just an over-egged post created to make people feel anxious. While the pandemic was one major hotspot for misinformation, online you can find fake and manipulated photos, text, and claims about a wealth of topics. The pandemic just showed how quickly social media enabled a specific misinformation movement to emerge, evolve and impact in real life, and how the different apps and platforms gave it new ways of catching attention. Misinformation and disinformation show us that information is something that can be, like a piece of plasticine, shaped and moulded at the owner's will, made into whatever form they desire. It makes it hard to trust what you're reading, and makes being online feel like a game where there are baddies around every corner, where information is no longer something concrete.

It feels like over time we've lost the vision of the positive things that the internet can give to us, Aoife Gallagher tells me. The way the algorithms work, the never-ending scroll, the sheer volume of the amount of information we're fed every day – it's not a light space in which to be. Adding misinformation into the mix makes the internet even more difficult to stomach. It means you always have to be a little bit suspicious, and that doesn't make for an overly pleasant experience. But life online during the pandemic wasn't all Twitter fights and misinformation. To share something vulnerable with others online is to offer a piece of yourself tenderly, to hope for care in return. And so among the posts about fake viruses, the torrents of terrifying news articles and doom-laden data charts could be found tweets, TikToks and posts about loneliness, frustration, isolation, fear. Online, you could begin to process what was going on with Covid-19, to share your longing or sadness, or show off the new skills you learned during the lockdowns.

For most people I knew, misinformation wasn't the greatest part of their social media stream, which was why it was so jarring to realize how huge it was in some communities. For some people, much of their time online was spent reaching digital hands out to others. It was proof of existence. It was a literal light in the dark, a glowing portal to friendship and connection. It was how people tracked their obsession with baking banana bread or cultivating tangy sourdough starters, both things which became 'communal experiences' through being shared digitally. We weren't in each other's homes baking, but we could witness the fruits of our labour online. I found Twitter and Instagram a safe and even necessary place in those early lockdowns, when the world had shrunk to an unimaginably small size. I didn't see my family for months, and watched the view outside my spare room, where I spent most of my time working, changing infinitesimally. Online, I could find variety, comfort, and vitality.

Social media could bring solace. Tragically, WhatsApp was even used by some people to say their last words to loved ones, with phones held over hospital beds. The impact of this upending of our world and separation from loved ones will be felt for years, as necessary as the public health regulations were. This strange new reality can also account for why people were drawn to misinformation which purported to give them answers, to make them feel like this was all a big plan. That way, they could be angry at a government or powerful individual rather than at a virus (though some people who didn't believe in misinformation were unhappy about public health decisions). The pandemic forced us to collectively grasp for facts in a world that no longer made sense. With normal activities and relationships now resembling those in dystopian fiction, there was a need for clarity. It was that which led some people directly into the world of misinformation – on apps and sites that were unprepared for how to deal with the consequences. There was no vaccination to make pandemic misinformation evaporate. Users can only hope that the learnings from Covid-19 will mean Facebook, TikTok et al. are more prepared for the next big wave. But while we're waiting, the small waves keep rolling in.

GHOSTS IN THE MACHINE

Broadcast yourself.

*

We have a zero-tolerance policy to any content that is abusive,
hateful, harmful and a team of moderators online 24/7 to remove
any content that breaks our strict rules – often in minutes.

*

Our rules are to ensure all people can participate
in the public conversation freely and safely.

*

These guidelines will continue to evolve over time. This means
we may take action against a user, server, or content that violates
the spirit of these guidelines when we encounter a new threat
or harm that is not explicitly covered in the current version.

The Other Side of the Screen

I

The world of widespread Covid-19 misinformation that we found ourselves inhabiting in 2020 would have seemed dystopian twenty years earlier, but it's not as if there weren't signs that it could happen. In the early days online, maybe we were naive or just innocent about what people could be capable of on the internet. But we can't say that the social media companies themselves couldn't have known by the early 2000s what their products could potentially foment in the quest to provide the world with its own online public square. Here in Ireland, we've had a front row seat to watching the tech companies grow, as they've set up their European bases in Dublin. But this country is also one of the places where moderators who do the unenviable job of trying to keep social media sites clean actually work. Yet it was only relatively recently that moderators in Ireland spoke publicly about what their job involves, and as a consequence those of us who benefit from their work have had to reckon with its impact on them. Since then, moderators have started taking court cases in Ireland against the tech companies who they provided moderation for, saying that the work led to post-traumatic stress disorder. Looking back, it feels like an inevitable end to a situation that started off relatively simply.

The job of a content moderator isn't a new one, but over the years it has evolved to fit whatever the internet requires of it. It all started with human behaviour. Back when I was in my teens and early twenties eking out a 'presence' online and building my relationship with the internet in fifteen-minute slots and euro coins, I witnessed the wide spectrum of behaviour on the internet. I would often find myself surprised at what people were willing to say online – how some were happy to cross a line, to get into fights, to make themselves look bad. When I met some of them in 'real life', they often weren't anything like they were online. As we know from looking at anonymity and pseudonymity, the internet can make normally nice people do some very strange or damaging things. I found it curious how being online was like a heightened version of everyday life, but politeness wasn't a guaranteed part of your experience. Sometimes, people would post links in forums to off-colour websites like Rotten.com, a site where you could view awful things like autopsy details, photos of dead bodies, and lo-fi videos of car crashes. I learned that what I avoided online was what some people were drawn to. That some content that was disturbing or untouchable to me was sought out and shared by others; that this occurred because of the variety of people the internet attracted, and the opportunities it offered for sharing information. I also soon learned that people on the internet would find their own ways of dealing with this.

By the time I got my first proper job as a journalist in 2008, Facebook had become a big part of my online life. That same year, the company announced it would be opening its Dublin offices. By that time I had also joined a forum dedicated to a British comedy duo I was a little obsessed with, called The Mighty Boosh. The forum ended up playing a big role in my online life for a while and, without me realizing, teaching me about the value of moderation. When I joined the forum, I was living in Kildare Town after a period of residing in Cork and Galway. Looking back, I remember feeling quite low, though that wasn't the fault of where I lived or worked. I just couldn't seem to get a foothold in this new county. I knew no one except my friendly and welcoming colleagues, but our office was in a different part of the county to where I lived. I got a train to work, which felt faintly exotic – but changed to ennui after I was mugged and broke my arm in the train station car park, on two separate occasions. At night, I ate packets of sour sugar-coated jellies in my rented bedroom and browsed the internet, because where I was able to get a foothold was online, in my little worlds on the sites I frequented.

In my bedroom in a housing estate next to a GAA field, I'd spend hours chatting on the Boosh fan forum and watching glitchy video clips, getting an education in offbeat British comedy series of the late twentieth century. Through my bulky silver laptop, I was able to have some sense of me and who I was outside of work and the small town I was living in. I'd spent a lot of my college years on a forum for a local nightclub, but though still niche, this forum was a much bigger deal. It felt like the comedy duo were on the precipice of major success, so we watched their actions closely. (They did end up becoming very famous, with one of the members, Noel Fielding, eventually co-hosting *The Great British Bake Off*.) The members were generally well behaved, but there were also the occasional fights, fractious discussions and emotional outpourings that I was familiar with from my years online. The only way to maintain harmony there was to have people work as moderators, or mods.

Moderating was a volunteer job, done out of dedication to making the site a nice place. Having a bit of hierarchical power helped draw people to the role too. I looked up to the mods on the comedy forum, because their presence meant that things could never get out of hand (they could delete comments, ask people to calm down, or even ban members if necessary). One afternoon, I was asked if I would be a mod myself, based on the fact I was able to 'diffuse things nicely'. I didn't spend a lot of time, though, thinking about my role in moderation online as a whole – why moderation was needed; how it helped relationships; what the pitfalls were; whether as the forum grew moderation would have to evolve with it; what it meant to have the power I had. I didn't ask myself, either, whether it was possible to have a site without moderation. If you'd asked me, I'd have said no, because I knew from other forums that no matter how small the membership, there were always bound to be fights online. It was like a family – I felt you needed at least one parent or guardian to keep an eye on everyone.

After I took on the role, I found that moderating could be rewarding, but it could also be stressful. It was indeed like being the parent/teacher/ manager of a large group of people, who would often have opposing ideas on what was right or wrong. It wasn't that the people on the forum were not nice people. It was a pleasant place to be, and I could spend hours private messaging some of the friends I made on there. We met up at events. We cared about each other. We shared secrets. Romantic relationships were sparked on there. It was a privilege to get to be a mod, and I took the decisions I made seriously. But I hadn't anticipated how I'd feel about the fact people could message me to complain about others, and that I'd have to make decisions on members' behaviour. When you're moderating, you only have the context of what you're seeing online to guide you in making a decision – you don't know why someone is acting out or posting certain things. I remember sitting at a friend's kitchen table in Dublin on a trip to see her, and being stressed out because I felt I needed to be on the forum to deal with an issue. But within a few years, as The Mighty Boosh got famous, the tight forum membership of the early days began to dissipate. People moved on in their real lives and had less time to spend there. Eventually, I left the mod role and then left the forum itself. The forum is gone now, and all of those conversations, all of the speculation and discussion and confessions and laughter and imagination, are digital dust.

It might have felt like small fry, but on that comedy forum we were part of a long history of websites finding their own way of dealing with user behaviour. What happened on that site was an echo of how the early bulletin boards, forums, Usenet groups, and blogs had to figure out how to make things work as peacefully as possible. (That's not to say that every community online is moderated – some deliberately aren't, and others, like controversial bulletin board sites 4Chan and 8Chan, claim to have moderators but have been the source of some of the internet's worst behaviour regardless.)

Social Capital

During the very early days of the social internet, known as Web 1.0, it was all about using the World Wide Web as a resource for information. The next phase, Web 2.0, meant blogging and joining social networking sites, connecting more with people, and putting content online that was visual. It was, the experts said, all about us and what we posted online. In this phase, the internet was expanding and users were becoming more important because we were the ones generating what was being called 'content'. The sites asked us to give them information about ourselves, and we freely handed over our names, faces, images, thoughts, ideas, dreams. We became eager to spend more time online. Websites started to look more enticing, and more sites were emerging that answered questions we hadn't realized we were asking about the potential the internet had: can I store my photos online in a personal account? Can I have people comment on my blog? Can I put my videos online? Can I talk to thousands of strangers in an easier, more immediate way than on a bulletin board? 'Yes' became the answer to all of them.

As the internet became more exciting and more useful, more people started to use the internet, helped on by broadband and Wi-Fi. The more people were able to communicate, the greater the variety of voices and opinions that were able to be read, and the wider that content was able to be shared. Now, it wasn't as though the internet hadn't been used as a place for toxicity, dodgy behaviour, or bad actors up until this point. But as Web 2.0 became the new online mode, and sites like Facebook and YouTube began hoovering up users by the billions, the problems with having so many voices and viewpoints online became visible. Anywhere people could gather online you could be sure you would find something troubling, and as these sites pulled us via their algorithms to spend more and more time consuming and creating content, the troubling things started to pile up.

For me, the first major signs of this new type of toxicity came with Facebook. First it was the arguments in Facebook comment threads, then it was the jokey, sometimes bullying Facebook pages that could be set up which were targeted at people. There were so many individuals gathering on Facebook that it was easy for things to get out of control. Making this more heightened was the fact it was obvious within a few years that Facebook was unlikely to disappear like MySpace had. It was clear that the intention with Facebook was stronger and more global than the early social media sites. It wanted to be a beast. It became a beast. But it also wanted to be a public square, to provide people with the chance to say whatever they wanted. Celebrities, politicians, and public figures of all types were able to create communities on there. People were able to set up their own communities and pages, and private and public groups on Facebook. There was a hunger to be on there and to see what it could show us, and the company came up with more and more ways for us to get hooked in. The number of users passed one billion, then two billion. Facebook was being talked about in the news because it was a company with heft. What happened on there mattered – people knew that to reach voters, consumers, and fans, you had to be on Facebook. But Facebook also wanted to be a place where people could say anything. Where it would not pass judgement on comments. Even though it was a site where you could find a multitude of content, some of it dangerous or toxic, Facebook didn't see its role as moderating that content. It was just providing people with a platform on which to communicate.

As we saw in previous chapters, this did not end well. It fed into allegations of interference and manipulation during the 2016 US presidential election, it led to a proliferation of pages, groups, and comment threads which spread and shared false information, misinformation or even defamatory comments. It meant people could share off-colour or offensive images, could set up groups dedicated to trolling people, and share non-consensual nudes. But Facebook wasn't the only site experiencing these issues, it was just the biggest social media site out there. All of the major platforms experienced similar problems. But Facebook is particularly interesting because it really, really does not want to be seen as the arbiter of truth, as having an opinion or a say on anything. Still, both it, Twitter, and every other social media site had to start hiring moderators to deal with the behaviour of their users.

I'm surprised that they didn't realize this was on the cards, given that we know moderation has been used on the internet for decades to deal with people's behaviour. But because sites like Facebook and Twitter became platforms and, particularly with Facebook, a utility, the problems they faced regarding moderation decisions have been extreme. Every new tool they introduced could be manipulated in a terrible way, because of the reach of the site and how its powerful algorithm amplified certain content for engagement purposes. Both Twitter and Facebook wanted to connect the world. This was a nice idea in theory, but in practice it meant that, for example, in the early 2010s both sites began being used as recruiting tools by terrorist organizations like ISIS.

The sites were at their best when used to broadcast political change, like when the Arab Spring protests took place in the Middle East and North Africa from 2010–12. I watched several of the events livestreamed online, history taking place on my laptop on a kitchen table. It was invigorating to be able to witness it as it happened – no need to wait for it to be written about, I could watch footage from someone's mobile phone shared on social media. But while pursuing the fairly noble aim of connecting people globally, the biggest social media sites were 'thrown into the complex world of geopolitics, mixed with arguments over freedom of speech', as Charles Arthur wrote in an article for *The Guardian* in 2014. He compared removing the recruitment posts by ISIS to a game of 'Whac-A-Mole': as soon as one was removed, another popped up. These posts were being blamed for a slew of young people travelling to the Middle East to go fight for ISIS or marry ISIS fighters.

In a high-profile case in 2015, three British schoolgirls, Amira Abase, Kadiza Sultana, and Shamima Begum, flew from London to Istanbul and then travelled to Syria, where they met with ISIS operatives after connecting online with another girl who had joined ISIS.[1] All three teenagers were believed to have been influenced by ISIS propaganda online. Sultana is since understood to have died, while Abase's whereabouts are unknown.[2] Begum is living in a refugee camp and trying to have her British citizenship reinstated. You can assume that the founders of Twitter and Facebook had no idea that their sites would be used for such things.

But the terrifying consequences of the always-on social media world kept coming. Another flashpoint was when livestreaming on Facebook began being used by people to stream themselves taking their own lives, self-harming, or committing mass murder. One of the highest-profile incidents was New Zealand's Christchurch massacre, in 2019, when a white terrorist livestreamed his killing of fifty Muslim worshippers. There were immediate calls for Facebook to examine how it was moderating such an obviously problematic feature. Two weeks afterwards, chief operating officer Sheryl Sandberg (who has since left Facebook) wrote a letter to *The New Zealand Herald*, where she outlined what steps Facebook had taken to remove the video and prevent its spread. 'We have heard feedback that we must do more – and we agree,' she said. She outlined what Facebook would be doing to deal with such incidents in the future, and added: 'People with bad intentions will always try to get around our security measures. That's why we must work to continually stay ahead.'[3] Even though the company cracked down on that video, removing millions of pieces of content related to it, a report in *The New York Times* in 2022 found that the Christchurch footage is still available online, across every major social media platform.

The decisions around what Facebook Live content to remove and what to leave up were becoming very public, and showed how the company strained to make the 'right' decision. For example, while it eventually removed the Christchurch shooting video, it chose to leave up a video of the aftermath of the shooting of Philando Castile. Philando was shot seven times by police officers in Minnesota during a traffic stop, and his girlfriend Diamond Reynolds took to Facebook Live to capture the horrifying aftermath as he lay dying.[4] The video was disturbing, but through it Diamond Reynolds was able to show the world the treatment of a black man at the hands of the police, feeding into the Black Lives Matter movement.

There have been different waves of problematic posts and content online – a new one will appear, the sites will find a way to try and deal with it and it will die down or not feature in the media as often; a little while later another one will appear. While there was a lot of media attention on the terrorist groups and their recruitment methods in the mid-2010s, it's not an issue that has gone away. The companies running the sites have had to put counter-terrorism teams into action to deal with it, which has helped to curb the spread. They have been investing more time and money in the right staff and policies to try and deal with what's happening, but it must feel Sisyphean at times. In an article in 2020 in the US publication *Military Review*, Victoria Fassrainer wrote: 'the weaponization of social networks as information hubs is a preferred tool amongst terrorist organizations operating in today's battlespace, with roughly 90 per cent of organized terrorism on the internet carried out through social media.'[5] No matter how much the platforms crack down on certain content, it will continue to seep through the cracks. The lessons Facebook learned from the recent 'fake news' and misinformation eras taught it about how to approach the 2020 US presidential election. But these lessons were learned the hard way. It took the weaponizing of Facebook groups for it to do anything about dealing with the content on them – for example, it eventually banned QAnon pages, but after a period of years and countless articles discussing the real-life impacts of QAnon conspiracy theories. Facebook now puts the responsibility for moderation of private groups into the hands of those who run them, with the threat of suspension if they don't behave.[6]

While sites like MySpace had moderators in house back in the early days, it was Web 2.0 that lead to more serious moderation. That in turn led to companies contracting the job out, and then to the introduction of AI moderation to proactively find content and remove it quickly – which is especially handy with terror and porn content, and with hate speech. Facebook says AI helps it remove 90 per cent of hate speech before it's flagged.[7] But this way is not without its problems. In 2018, mainstream news outlets reported that images of historical figurines such as the Venus of Willendorf were being removed from Facebook because they were being automatically flagged as pornographic. Sometimes their moderation could go too far. But while the platforms had to begin admitting they were using human moderators due to issues like the livestreaming and terror recruitment, they didn't provide information on what it was like to do that job, or how moderators were treated, or even where they were based. Users didn't have to mull over what content moderation even meant for the moderators. All they knew was that the job was being done.

When the look behind the curtain came, it was damning. One of the first major exposés of content moderation and its impact on the workers was a 2010 *New York Times* article, which called the role an 'obscure job that is repeated thousands of times over, from office parks in suburban Florida to outsourcing hubs like the Philippines'.[8] In that article, the moderators are referred to as 'screeners'. One of the interviewees, Ricky Bess, is described as spending eight hours a day 'viewing some of the worst depravities harbored on the Internet'. Another interviewee, Hemanshu Nigam, the former chief security officer at MySpace, says that some screeners signed up because they thought it would be a chance to view pornography. 'They have no idea that some of the despicable and illegal images they will see can haunt them for the rest of their lives,' he tells the reporter.

In addition, while myself and the other comedy forum mods were visible, wearing a badge on our profiles that declared our roles, this new generation of moderators was being employed in a hidden, lesser talked-about job. They became the ghosts in the machine, and so the impact of the work they do took years to become public. Undoubtedly, many Irish people didn't know that moderators were even working here until they read about some taking High Court cases over claims the job gave them post-traumatic stress disorder. Until some of the staff broke the non-disclosure agreements (NDAs) they were told to sign in the early 2020s in order to speak out about their conditions, people might not have realized that the wages paid to the moderators in Ireland are a fraction of that of the actual staff at the platforms they clean up.

Early on, it was Facebook staff in Dublin who reviewed content in Ireland, but since then the company has outsourced the work to companies including CPL and Accenture (the bulk of moderators work for CPL). Altogether there are thousands of people across the world moderating the most popular platforms. Their existence is hugely important, but the stories that have been published about their experiences show that their job is taxing on body and mind. They work in a shadowy online world where they are so essential that things would collapse without them, but where they must not go public because they are a reminder of the worst side of the internet. A job spec I saw in 2022 for a role as a content reviewer (moderator) at Covalen, which is owned by CPL, on LinkedIn said: 'Due to nature of the role, candidates must be fully confident in dealing with sensitive content.'

II

After the initial articles online, like the *New York Times* article on 'screeners', there followed more exposés about the role. Adrian Chen is a prominent tech writer who has long explored the truth of what content moderation is. His first article about the industry was published on the website Gawker in 2012, and had the unwieldy yet pointed headline of: 'Inside Facebook's Outsourced Anti-Porn and Gore Brigade, Where "Camel Toes" are More Offensive Than "Crushed Heads"'. He had been leaked documents by a former content moderator, which showed how staff had to make decisions about which reported content to remove, leave, or escalate further up the chain. They showed the types of decisions that workers for the company oDesk had to make about images of nipples, drugs, nudity, hate speech, and crushed limbs. As the headline alludes, the documents also illustrated how difficult it was to classify what content to leave up or take down. Someone had to rank what was more or less offensive: an almost impossible job.

Within a few years, Chen had teamed up with an Irish documentary maker, Ciaran Cassidy, to share footage with the world of content moderation in action. Their documentary *The Moderators* looked specifically at workers who were moderating dating sites based in Europe, rather than strictly social media sites, but the inference was clear – no matter what site or app you were on, you could expect that moderators were dealing with objectionable content.[9] When it came out in 2017, it took content moderation from a 2D, imaginary job to a real role involving real people. It made me think deeply about who was making the internet safe, and make the link back to my moderation experience. It showed that on any app there could be content that would need to be removed, and that the people removing it could be based thousands of miles away from you. It did give a sense of safety, knowing the job was taking place, but it was clear the job was relentless and not very well paid. I knew that there was unsavoury stuff out there online, but 'out there' felt like the operative words – out there, somewhere, where I didn't have to think about it. I had experienced moderating on the forum, but we weren't dealing with porn images, child abuse or violent threats. This was another level altogether.

Chen's writing and *The Moderators* helped highlight that the job was one that was being kept quiet. They also showed that the people doing the difficult job of sorting through reported content and deciding – based on the site's community guidelines – if it should be removed were often in countries which were far away from the glittering tech hub of Silicon Valley. The sites themselves had gutsy origin stories, often said to be born in a self-created fount of tech genius and power; their dark sides were cleaned up by lower-paid workers in countries across the globe. In a 2014 article for *Wired*, 'The Laborers Who Keep Dick Pics and Beheadings Out of Your Facebook Feed', Chen wrote that content moderation was 'soul-crushing'. He pointed out that as more grandparents started to use sites like Facebook, the company understood they wouldn't want to find footage of killings as they scrolled for updates on their grandkids. Advertisers wouldn't want their potential customers to be appalled at seeing Russian dashcam footage of car crashes or pornographic content which might distract them from the ads. Chen called the workers in the Manila office of the third-party company TaskForce an 'invisible pool of human labour', who kept social media a better version of itself. But as he explained, these moderators had to view every single item that it wasn't deemed appropriate for the site's users to see. They had to watch the ISIS videos of murders in cold blood. They had to decide whether an image of a child and an adult was actually depicting child abuse. Chen's work was a flashlight shining on the signs pointing towards a dehumanization of people doing such a difficult job. 'Adrian was writing years before workers started suing tech companies and having PTSD [post-traumatic stress disorder], but I think he was able to see what was coming down the line,' Ciaran Cassidy tells me.

Chen's writing on content moderators in the Philippines appealed to Cassidy because it wasn't judgemental. He got in touch with him, and that led to them working on *The Moderators* together. They wanted to show through their documentary that the job of content moderation exists, and what it involves. 'Social media can grim me out – and I'm using it *after* it's been moderated,' says Cassidy. He'd started to think about this while he was online, the question of what it was like for the people on the 'other side' tugging at his mind. He wondered about the rights of the moderators, and suspected that while he was visiting a site there could be somebody earning very little on the other end of it, mopping and rinsing. He tells me he realized that when he saw something objectionable on Twitter, he held a power the moderators didn't. He could look away. He began to feel as though the social media sites wanted the act of using their products to 'feel like magic'. That duality both fascinated and bothered him. Through their documentary, he and Chen wanted to make the unseen seen, just as the moderators wanted to do the inverse: disappear images before people got to view them.

As Adrian Chen had already highlighted in his reporting that content moderation was happening in developing countries, where staffing costs were cheaper, the pair decided to film in India. The company they filmed at was 'strangely open' to the idea, perhaps because it was a small outfit, says Cassidy. The filming took place in offices on the second floor of a nondescript building in Bangalore. The crew agreed they wouldn't film the entrance. The only sense viewers got of what was outside the walls was from the bustling street sounds leaking through the open windows. The workers were all young, educated in different parts of India, but had migrated for work to Bangalore. The company dealt with a lot of popular European dating sites, and so operated on a twenty-four-hour cycle. The managers told the pair how they treated employees, and they took them at face value. 'But it's a very, very wide industry,' says Cassidy.

The documentary focused on a week-long training for new recruits, who had to sign an NDA before starting their work. There wasn't a lot of talk about the content moderators' mental health while they were filming, though the training instructor is seen in the documentary telling trainees to separate themselves from their work and to try not to take it personally. But this might be a bit too theoretical, says Cassidy. 'Even if you do have that very focused approach that the instructor would have had, I feel deep down it would still affect you,' he says. The speed of work was 'relentless'. 'You had a fraction of a second and you're on to the next image,' says Cassidy. Workers often faced a stream of disturbing or obscene images that they had to make a decision about. 'I remember we sat down to talk with one worker, and it was just dick pic after dick pic,' says Cassidy. When it came to these explicit images, the rules around what to do depended on the site. On some, any picture of an erect penis was removed, but others allowed such images. The decisions the moderators made were based on what the client wanted.

The Moderators was followed by a 2018 feature film *The Cleaners*, directed by Moritz Riesewieck and Hans Block, who filmed content moderators in the Philippines. The workers weren't allowed to say who they worked for, but it was clear they were employed to do work for major social media companies. In the documentary, the moderators who showed their faces had all left their roles, enabling them to appear on screen without endangering their employment. One of the moderators said the reason they spoke to Riesewieck and Block was because they wanted to say, 'we are here'.[10] They wanted people to know who they were and what they did.

Although they detailed seeing horrific things – dead bodies, abuse – they weren't ashamed of their job. The directors said in an interview afterwards that the moderators wanted to speak to them because they were proud of the work they did. The social media companies were contacted by the directors about the claims made in their documentary, but didn't have a response for them.[11]

In the years since both of these documentaries were made, because of the issues that the sites were newly dealing with, they began pledging to hire more moderators. Hiring moderators became the answer to 'what are you going to do about this major problem on your site?' But while there are content moderators in Ireland, working for companies and contracted to work for social media giants, you don't know exactly where the person who deals with your reports or complaints lives. The mystery and silence that has long surrounded the role has fed into an idea that content moderation is being done far, far away from Irish social media users. It's a place where people's prejudiced impulses and unconscious biases can spring up and happily ferment. You can get used to thinking of content moderation as something that others should do – others far away from you.

In her in-depth book about the emergence and growth of commercial content moderation, *Behind the Screen*, Sarah T. Roberts writes that while moderation is increasingly outsourced to countries like India and the Philippines, Western workers in turn 'find themselves "outsourced" in their own countries of origin, and compared directly to as well as competing directly with counterparts they likely consider a racialised Other halfway around the globe'.[12] The outsourcing abroad can keep moderators at a distance from the content they're moderating, as they might be dealing with content that's not from the country they live in (for example, workers are hired in the Philippines because of the country's cultural ties to the US). This can mean that both they and the people benefiting from that moderation don't recognize each other in it. They can be disconnected from each other.

Because we can start to think of content moderators as 'other' based on where they work and the type of work they do, it can also mean that when it's revealed that content moderation is happening in Ireland's capital, you can slip into 'othering' those people too. The factors surrounding the role might mean people not seeing the moderators as individuals who deserve the same treatment as if it was them doing that job. In the act of othering a moderator, you can fail to think about the impact of the job on them, and about what it does to their psyche to deal with other people's filth. But just like their peers in the Philippines, the US, Kenya or India, Irish content moderators are on the frontlines of how social media tackles the issues created by its own existence.

III

When I speak to former moderator for Facebook Chris Gray, he doesn't want to have to tell me the same stories that he's told multiple eager journalists. He worked for the company CPL as a content moderator for Facebook in Dublin. He's been here before: sitting in front of a stranger, waiting for their questions about how terrible it was to do the job, what grisly things he saw, and what the impact was on him. He's not sure he wants to go through it all again. We're on Zoom – he has Covid-19, but feels well – and he's wearing a fluffy dressing gown. For his background he has chosen a GIF of a sandy beach, with shimmering waves and a palm tree swaying in the wind. Together, we can pretend we're chatting in an exotic clime, and not a locked-down Dublin. I wanted to talk to Gray to find out what he experienced as a content moderator. It was hard to get hold of him – it was hard to get hold of any content moderator. The others I contacted did not want to go on the record. Gray stands out because, having left the job, he has spoken to the media about what it was like working in Dublin for CPL, and he's also taken a High Court case over the PTSD he says he suffered as a result of the work.[13] But as we discuss the parameters of what I want to talk to him about, he asks me: 'What's the point?'

It feels like the point is obvious, but as I speak more to Gray I see how the complications around moderation go beyond how the moderators are treated and what the impact on them is. Yet even this aspect is troubling. An article about Gray in 2020 quoted him as saying 'people are awful. This is what my job has taught me'. It described a talk he'd given about his gruelling work as a moderator – how he had seen stonings; executions; an image of a child dressed up as Adolf Hitler; topless photos; inhumane and graphic images.[14] He talked too about having to make the 'right decision' when moderating, the hundreds of 'tickets' (moderation jobs) he had to deal with every day, and what a minefield it was, as well as the high targets moderators had to reach. After six months in the job, it had started taking its toll, and after he left he was diagnosed with PTSD.

He makes it clear he doesn't want to rehash his own trauma again and again. He doesn't want to answer my questions about what he saw while sitting at his computer terminal. I fear the interview is over but he keeps talking. He tells me he's angry that despite the fact he has bared his soul to the media about what he has experienced, and though Irish politicians have claimed to listen to moderators like him, nothing has changed. He tells me he doesn't think that detailing the trauma to me for a book will change anything either. (Gray has since written his own book about his experiences, which was published in late 2022, but it's only in the afterword that he details any of the more traumatic things he dealt with.)[15]

Gray has initiated High Court proceedings against both Facebook and CPL Solutions over claims of psychological trauma while doing the job from 2017 to 2018. (The case is ongoing at the time of writing.) His is one of around forty cases being taken in Ireland by content moderators based both here and in Europe. The cases have to be taken here because Facebook's European HQ is here. In Ireland, we don't have class action suits, where one case can be taken by multiple people, so all the moderators who take one do so separately, in the hope that a judge might deal with them in some way together. In May 2020, Facebook settled a class action case in the US with moderators who said they had developed PTSD on the job. Facebook paid out $52 million in total, but by the time the payment was distributed to the current and former moderators (11,250 of them took the case), and legal fees were paid, the final sums given out weren't huge.[16] The claims were settled without Facebook being found liable for the alleged harms; it denied liability and said it settled to avoid the expense and distraction caused by the case.

Gray believes that content moderation and associated issues took Facebook by surprise. A lot of moderation and related problems are down to people being offended, he says, but the problem is that not everyone is offended by the same things. People report things that offend them, expecting moderators to deal with it. But different things offend different people. 'You will see people advertising puppies for sale on Facebook, and somebody will report that, because they're offended by the idea of people owning animals. Or offended by people eating animals,' he says. 'People are always going to be offended by stuff. So the stuff getting reported is always going to be there.' The question is what to do if you accept this is just part of online life. You still have to respond to the reports, says Gray, but it's a constant derring-do with no end to the tale in sight.

He says that there will always be things that people are offended by online, and I know he's right on this, having seen offence expressed over what I thought were quite minor things (of course, they might be minor to me, but major to the offended). Plus, there will always be some people who want to behave in a way that pushes against what's deemed acceptable, and that is something that's been present online since the very early days of the internet. Creating a new world means that you can subvert even its rules. Whatever a social media platform's rules say, it will still need content moderation, says Gray. 'It's a never-ending battle. Because there are always going to be people doing things that other people are offended by. And even if you push the rule, that pretty much anything goes, there are people who want to push it a little bit further. So whatever your rules say, you still need content moderation. That's your first problem – that we can't agree on what's acceptable [behaviour] or not,' he says. Not being able to agree on what's acceptable means the moderators are trying to make difficult decisions, at the behest of an organization that's attempting to balance its own aspirations of free speech with complaints from users.

These billion-dollar tech companies know they have a responsibility to their users – and advertisers – to keep their sites as clean as possible. But moderation is fraught for them because they don't see themselves as publishers. Instead, they see themselves as platforms for other people's thoughts. Their First Amendment 'free speech' mindset is joined by the fact that, in the US, the companies are protected by Section 230 of the Communications Decency Act, which means they can't be taken to court over what their users say on their platforms. But as tech regulation becomes less of a fringe topic and part of mainstream conversations, Section 230 is under threat, with some US politicians wanting to remove this protection. We don't have Section 230 in Ireland but neither do we have regulation which deems social media platforms to be publishers.

While the sites have been trying to figure out how to do enough to make a difference, but not so much that they're operating a censorship regime, they have been making mistakes, because moderation is an imperfect thing. Moderators often have to cater for a wide sweep of cultural practices and beliefs, and what might be seen as normal in one context might be deemed offensive in another. In 2011, for example, Facebook apologized after removing a post that contained a still from the show *Eastenders* of two men kissing.[17] In another example, an Instagram user in Brazil shared a post in October 2020 to raise awareness of signs of breast cancer. The post featured eight photographs that showed breast cancer symptoms: five of the photos had uncovered female nipples in them, and the post was removed after being detected by AI trained to identify nudity in photos. Although Facebook reinstated the photo after an appeal, its own Oversight Board said that the removal went against Facebook's community standards, which allow uncovered female nipples if they are being shown to advance breast cancer awareness. It said the image's incorrect removal indicated a lack of proper human oversight, which in turn raised human rights concerns. This Oversight Board is Facebook's way of kicking decisions about freedom of expression to a group of independent people. Users are able to appeal moderation decisions to the board, and have its members make a (binding) decision on whether Facebook's decision should be changed or not.[18]

These sorts of appeals happen because social media platforms can't avoid making unpopular moderation decisions. They aim to have a safe space for their users, but no two of their users might have the same opinion on what a safe space is. One might want their feed full of the same sort of content their neighbour might find highly offensive. A person might share a video of a child being bullied as a way to raise awareness about bullying, or they could share the very same video to get a kick out of it. And on top of this, Chris Gray says that a moderator won't always reach the same conclusion as the content moderator sitting next to them.

Before talking to Gray, I believed that the content moderator's job is to catch things quickly, shut them down, and stop toxic behaviour. But his way of thinking about it is more fluid. He believes the job of the content moderator is to keep things moving, 'to keep everybody engaged and keep everybody there so that [the company] can show them ads and sell them something, make some money out of them'. He believes that it's not about protecting society from someone's opinion. He even suggests we need to give up the idea of moderators making a right or wrong decision. The right answer, he says, is whichever one keeps the community in motion.

'Facebook's business is to maintain a safe space, the town square, a place where people can congregate and talk and so that's what they do,' says Gray. 'Now all the technology is really just a service to that, they're not a technology company at all – they are a company whose job is to manage human behaviour, human interactions. To me that's what Facebook is.' Because the moderators do such an essential job with this, he says they should be paid far more than they are. 'Really the content moderators should be the people that are on €150 k,' he says, instead of the Facebook staff who are highly paid. But as moderators have shown, their salaries are far, far below those of the people who build and work at the social media sites – and their working conditions are different too.

The Future of Moderation

In 2019, leaked audio from two open meetings of Facebook staff with CEO Mark Zuckerberg was published by The Verge, a tech website. In one clip, he was asked about the reports on what content moderators for the platform were experiencing. His answer appeared to underplay what the moderators themselves had been describing. 'Some of the reports, I think, are a little overdramatic,' said Zuckerberg. 'From digging into them and understanding what's going on, it's not that most people are just looking at just terrible things all day long. But there are really bad things that people have to deal with, and making sure that people get the right counselling and space and ability to take breaks and get the mental health support that they need is a really important thing.'[1]

His comments were not well received by those within the content moderation world. They seemed to indicate that he didn't realize the full impact of the work on the people contracted to do it. A year later, the pandemic led one group of moderators to write directly to Zuckerberg. In November 2020, over 250 Facebook moderators (working for the companies CPL and Accenture, and just a fraction of the thousands of moderators globally at the time) wrote an open letter to the Facebook CEO, asking him to reconsider making them work in their offices. The pandemic was showing yet another way moderators were treated differently to the staff working for the social media sites. Content moderators for Facebook aren't Facebook employees. They're third-party employees contracted by Facebook, so they don't benefit from all the perks that its direct employees do.

'Before the pandemic, content moderation was easily Facebook's most brutal job,' these moderators wrote. 'We waded through violence and child abuse for hours on end. Moderators working on child abuse content had targets increased during the pandemic, with no additional support.' With the added complication of Covid-19, they were fearful about their physical safety. They were worried they might take the virus home with them, having picked it up in the office. Some had vulnerable family members; others were vulnerable themselves. But without their work, they told Zuckerberg, his 'empire collapses'.[2] They knew their worth: they could do the job better than AI; they could spot the cultural quirks and neologisms, the shorthand and slang. They made moderating better. They made Facebook better. CPL and Accenture released statements recognizing the moderators' work, but said that it had to be done in the office due to its sensitive nature, and because it was essential work.[3] Facebook also claimed that many moderators were already working from home anyway. Meanwhile, it was reported in the US that Facebook staff were given a stipend to help set up their home offices.[4] The pandemic showed exactly how big the gulf is between how these contractors are treated and viewed, and how staff of the social media companies are.

The following year, in May 2021, content moderators in Ireland brought their stories to the public by speaking in front of an Irish government committee. The speakers included content moderator Isabella Plunkett, lawyer Cori Crider from Foxglove, which advocates on behalf of moderators, and Fionnuala Ní Bhrógáin from the Communications Workers' Union (CWU). Plunkett detailed the impact of moderating on her mental health: the 'horrible lucid dreams' she had been having about what she'd seen while working, and how she needed to take antidepressants as a result. She said that the company offered wellness coaches to moderators: 'They suggest karaoke and painting, but frankly, one does not always feel like singing after having seen someone be battered to bits,' she said.[5] Just like the workers Ciaran Cassidy and Adrian Chen met in Bangalore, Irish content moderators sign documents that state they won't talk about the content they deal with. Fionnuala Ní Bhrógáin of the CWU claimed that these NDAs had a 'chilling effect' on the workers in terms of speaking out about conditions.

Plunkett gave an insight into the conditions where she worked. She said that the starting salary was €27,000 per year, with a €1,000 pay rise after a year and an eleven-month probation period. The average wage at Facebook is a few multiples of that. Many of the moderators came from different backgrounds, said Plunkett, with some training to be doctors, lawyers, or in hospitality. Some of her team were college students, looking at the internet's underbelly to earn cash between lectures. That same year, Ibrahim Halawa spoke to the then Tánaiste Leo Varadkar about his content moderation job at the company Covalen, which is part of CPL. He had last been in the press after being freed from an Egyptian jail while in his teens. The irony was that Halawa was just seventeen when he became a political prisoner, and his story was widely discussed on Irish social media, making him the subject of trolling and abuse. Ahead of the meeting, Halawa told RTÉ *Prime Time* that moderating was an essential job. Even though he wasn't allowed to talk to the media, he wanted to speak out about his work issues. Remarkably, he wasn't speaking out because he wanted to leave – he saw his job as a way of helping make social media safe.[6] Like the moderators in the Philippines who featured in the documentary *The Cleaners*, he was motivated by what moderators can achieve through doing what they do. But he knew that while mentally he could deal with the job to an extent – in part due to his experiences in jail in Egypt – not everyone would be as capable.

Cori Crider is the co-founder of Foxglove, a non-profit led by lawyers which helps content moderators speak out about the conditions they work under. Crider told the Oireachtas committee that Facebook designs the software used by the content moderators and sets the production targets. She told the assembled politicians that a large proportion of content moderators working in Ireland are non-nationals, hired to work on various streams and in multiple languages. Moderators are needed for their specific languages, ethnicities and cultural knowledge, so that they can look at content from across different countries. But this could also make the workers vulnerable, due to their possible lack of knowledge of their rights and entitlements in Ireland. During the pandemic, there had been applause and signs draped out windows to show support for frontline workers. To Crider, content moderators are frontline workers too, playing a critical role in society, doing work that just isn't valued enough. But there were no flags for them.

Because the workforce isn't unionized, Foxglove hears from workers who say they're fearful about speaking out. Martha Dark, who also works at Foxglove, tells me in a separate conversation: 'For too long, the back end, or the "production line", of social media has been hidden and separated from issues in front-end content moderation. And I think that's problematic.' In describing why people do the job, she reiterated Halawa's sentiment when she said, 'Pretty much every content moderator I speak to does that job because they want to make a contribution to the safety, security and effectiveness of the monitoring of the public square.' But almost all the moderators she deals with have serious mental health conditions. She believes that the longer people do the job, the more likely they are to be impacted – physically or mentally – by what they've seen. People have told her about panic attacks, certain sounds triggering them, anxiety, and depression. Depending on the area of the world they moderate the content from, moderators might be dealing with more or less extreme content. 'Some see beheadings and extreme violence and sexual violence,' says Dark. 'But I think fairly consistently, they're saying that they see very graphic content that keeps coming.' Some staff have told Dark they're afraid to take the wellness breaks they're entitled to if they're behind on reaching their target.

As more calls are coming for moderators to help clean things up online, some experts are highlighting that the solution might not be moderating at scale, or that even if you try to moderate larger volumes of content successfully, you won't be able to do a good job of it. In 2019, TechDirt writer and content moderation expert Mike Masnick proposed what he called Masnick's Impossibility Theorem: content moderation at scale is impossible to do well.[7] He wrote that his theory isn't an argument to do nothing, and it also doesn't mean that companies can't do a better job of content moderation. But he says there's a huge problem, in that many people seem to expect that companies should strive for a level of content moderation that is simply impossible to reach.

Masnick suggests that content moderation 'will always end up frustrating very large segments of the population and will always fail to accurately represent the "proper" level of moderation of anyone'. For starters, he says that the people whose content has been moderated will be unhappy. They thought their content deserved to be online, after all. Then there's the fact that moderation is a subjective practice, and it's impossible to have it be more scientific or objective. It's going to rely on judgement calls, and that will involve grey areas. But the solution to all this isn't *no* moderation, as people also don't want that, he says. And as we've seen in this book, there are many reasons for this. Given all the challenges, he believes moderation at scale will never reach the high level that people would like it to reach.

Masnick has highlighted for years that one of the problems of content moderation is that you often need a lot of context to make a moderation decision, and there's no way to adequately provide that at scale. When dealing with large volumes of content that need moderation, you need to set rules, but he says rules don't always leave room for understanding and applying context.[8] The documentaries on moderation did show that the moderators have many tickets to go through every day, and it didn't appear like in-depth conversations could happen around every decision. Instead, the staff turn to the guidelines and rules that the company provides them. Given that there isn't a lot of room for applying context, the sites can end up with lots of edge cases, which really don't look great.

Masnick also says that scaling up content moderation means that the greater the volume of things to moderate, the higher the number of 'mistakes' that will be made. You might reach 99 per cent accuracy, but when you're moderating millions of posts a day, that means that 1 per cent is still going to be a large number. This in turn can make the companies look like they're not doing much, even if they've successfully dealt with millions of offensive posts and videos.

Masnick details an experiment carried out in 2018, at a content moderation conference in Washington DC, to show how difficult content moderation is in practice. The audience spent an hour behaving as a trust and safety team who had to deal with reported content on a (fake) social media platform. They could choose four potential outcomes. The result was that there was at least some disagreement on what the moderators should do with each reported item. No matter what the person chose for each example, they couldn't keep everyone happy. And so Masnick concludes that there is no perfect solution to content moderation, and any company, 'no matter how thoughtful and deliberate and careful', is going to make mistakes.

It is obvious that seeking perfection from content moderation is futile. In the distant future, perhaps it could approach a much higher level of infallibility than it currently reaches. The platforms are trying to move more towards using AI instead of relying on human moderators, but AI is an imperfect solution, and as long as there are humans doing the job of moderating social media, they will be exposed to the worst of human behaviour. Once there is a person in charge of deciding what should and shouldn't stay on a website, there will be an impact on them. Compared to a decade ago, the role of the content moderator is better understood. It's gone from people not knowing the job exists to politicians pledging to speak to moderators' employers about improving their working conditions. But despite the High Court cases, interviews, talks with the public and with politicians, Chris Gray says nothing has changed for moderators like him. 'It doesn't achieve anything,' he says of the speaking out so far. 'It's almost like we're all just participating in theatre.'

He worries about people who have been 'harmed' being used for other people's agendas. 'When politicians jump up and down saying: we want Facebook to do more about hate speech or bullying or vaccine misinformation? Well, there's no concrete proposal. There's no real understanding of what that means,' he says. 'They're not really engaged with the topic. It's just political theatre to make them look good.' When we say we want Facebook to do more to fight misinformation or harmful content, what we mean is we want more content moderators to be hired. Gray pictures the result being 'more people in a sweatshop being harmed, working to meet impossible targets in ridiculous conditions'. When I ask Martha Dark what the group Foxglove, which advocates for content moderators, thinks would make life better for the workers, she tells me the companies should provide proper, meaningful mental health care; the government should force the companies to end overly restrictive NDAs which slow worker organising; content moderation should be better regulated; and all social media firms should be made to bring content moderation in-house. Given that their role is so important to the safety of the internet, and there are only going to be more content moderators hired in the coming years, Dark said these steps must be taken to make this work safe and fair for those doing it.

It is hard to speak out. The content moderators who have been interviewed for documentaries like *The Moderators* and *The Cleaners* were brave. In their voices being made public, the ghosts in the machine have transmuted into full-bodied people. Their experience has been aired, and social media users can't live in ignorance any longer – they now know the human impact of making their favourite sites safe. Whether the platforms will listen to the workers' demands, and transform their conditions, should concern anyone who benefits from the online space. But until things change, the moderators will continue to invisibly do doing the internet's most difficult job.

TECH AND THE CITY

Friend just sent me this. Property company advertising
'annual rent inflation of 8.7%' in the silicon docks.
Isn't that, yanno, illegal?

*

If you unironically use the term 'Silicon Docks' you deserve
to have your pockets filled with old Millennium 50p coins
and then be thrown into the Liffey.

*

In one brazen invasion of sovereignty, Google renamed
Grand Canal Dock as 'Silicon Docks' on Google Maps. Granted,
it's not quite 'Londonderry,' but these things are a slippery slope.

Big Tech Constellation

It's 24 degrees as I sit in Merrion Square in Dublin city centre and plan my walk, a mini tech pilgrimage of sorts. It's an unusual Sunday in an unusual summer. Ireland is at the tail end of a heatwave and while sitting in the park, insulated from the city traffic and the worst of the heat by the trees, I feel for a moment like I'm somewhere more exotic. I plot my route in my notebook and eat a slice of banana bread studded with melting chocolate chips. Ahead of me there are people ordering ice creams from a truck, sitting on benches chatting, walking dogs, and eating lunch al fresco.

The Georgian square is significant because of its past – locals who lived in the tall houses that line the green space included Oscar Wilde and Daniel O'Connell – and as I get up to leave I wonder if the park was sentient, what it would say about what it has seen. The square has thankfully been untouched, but just around the corner buildings have been knocked and built, and if you walk in any direction from it you'll see signs of how Dublin has evolved. I use Google Maps to figure out where the offices of Twitter, Google, and Meta are, and star each one of them. Together they make a small constellation.

Around the corner from the square, things are less serene and more like the regular Dublin city I inhabit, with apartments and busy restaurants, corner shops and offices. As I head to where I know the Twitter headquarters are, I stop to take a photo of a sign on one of the apartment blocks, St Andrew's Court, which memorializes the death of Linda Byrne and Marion Vardy, two young girls from Holles St, who died in 1963 when a tenement building collapsed on Fenian St.[1] This and a similar incident sparked an inquiry and led to the clearing of inner-city tenements.

The plaque says that the population of the Westland Row parish fell within a decade from 20,000 to 6,000. 'Their sacrifice should not be forgotten,' reads a line in capitals at the bottom. Across from that spot now are flats, all boarded up at the bottom. Down the road and opposite them are modern apartments and an Italian restaurant; further up I see a fancy bistro, and then on the right hand side, on Cumberland Street South, is the six-storey-tall Twitter building. It doesn't look as glass-boxy as some of the latest office buildings that have been built in the city, as it has lines of what might be wood vertically bisecting the floor-to-ceiling glass.

The street is quiet; the offices are quiet. I can see no one through the windows, and empty chairs are visible in the small café at the front of the building. I recall being in there once, for an event about women in politics. The office didn't feel as flashy as somewhere like Google, where I had visited for lunch at least a decade previously. Back then, I was impressed by how slick everything was – and how free everything was. Inside, you could pretend money didn't exist. Twitter didn't look as swanky, simply because by the time of visiting I was used to seeing offices like that.

If I didn't know what the Twitter building was, I wouldn't guess today that it belonged to the company which runs the app where I spend too much of my time online. It's just there, part of the landscape of modern Dublin, modest but taking up considerable space. As I walk away I see that along Bass Place, next to the office, is a row of derelict houses, with yet more derelict houses up ahead, and when I round the corner onto Sandwith Street, I see even more derelict houses. If you wanted to make a bald point about the state of housing in Dublin, you could opt for taking a photograph of that scene.

Walking down Sandwith Street I look towards Pearse Street ahead of me, a long stretch that has Pearse House on one side, designed by Dublin

Corporation architect Herbert Simms in the Thirties after the tenements were cleared out. The rest of the street is home to offices which are side by side with local businesses – like Mattress Mick's mattress shop, and the Pig & Heifer deli. I walk past the enviable Victorian park at Pearse Square and on towards the bridge over the canal. The sky is blue and fresh. I turn right just before the bridge.

Here is where it all began, on Barrow Street, where Google opened its offices in 2003. Tourists are taking photographs of the pretty canal boats with the tall Boland's Mill in the background, the painted signs restored after building work saw the old silos knocked and new offices built for Google.[2] Ahead of me now I notice, Barrow Street, looks shorter than usual, as if it's been fenced off. It transpires there's a huge hoarding there, covering a new development underway opposite the Google offices. Across the way again is an empty razed lot, where more construction is set to begin. A year after the Google offices were opened, an article in *The Irish Times* described the street as having been 'once bleak . . . filled with disused warehouses'.[3] The Google offices, just like Twitter's, are tall and impressive, but still quite unremarkable from ground level. They are as humble as a multi-storey office building can be. The inside looks intriguing and colourful. Before I go back towards the Meta offices, I walk past the hoardings and under the nearby railway bridge, which is one of my favourite spots in this area, despite the fact it's very low and gloomy under there. It's like going back to Victorian times. But the reminder that I'm walking the cobbled street in 2022 comes when I see a blue two-person tent set up under the bridge.

To get to the Meta offices I turn back and head towards the bridge by Grand Canal Docks again. More tourists are milling around now, and the area is warm, bright, and colourful, despite the greyness of the tallest buildings. Retaining some of Boland's Mill has allowed the area to keep a sense of character and history, something that feels alive. So many of the newer offices and buildings these days in the city feel to me to be blank, unemotional; ciphers standing in for buildings, not absorbing the world around them. The older buildings interspersed among the new make the place feel like it's tethered to reality. Those glass boxes have come to symbolize a type of future-forward thinking in Ireland, construction with an eye for what works best for business and capitalism, not necessarily what works best for people. That might not be the intention, but that's how it can feel as you pass. Perhaps I'm too much of a romantic, assigning these emotions to bricks and mortar, but I know I'm not alone in holding these ideas close.

I cross the road into the Grand Canal Dock area, the water bringing a cooling effect to the hot day. In the distance are colourful smudges: kayakers. People are everywhere here: sitting on the water's edge, outside cafés, in the shops, on benches, laughing, talking. The former docklands was a shell of a place before it was developed. On a neat road at the corner of Macken Street and Misery Hill – believed to have been gifted the moniker either because it was where bodies were displayed after being hanged at the nearby Gallows Hill, or because a leprosy hospital was nearby – are the offices of Meta. The company sign has the Pride rainbow on it the day I visit. The building fits in well with this part of the docklands: tall, angled, and mysterious, with long glass windows. Through the windows I can see a large blue neon tubular sign spelling out 'dream big', and another large sign which has 'What's on your mind?' written on it. Nearby are more offices, apartments, the Bord Gáis Energy Theatre, which was designed by the Polish American architect Daniel Libeskind.[4] When I think of this area I think of progress, of constructing something new, of remaking a city.

This area is often referred to as Silicon Docks, a minor-scale take-off of Silicon Valley. Out of the death of the docklands came this area, a new space to build a new future for Dublin. A few months before my wander I spoke to Dolores Wilson, a community activist who lives near the Meta offices on Macken Street. 'It's only the likes of auctioneers and the big tech companies that call it Silicon Docks. Ordinary people on the ground don't call it that,' she told me. 'It's just a marketing tool.' Locals like her have witnessed how this area has changed. While I'm a blow-in, she grew up here, playing on the streets with friends as a child. 'It's amazing in fifty years what's happened, but some of it has been good, some of it not so good,' she said, even though she's not a NIMBY and certainly not anti-development. The reimagining of the docklands was very exciting at the start, she said. She was a member of the Docklands Oversight and Consultative Forum, alongside fellow locals, community workers, business owners, and local politicians.

I find a video on the RTÉ archives website from 2001 of her talking to a journalist about a new bridge that was due to be built over the Liffey and onto another part of the docklands, which some locals opposed (it was eventually built anyway).[5] Aerial footage of the docklands in that 20-year-old news report shows a tetris-like space, filled with grey and blue squares and rectangles of flat warehouse roofs and empty yards; large ships sitting in a row along the side of the Liffey. I hold the images of this earlier time in my mind, transposing the places where I'm walking now over a map of what it was like then. The old yards at the very end of the docks are now a children's park and home to Brewdog pub, with grass growing where only concrete once lay.

On the quays I see the orange diving bell designed by Bindon Blood Stoney, who also designed the quay walls of the Liffey. During the re-development, the city tried to keep as much history as possible alive in the area, so you can bump into unusual remnants of the past sitting atop something new. I stop and look around at both sides of the quay, the harp-like Samuel Beckett Bridge to my left. Where once there would have been dockers unloading grain and bananas off boats there are now people cycling and walking, and where once there were busy warehouses and yards there are office buildings, the Convention Centre, headquarters of law firms, apartments. A buzzing hive of business.

The docklands have seen locals leave over the decades: like after the tenements collapsed, and after ships started using containers, reducing the need for dockers. Dolores Wilson says the North Inner City locals have fought to survive. The population continued to drop over the decades, and so the locals didn't want it to drop further as tech companies moved into the docklands and the area was built up. Out her window Wilson can see the site where a new ten-storey building is due to be constructed by the company Bartra, set up by Richard Barrett who was formerly in business with Johnny Ronan, of Ronan Group Real Estate, which is behind new Facebook offices being built in Ballsbridge on the city's south side. Residents of Macken Street thought they were fairly safe in terms of not getting much development near them, said Dolores Wilson. But now they can feel it encroaching. Complicating things, during the pandemic came the worries about whether there would be enough workers eager to leave home and use these new office developments.

After the economic decline of the docklands, into the early Eighties' the question was what to do about the area. Before my wander I went down a rabbit hole online of archive reports about what was planned, and noticed that there was some focus on cultural development, like promises of a museum, an archive, and art galleries.[6] There were pledges that it wouldn't just be a place for office blocks.[7] And yet I don't see many cultural buildings – save the Irish Emigration Museum and Bord Gáis Energy Theatre – near that part of the quays now. There's a continual push and pull in Dublin city over what's to be built and where, and how to best serve the city and its future. In the past ten years, the question of how many hotels and student apartments are planned for the city has been a particular bugbear of some of its residents, even as tourism organizations say there are too few hotel rooms to cater for visitors.

The development in the docklands area I'm walking around is in large part down to initiatives like the Custom House Docks Authority (launched in 1994) and the Dublin Docklands Development Authority (DDDA) launched in 1997, which Dolores Wilson was involved in. She told me that the DDDA felt like the first time locals could have proper input into what was going to happen. A lot of good things came out of the DDDA, she said, social benefits like educational programmes, and a jobs placement scheme that got some locals working in financial services. They also got 20 per cent social affordable housing on the south side of the docklands, which would contribute to enabling locals to stay in the area.

The DDDA said after it wound up that it created 40,000 jobs, built 11,000 new homes, and saw the population grow to 22,000 by 2008. After that came the Strategic Development Zone for North Lotts and Grand Canal Dock in 2013. The locals got nothing out of it, Dolores told me. Certainly not the social housing and accommodation they had hoped for. The social housing requirement for new residential developments was brought down to 10 per cent from 20 per cent under the SDZ. When it comes to the development in the area, Wilson said that a lot of people are fearful, particularly those who live in the flats on her street, about what's next. People don't have the sense that they can actually change tech companies' plans if they are set on doing something in the area.

I walk onto the Samuel Beckett Bridge and look out at both sides, at the Liffey that flows under where I'm suspended, past the docklands and out to the sea. I'm on the side reserved for pedestrians, and next to me are cycle lanes that would bring me all the way to Phibsboro and beyond if I followed the canal. The city just happens, doesn't it, I think to myself: it just lives and moves and breathes. The people work and walk and talk and sleep, they shop and love and pick up rubbish and toss rubbish, they drink and they take drugs, they bed into the city and they ignore it. Every year brings more changes to the city, new layers built on, new buildings opened and closed, new cycle lanes and new tarmac melted onto old roads.

Most people aren't examining the city around them as they make their way through it. We often have to be jarred into opening our eyes and re-alizing where we are by spotting something new or unexpected. As I walk away from the river I watch children in wetsuits jumping into the old canal, and a teen racing down the cycle lane on a small, child-sized motorcycle, doing wheelies. This particular stretch is a strange combination of similar modern-looking apartments and office buildings baking in the sun, and old parts of the docklands standing proud, like the rusting metal hulk of machinery that looms over a bridge bringing people onto Sheriff Street Upper. I love that piece of machinery, the unexpected heft of it, how it has been allowed to stay even though it's past its point of usefulness. It overlooks a huge bust of the singer Luke Kelly, who grew up locally, his mouth opened as though he's mid-song.

I go straight on, up the Royal Canal Greenway. I spot two herons standing near each other by the water, unmoving. A few months previously I had visited a shop nearby called K&A Stores on Seville Place. It was spring, and cold. The owner, Gerry Fay, and his son Mark were working behind the counter, sorting stock and dealing with customers, when I arrived. Gerry Fay took over the corner shop over in 1980 and in a charming way it looks like it hadn't changed since. Its white counters were home to piles of packets of crisps, chocolate bars, and crusty bread rolls, and under the window were bags of potatoes. When I sat down to talk to Gerry Fay in his office, behind him were tacked up articles about dockland development, like one about big tech firms looking for office accommodation, and another about a proposed swimming pool. There were planning ads for developments also on the wall, along with photographs of him as a young boy with Luke Kelly, who was one of his classmates. In one image, the young boys are wearing ties and child-sized trench coats. Gerry Fay grew up around the corner from his shop, on Sheriff Street, and has been involved in local community action for decades. Like Dolores Wilson, he has watched with a keen eye how the docklands has been rebuilt.

When I asked Fay about the pieces of paper stuck to the wall behind him, he said, 'Basically, we're not against development as such – you can't be against development. And things never stand still. But the developer has to have regard to the concerns and the fears and the aspirations of the indigenous community.' He sees the policy around the docklands' development as being 'the policy of gentrification and dislocation'. What's happened to the community has been a violation of basic human rights over the last thirty years, said Fay. 'Thirty years of social deprivation.'

Walking on, I think about what he told me about the various changes made to the docklands area over the years, the strong local community, the socio-economic problems, the unemployment rate that averaged

30 per cent in the late Nineties. Today, it's typically reported that around 40,000 people work in the docklands area, and that around 27,000 live across the various communities on both sides of the Liffey (the docklands is split in two by the river).[8] I read in the local estate agent Owen Reilly's docklands residential report for 2021 that the average selling price for a home was €430,143.[9] What's happened to the working class docklands area as it has been developed over the decades has left Gerry Fay and his son Mark wary – they simply can't afford not to be on the alert about what could be coming down the tracks. They told me, like Dolores Wilson, that they were happy for development to happen, and welcoming of change, but things that have occurred in the past can be a cause for worry. When we spoke, they were particularly worried about a new development planned for Sheriff Street. Mark said they couldn't but be reminded of what happened to the old Sheriff Street flats, which were demolished in the Nineties to the shock of locals, and whether the current flats were at risk. I see that when new development is planned near them, they have to ask: will it create a further divide in the community, marking out the haves from the have-nots? Or will it be an opportunity for local employment, and give the place a boost?

I found an *Irish Times* article from the late Nineties online about the proposed development authority, and Gerry Fay was quoted in it, saying he was optimistic about the integration that was to be part of the plan. He described it then as a chance to breathe life back into the area.[10] The Sheriff Street flats' destruction was the first sign for him and others that the redevelopment of the docklands could mean an impingement on the lives of locals. Sheriff Street has developed unequally, and one part, Sheriff Street Lower, has an unenviable reputation for crime and drug use. I went on to YouTube and searched for videos of Sheriff Street. I found one where an interviewer spoke to children there in the Seventies. He called the area, home to many families and bright young children, a 'ghetto'.[11]

Gerry Fay described a docklands that I would never see, one that he grew up within, which had all kinds of shops, timber yards, factories. I wonder what bits of them are left behind; on the greenway I can see that on the other side of the canal from me there's still the rubble and detritus of what must be dockland life. After 'containerization' came in in the Fifties, where containers began to be used by cargo ships, fewer dockers were needed for loading and unloading goods. 'The decline set in,' said Fay. The government at the time offered people a grant to relocate out to the new emerging housing estates. Dublin's movement of people into and out of the city for accommodation has come in waves. Suburbanisation was an important part of Ireland's housing history, but by the Eighties the capital was in decline.

A visit from Ted Johns, a former British Labour councillor who died in 2004, to the docklands has always stuck in Gerry Fay's mind. Johns lived on the Isle of Dogs, a peninsula off the Thames in London, where Canary Wharf is – another docklands area which suffered after container- ization came in. In 1970, when Johns and others grew tired of the lack of government support and amenities in their area, they temporarily cut the Isle of Dogs off from the rest of London using a 'people's barrier' across both bridges into it.[12] Just like the Dublin docklands, in the Isle of Dogs there were similar concerns about how the locals were treated as the place was regenerated. 'Ted said even the local pub was bought and you had to be wearing a tie and a shirt and everything else,' said Gerry. 'They didn't want the locals in.' Johns told him that people in charge of development always talk about the future, and all that will be available then. But tomorrow never comes.

People say there are a lot of social problems and anti-social behaviour in the area Gerry and Mark Fay live in. But Gerry told me that most of these problems are related to how the area has developed. He said that 'official vandalism' is his top subject. 'I acknowledge that we have the vandals, but it's the official vandals, the people in the suits that meet in these offices and make decisions that impact on and affect people's lives,' he said. He has seen how the personal impact of decisions made in the boardrooms. Before I left, we spoke about all they did have in the area: the school, the community hall, the soccer teams, the women's centre, the preschools, the afterschools, the after-care recovery group, the Girl Guides,

258

the credit union, the Dublin boxing club, the GAA club. The many volun-
tary workers, the people the community is built on and by. Gerry could
see the gentrification and dislocation, but also the precious parts of the
community that they want to protect. 'We'll fight the battle and we'll still
be here. We're not going anywhere,' he told me.

If you turn right at the bridge onto Sheriff Street Upper instead of going
up the greenway, and walk under the hulking old machinery, head towards
the river and you'll soon get to another part of the docklands that's a
controversial symbol of development: Mayor Street Upper. I walked over
there around the same time I met the Fays, and every time I'm in the
area I think about what I saw and heard. The area is a great example of
the docklands' success – there's a college, apartments, restaurants, shops,
businesses, cafés, hotels. On Mayor Street Upper is a short, neat row of
six terraced houses, and in number one lives Tony McDonnell. The front
door to his home is temporarily boarded up pending an application to
An Bord Pleanála, but you can access a new door through a metal gate
to the side. Just a few feet in front of his home are the Luas tram tracks,
and even when you're inside you can feel the deep whomp-whomp of
the tram as it glides by. He tells me that no sound insulation was ever
offered or provided when the Luas was developed. Across the road in
front of his home is a hotel that completely blocks the chance of any sun.
Behind his home and to the left-hand side is a build-to-rent and co-living
residential development being delivered by Ronan Group Real Estate.
Nearby is the huge Salesforce Tower offices, also being built by Ronan
Group Real Estate. Salesforce is a US tech company that specialises in
cloud computing.

Tony told me he and his wife moved to Mayor Street Upper in 1992,
as they had five children under four (including two sets of twins) and
their nearby home was too small. With Mayor Street, they had the chance
to live on a peaceful cul de sac. It was unusual in that it was a quiet road,
despite being in the city. The terrace was south facing. But within a few
years, there were soundings about the docklands being developed.

Between 1992 and 1998, living on the terrace was 'bliss'. 'The only thing that went out there,' said McDonnell, gesturing to the road outside, 'was a stray cat.'

But once 1998 came along, there was the Conference Centre, the Spencer Dock development, and apartments to be built for starters. Then, in around 2008, things went bust due to the downturn. As the economy cranked back up, development work began again. Part of making the docklands attractive to big businesses was improving the public transport in the area. The Luas tram line extension to the Point, which was opened in 2009, necessitated a wall, just feet from McDonnell's home, being knocked. No more did he live in a cul de sac. The Luas now sails past his front door hundreds of times a day, starting at 5.30 a.m. and finishing up around 12.30 a.m. Residents feel wide open to anti-social behaviour, as there is no defensible space, particularly when there are large crowds attending concerts in the nearby 3Arena.

McDonnell told me he'd seen the glossy brochures that outlined the great plans for the docklands developments, but that the reality has been different for people like him. 'There's been times where it's been like a talcum powder factory with the amount of dust,' he said of living through the construction process for various projects. The south-facing view is now completely blocked. When I visit, the lights are on in the front room. 'It's been death by 1,000 slashes. If you can point out to me in this area, with all the billions that's gone into the building, a child's swing. If you show me a tree that's been planted. There's nothing. There's a concrete jungle,' said McDonnell. He's had people ask – well if it's that bad, why not move out? 'Who'll buy the homes? Where do we go?' is his reply.

We walked into his back garden, which was overlooked by the balconies of the under-construction Spencer Place North build-to-rent apartments. 'As one person said to me, 'God, this is like being out in the exercise yard of a prison,' said McDonnell. One entrance to the apartments is two metres away from his home, on an elevated walkway that goes from parallel to the side of his house, to right opposite the rear of the terrace. People walking over it will be able to look down into his back garden. He told me that 'the State put public transport to the front of my home, and now pedestrians to the side'. The apartments are part of the growing build-to-rent category of apartment living that's become popular among developers in Ireland. It was preceded by the short-lived co-living, and both were clearly influenced by the new tech workers living in the country, due to a stereotypical view of them as being young and uninterested in settling down.

Due to the uproar among people and politicians about their allotted dimensions for tenants, new co-living developments were banned in 2020.[13] On their heels was build-to-rent, with its marginally bigger homes. It doesn't feel like a coincidence that two of the most controversial forms of housing in Ireland over the past decade have been co-living and build-to-rent, neither of which are aimed at people putting down roots in a community, and both of which – overtly or not – seem aimed at the tech sector in particular. They seem to be pointed towards people who earn high wages, are young, and will be moving on soon. Out of this comes the suggestion that they were aimed at this specific cohort, and that catering for the tech sector influenced housing policy. 'You can more than definitively say it, we can prove it,' Lorcan Sirr, a senior lecturer at TU Dublin and a housing policy analyst, told me before my visit to Mayor Street. 'There is a whole set of planning guidelines for build-to-rent that were designed specifically for young international mobile workers. It says in the actual guidelines that they were designed for these people. And they have lower standards than normal apartments.' He tells me that Ireland has created 'a whole system of accommodation, specifically for people on six figure annual salaries, with a narrative from economists and the development lobby that these workers would love to live in this purpose-built accommodation.' But he he says that this presumption – that tech workers want to live in smaller places as they'll be moving on soon – is incorrect. 'Actually, what you find is particularly couples, but a lot of these highly paid people want to live in established communities such as Phibsborough and Dublin 8, where there are proper Dublin pubs and bakeries and butchers', he tells me. Neither co-living or build-to-rent offer what tech workers might actually want, only what lobbyists conveniently assume a stereotypical tech worker might desire, he says. As I leave the docklands area on that sunny summer day, I think about what he said, and about how at the end of the day, people just want community. The residents I had spoken to saw their local community as an important bolster in their lives. They wanted their community to be listened to and respected. The idea of tech workers somehow rejecting community feels speculative. Underneath the titles we like to give people, 'docklands resident' and 'tech worker' are both the same: they are people.

While sitting in Merrion Square I had opened Twitter, and saw someone sharing a TikTok video on my timeline. 'Another deeply depressing look at the Dublin rental market' was the tweet. The video was of an American woman viewing three apartments in the city. One had a bed in the kitchen and cost €1,000 a month to rent. The ongoing squeeze on housing in Ireland has led to higher rents, young people leaving for cheaper pastures, and fears about a post-millennial generation not getting on the property ladder. It's a conversation that has been playing out on social media, with young people sharing listings for grim apartments to highlight just what the reality is for people looking for a home. On the dull winter's day in Mayor Street Upper, I could hardly believe what I was seeing, and how much the rejuvenation of the docklands was affecting one family in their own home. The issues on that street are interconnected with the experiences of young people searching for affordable rent; with the lack of progress on building homes in a country that badly needs them; with the power that developers and lobbyists hold to influence the direction of a city or country's housing policy; with the need to attract new big business to a capital city. It felt like the little person was getting lost in the greater battle to balance the competing needs of continual progress, versus supporting existing communities. In the journey to make Ireland bigger, glossier, and more appealing to tech companies in particular, I could see what was being lost, and how individuals felt discarded and ignored. I recalled what Sirr told me about how post-recession Ireland could have been an opportunity for the country to do things differently when it came to housing. But Ireland didn't take that opportunity, he said – instead, it doubled down on what was there before.

Out of Silicon Docks and back in my own patch of Dublin, I kept walking down the canal, aiming towards home. I felt the luck of being a homeowner like a pebble in my hand. It had weight and power, and I didn't want to lose hold of it, because of what it represented. It stood for what I had that others didn't. I felt that to lose sight of this – that we are not all given the same luck and privilege in life, especially when it comes to our own home – was what could lead to decisions being made without a thought for their impact. It could lead to policy utterly disconnected from the individuals whose lives it would affect.

The Silicon Docks is a handy bit of shorthand for saying that tech companies have had, and continue to have, a major impact on the development of Dublin's docklands. Without them, there wouldn't be the magnetic pull for other companies to locate in an area that just a few decades ago was full of empty warehouses and dusty yards. With my own home in sight, I continued to tease apart my thoughts on the area's development. Yes, it was good to see a formerly unused space being redeveloped. Yes, Dublin needs better transport for its residents. Yes, it was impressive to be able to compare what was there now to what had been there before, and to see the power the tech companies had to help rejuvenate the space, to bring people in to live and to work. To leave the docklands empty and unused would be wrong.

But I had learned through speaking to locals about the impacts on those living there, and wondered about the price that was being paid. I don't like the stereotype around the type of employee who is drawn to working at the likes of Google and Facebook, knowing that it is reductive. I also don't love the assumption that Ireland needs more accommodation for so-called 'transient' workers (a strange and loaded phrase used to describe tech workers who it is presumed won't be staying long in the city), leaving developers to go hog wild putting in planning permission for co-living and build-to-rent developments.

During my walk around the points of the tech constellation, I could see how natural the offices of the tech companies felt where they were. They didn't stick out; they didn't seem unusual. They might have at one point, but their presence attracted more development, and they helped kick off a completely new phase for this part of the capital. They are symbols of progression. Inside of these offices are people who work hard, who are doing unseen work to keep people like me using their free apps and services. For the docklands residents I met, it is impossible to unravel what has happened since Dublin opened to tech companies, and they must live with where things are now. They can try to be heard, but it is not guaranteed their input will be taken on board. This leaves them with a level of fear about what will be planned for their localities in the future. They can never presume the worst isn't waiting to be unveiled.

And yet. One night, Dolores Wilson told me, she was in Grand Canal Square with two friends who were also involved with the Dublin Docklands Development Authority. They looked around them, taking in how everything had been transformed. The yellow lights shining out from the nearby offices and hotel, the clatter of plates and wine glasses in the restaurants, the planters lush with vegetation, the cosy apartment blocks, the glowing red poles that light up the edge of the canal. 'We said: my God, look what we were involved in. Isn't this wonderful?' she recalled. They all remembered what it used to be like: dark, cold, and a bit desolate. Now, it was beautiful.

References

Introduction

1. Conger, Kate, and Hirsch, Lauren, 'Elon Musk Completes $44 Billion Deal to Own Twitter', *The New York Times*, 27 October 2022
2. Conger, Kate, and Mac, Ryan, 'Elon Musk Begins Layoffs at Twitter', *The New York Times*, 3 November 2022
3. @joinmastodon [tweet], 'Why choose Mastodon? Because its decentralized and open-source, it can't be sold and won't go bankrupt. It respects your privacy and gives control over the network to the people. It's a product on top of a protocol, the way Twitter should have been.' 11:11pm, 27 October 2022
4. Turner, Fred, *From Counterculture to Cyberculture* (University of Chicago Press: 2006)
5. Berners-Lee, Tim, *Weaving the Web: The Original Design and Ultimate Destiny of the World Wide Web* (HarperCollins: 1999)
6. Murphy, Niall, 'The History of the Irish Internet', Internet History, 2016.
7. Barlow, John Perry, 'A Declaration of the Independence of Cyberspace', Electronic Frontier Foundation, 8 February 1996

Aoife Barry

INFLUENCE

The Protest

1. Barry, Aoife, 'Schull teens travel to Dublin to tell Facebook to 'face up' to the impact of algorithms', The Journal, 10 November 2021
2. @TJ_Politics [tweet], 'These lads are outside Leinster House saying marriage should be between males and females #marref', 12:57 pm, 20 May 2015
3. 'About Us', Uplift, 2022
4. Horwitz, Jeff, 'The Facebook Whistleblower, Frances Haugen, Says She Wants to Fix the Company, Not Harm It', *The Wall Street Journal*, 3 October 2021
5. Wells, Georgina, et al., 'Facebook Knows Instagram is Toxic for Teen Girls, Company Documents Show', *The Wall Street Journal*, 14 September 2021
6. 'Whistle-Blower Unites Democrats and Republicans in Calling for Regulation of Facebook', *The New York Times*, 5 October 2021
7. Raychoudhury, Pratiti, 'What Our Research Really Says About Teen Well-Being and Instagram', Meta, 26 September 2021
8. Newton, Karina, 'Using research to improve your experience', Instagram, 14 September 2021
9. Cadwalladr, Carole, ''I made Steve Bannon's psychological warfare tool': meet the data war whistleblower', *The Guardian*, 18 March 2018

The I in Everything

1. Tolentino, Jia, *Trick Mirror: Reflections on Self-Delusion* (HarperCollins: 2020)
2. Bilton, Nick, *Hatching Twitter: A True Story of Money, Power, Friendship and Betrayal* (Hachette: 2013)
3. Frier, Sarah, *No Filter: The True Inside Story of Instagram* (Simon & Schuster: 2020)

266

4. Deegan, Gordon, 'Profits at blogger turned businesswoman Suzanne Jackson's companies soar', *Irish Independent*, 8 December 2021

5. Deegan, Gordon, 'Revenue at Pippa O'Connor's fashion business increases to record €2.7m', *The Irish Times*, 23 July 2021

6. 'TikTok Creator Spotlight: @lagomchef', TikTok, 4 November 2022

7. Moreno, Johan, 'Google Is Evolving Search As Zoomers Use TikTok, Instagram To Find Things Online', *Forbes*, 19 July 2022

8. Brennan, Martha, 'For the gram: what it's really like to work as an Irish "influencer"', *Irish Examiner*, 29 March 2021

9. Statista Research Department, 'Influencer marketing market size worldwide from 2016 to 2022', Statista, 6 January 2023

10. 'Advertising Standards Authority for Ireland calls on bloggers and influencers to fully declare marketing communications', Advertising Standards Authority for Ireland, 24 January 2017

11. Daly, Adam, 'Complaint upheld about blogger's "misleading" Instagram image', The Journal, 26 June 2018

12. 'Over half (51%) of people in Ireland say they are concerned by a lack of transparency in influencer marketing according to research conducted by the Advertising Standards Authority for Ireland', Advertising Standards Authority for Ireland, 23 February 2021

The Backlash

1. Daly, Adam, '"Things have taken a nasty turn": Bloggers Unveiled account shuts down', The Journal, 2 August 2018

2. Fitzmaurice, Éadaoin, 'I Was The Target Of Bloggers Unveiled For 24 Hours – Here's What It's REALLY Like', Lovin' Dublin, 5 July 2018

3. Mooney, John, 'Bloggers Unveiled? I don't run this Instagram account, says frightened Tullamore beautician Ramona Tracey', *The Irish Times*, 29 July 2018

4. Armstrong, Kathy, '"The baying for blood makes me sick" – popular Bloggers Unveiled page removed', *Irish Independent*, 1 August 2018

5. Chapman, Michelle, 'To Close The Forum Tattle Life', Change.org, 2019

6. Cliff, Martha, and Hawken, Lydia, 'Mummy blogger Clemmie Hooper apologises for trolling friends and calling husband "class A t***" under fake profile', *The Sun*, 7 November 2019

7. Ronson, John, *So You've Been Publicly Shamed* (Riverhead Books: 2015)

NAMELESS, FACELESS

Anonymity

1. Fleishman, Glenn, 'Cartoon Captures Spirit of the Internet', 14 December 2000

2. Eoghan Harris, 'Eoghan Harris interview' , *Drivetime*, RTÉ Radio 1, 7 May 2021

3. @aoifegracemoore [tweet], 'This account sent me sexualised messages about whether Mary Lou McDonald "turned me on", the size of my arse and called me a terrorist from the month I started at the Examiner. Since then, I've had to go to counselling and the guards', 11:24 pm, 6 May 2021

4. Harris, Eoghan, 'Eoghan Harris: "Barbara J Pym was no trolling account"', *The Irish Times*, 15 May 2021

5. Cunningham, Francine, 'A tale of tweets, trolls and true courage', Ireland by Accident, 9 May 2021

6. Board of Management, Salesian Secondary College Limerick, and Facebook Ireland Limited, No. 1419, High Court, 19 May 2021

7. Molloy, Amy, '"Ball is in Facebook's court now", says solicitor after Miriam O'Callaghan receives "unreserved" apology over bogus skincare ads', *Irish Independent*, 26 February 2022

8. Carolan, Mary, 'Fastway couriers seeks court orders over "abusive" parody Twitter account', *The Irish Times,* 30 April 2020

9. XY v Facebook Ireland, NIQB 96, High Court of Justice in Northern Ireland Queen's Bench, 30 November 2012

10. Notopoulos, Katie, 'We Found The Real Names Of Bored Ape Yacht Club's Pseudonymous Founders', Buzzfeed News, 5 February 2022
11. Lorenz, Taylor, 'Meet the woman behind Libs of TikTok, secretly fueling the right's outrage machine', *The Washington Post*, 19 April 2022
12. Butler, Anita, and Parrella, Albert, 'Tweeting with Consideration', Twitter Blog, 5 May 2021

Aoife Martin's Story

1. 'Exposed: The Scale of Transphobia Online', Brandwatch, October 2019
2. 'Briefing note on the Lydia Foy case: The case that won recognition for Ireland's transgender community', Free Legal Advice Centres (FLAC), October 2015
3. Fairbairn, Catherine, et al., 'Gender Recognition Act Reform: Consultation and outcome', House of Commons Library, 17 February 2022

HATE AND HARM

A New Way to Bully

1. CyberSafeKids Annual Report 2020, CyberSafeKids, 2021
2. Cotter, Pádraig, and McGilloway, Sinéad, 'Living in an Electronic Age: Cyberbullying Among Irish Adolescents', *The Irish Journal of Education*, 2011
3. Information Society Statistics – Households 2020, Central Statistics Office, 7 October 2021
4. Milosevic, Tijana, et al., 'KiDiCoTi:, Kids' Digital Lives in Covid-19 Times: A Study on Digital Practices' (National Anti-Bullying Research and Resource Centre [ABC]: 2021)
5. Mayo Tusla Youth Advisory Committee, 'Social Media Use in Mayo's Teenagers', Tusla Child and Family Agency, November 2019
6. Social Media Report 2012: Social Media Comes of Age, Nielsen, December 2012

7. O'Neill, Brian, and Dinh, Thuy, 'Mobile Technologies and the Incidence of Cyberbullying in Seven European Countries: Findings from Net Children Go Mobile', *Open Access Societies*, 27 April 2015

8. O'Neill, Brian, and Dinh, Thuy, 'Cyberbullying among 9–16 year olds in Ireland', Digital Childhoods Working Paper Series (Technological University Dublin: 1 February 2013)

9. O'Doherty, Caroline, 'Ask.fm "thoughts" with family for suicide inquest', *The Irish Examiner*, 15 August 2016

10. Neville, Simon, et al., 'Ask.fm loses advertisers as Cameron calls for "irresponsible websites" boycott', *The Guardian*, 8 August 2013

11. 'Hannah Smith inquest: Teenager posted "online messages"', BBC News, 6 May 2014

12. ASKfm Community Guidelines, ASK.fm, 2023

13. McMorrow, Conor, 'Family says teen took own life after years of bullying', RTÉ, 19 January 2022

Without Consent

1. Stop NCII, Stop Non-Consensual Intimate Image Abuse, 2023

2. Hill, Kashmir, 'Revenge porn (Or: another reason not to take nude photos)', *Forbes*, 2 June 2009

3. Contrera, Jessica, '"Revenge porn" distributors are finally seeing legal ramifications. This Web site owner will go to prison for 18 years', *The Washington Post*, 5 April 2015

4. Hern, Alex, 'How revenge porn sites rely on legal loopholes and anonymity', *The Guardian*, 9 May 2016

5. Number of pieces of content removed on Reddit in 2021 by type violation, Statista, February 2022

6. Constine, Josh, 'Reddit Will Hide Indecent Content From Search and Logged-Out Users, Reiterates Harassment Ban', Tech Crunch, 16 July 2015

7. 'McEntee says anyone who shares intimate images without consent "will face serious criminal sanctions"', The Journal, 20 November 2020

8. @maevemctaggart [tweet], 'Knowing over 500 Irish men in a Discord server felt comfortable sharing 6000+ nude images of women and girls has left my heart a bit broken today – this is a culture problem + a rape culture problem', 11:32 pm, 18 November 2020

9. Gartland, Katie, 'We need to criminalise image based sexual abuse now', District Magazine, 20 November 2020

10. End IBSA Ireland, 'End IBSA Ireland Protest', Facebook, 20 December 2020

11. Barry, Eloise, 'Why OnlyFans Suddenly Reversed its Decision to Ban Sexual Content', Time, 26 August 2021

12. Steadman, Otilla, 'Everyone is Making Porn at Home Now. Will the Porn Industry Survive?', Buzzfeed News, 6 May 2020

13. Cole, Samantha, and Cox, Joseph, 'Inside the Underground Trade of Pirated OnlyFans Porn', Vice, 17 June 2020.

14. Ryan, Órla, 'Gardaí looking into allegations that large number of images of women were shared online without their consent', The Journal, 19 November 2020

15. McGrath, Pat, 'Man jailed for sharing explicit photos of ex-girlfriend', RTÉ, 13 June 2022

16. Deegan, Gordon, 'Father accepts in court "flashing" of intimate photo of ex-wife to their daughter was wrong', *Irish Examiner*, 9 January 2023

17. "Real People Not Pixels: Annual Report 2021", Hotline.ie, 21 December 2022

18. 'Best Leaks Discord Servers: Find Best Leaks discord servers and make new friends!', Discadia, December 2022

Hate

1. Schroepfer, Mike, 'AI gets better every day. Here's what that means for stopping hate speech', Meta, 11 February 2021

2. Rose, Steve, 'A deadly ideology: how the "great replacement theory" went mainstream', *The Guardian*, 8 June 2022

3. 'Anti-Corruption Ireland', Anti-Corruption Ireland, 2019
4. O'Doherty, Gemma, 'Historic Moore Street Now An African Ghetto Courtesy Of The Government Who Loves You So Much', Gemma O'Doherty, 21 November 2022
5. @lidl_ireland [tweet], 'After offensive and racist tweets from Gemma O'Doherty we have decided to block and report her to @Twitter. We are proud of our multicultural & diverse team and our customers. We are proud to work with, and serve, each and every one of them. Everyone is welcome in our store', 1:10 pm, 8 September 2019
6. Prohibition of Incitement To Hatred Act, 1989, Irish Statute Book (Office of the Attorney General of Ireland: 2007)
7. O'Mahony, John, 'Man cleared of online hatred against Travellers', *Irish Examiner*, 1 October 2011
8. 'Irish District Court dismisses Traveller Facebook hate speech case', Pila (Public Interest Law Alliance) 5 October 2011
9. Holland, Kitty, 'Couple in ad campaign left "shaking and fearful" after online abuse', *The Irish Times*, 27 September 2019
10. Submissions to the public consultation on Hate Speech and Hate Crime Legislation, Department of Justice, 26 October 2022
11. O'Brien, Carl, 'YouTube terminates Gemma O'Doherty's account over breach of "hate speech" policy', *The Irish Times*, 16 July 2019
12. Rogan, Aaron, 'YouTube received legal requests to delete O'Doherty's videos', *Business Post*, 21 July 2019
13. INAR's 2021 iReport.ie Reports of Racism in Ireland, Irish Network Against Racism, 2021
14. INAR's 2020 iReport.ie Reports of Racism in Ireland, Irish Network Against Racism, 2020
15. MacNamee, Garreth, 'FactCheck: No, George Nkencho was not a convicted criminal out on bail for attacking his girlfriend', The Journal, 4 January 2021
16. O'Loughlin, Ciara, '"Justice for George" chanted by protesters after Garda shooting', *The Irish Independent*, 31 December 2020
17. @emantreeman [tweet], 'Fuckfuck fuck', 6:05 pm, 9 August 2014

18. Anderson, Monica, 'The hashtag #BlackLivesMatter emerges: Social activism on Twitter', Pew Research Center, 15 August 2016

19. Cobb, Jelani, 'The Matter of Black Lives: A new kind of movement found its moment. What will its future be?', *The New Yorker*, 6 March 2016

20. Kang, Jay Caspian, '"Our Demand Is Simple: Stop Killing Us": How a group of black social media activists built the nation's first 21st-century civil rights movement', *The New York Times*, 4 May 2015

21. Ingle, Róisín, 'Black Lives Matter: Experiences of Racism in Ireland', Galway International Arts Festival, 5 September 2020

22. Nialler9, 'Listen to the Black Artists Who Are Absolutely Running the Irish Music Scene playlist', Nialler9, 8 June 2020

23. @DeniseChaila [tweet], 'Hey! Thank you for wanting to defend me, but it's fine that RTE aren't tagging this account in their posts. I've asked them not to. I need space from racism while celebrating my music once in a while. And I'm enjoying figuring out these boundaries. Love you family! D xx', 2:09 pm, 27 January 2021

24. Ní Aodha, Gráinne, 'Justice Minister condemns arson attack at Donegal hotel being prepared for asylum seekers', The Journal, 25 November 2018

25. Thomas, Cónal, 'Move quickly and misinform: How direct provision centres became a catalyst for far-right activism in Ireland', The Journal, 15 March 2021

26. Frenkel, Sheera, and Kang, Cecilia, *An Ugly Truth: Inside Facebook's Battle for Domination* (HarperCollins: 2021)

27. 'Annual reports, Special Rapporteur on minority issues', United Nations Human Rights Office of the High Commissioner, 2022

28. 'Ditch the Label Hate Speech Report Uncovered: Online Hate Speech in the Covid Era', Ditch the Label, 2021

Aoife Barry

WHO'S WATCHING WHO?

BOD

1. Bilton, Nick, *Hatching Twitter: A True Story of Money, Power, Friendship and Betrayal* (Hachette: 2013)
2. Frier, Sarah, *No Filter: The True Inside Story of Instagram* (Simon & Schuster: 2020)
3. Kunzelman, Michael, 'Internet troll 'Baked Alaska' pleads guilty in Capitol riot', AP News, 22 July 2022
4. 'Everyday Sexism Project', Everyday Sexism, 2023
5. 'Abuse and harassment driving girls off Facebook, Instagram and Twitter', Plan International, 5 October 2020

Feeling Watched

1. Odell, Jenny, *How to Do Nothing: Resisting the Attention Economy* (Melville House: 2019)
2. Bates, Laura, *Men Who Hate Women: The Extremism Nobody is Talking About* (Simon & Schuster: 2021)

TRUTH AND LIES ONLINE

Fool Me Once

1. Olson, Parmy, 'Inside The Facebook-WhatsApp Megadeal: The Courtship, The Secret Meetings, The $19 Billion Poker Game', *Forbes*, 4 March 2014
2. WhatsApp: penetration rate among global messaging app users as of April 2022, by country, Statista, May 2022
3. Hutchinson, Andrew, 'WhatsApp Partners with Indian Government to Provide Digital Identity Documents In-App', Social Media Today, 23 May 2022

4. Bohan, Christine, 'Why those messages you're getting on WhatsApp about coronavirus cases in Ireland are (probably) not true', The Journal, 28 February 2020

5. Horgan-Jones, Jack, and O'Connell, Hugh, *Pandemonium: Power, Politics and Ireland's Pandemic* (Gill Books: 5 May 2022)

6. @TheHarryMcC [tweet], 'I can confirm that @GardaTraffic have escorted a Brennans Bread van into Ballyfermot . . . #StormEmma #BeastfromTheEast' 4:25 pm, 27 February 2018

7. Fichera, Angelo, 'Facebook Users Wrongly Tie Dog Vaccine to Novel Coronavirus', Factcheck.org, 22 April 2020

8. Duffy, Rónán, 'Debunked: No, this tweet saying that all Cheltenham racegoers from Ireland are being put into isolation is not true', The Journal, 13 March 2020

The Infodemic

1. Iqbal, Mansoor, 'TikTok Revenue and Usage Statistics (2022)', Business of Apps, 11 November 2022

2. Distribution of TikTok users worldwide as of April 2022, by age and gender, Statista, 14 November 2022

3. Kang, Cecilia, 'ByteDance Inquiry Finds Employees Obtained User Data of 2 Journalists', *The New York Times*, 22 December 2022

4. Community Guidelines Enforcement Report, April 1, 2021 – June 30, 2021, TikTok, 13 October 2021

5. Gallagher, Conor, 'Facebook removes page of ex-UCD professor over Covid misinformation', *The Irish Times*, 13 December 2021

6. Gallagher, Aoife, 'How Facebook's Failure to Remove False Content Allows COVID-19 Misinformation to Spread', Institute for Strategic Dialogue, 2 November 2021

7. 'About fact-checking on Facebook and Instagram', Meta, 2019

8. @Microsoft [tweet], 'A joint industry statement on COVID-19 from Microsoft, Facebook, Google, LinkedIn, Reddit, Twitter and YouTube: [attached: a screenshot of an image reading 'We are working closely together

on our COVID-19 response efforts. We're helping millions of people stay connected while also jointly combatting fraud and misinformation about the virus, elevating authoritative content on our platforms, and sharing critical updates in coordination with government healthcare agencies around the world. We invite other companies to join us as we work to keep our communities healthy and safe.]', 12:00 am, 17 March 2020

9. Rosen, Guy, and Lyons, Tessa, 'Remove, Reduce, Inform: New Steps to Manage Problematic Content', Meta, 10 April 2019
10. Jin, Kang-Xin, 'An Update on Our Work to Keep People Informed and Limit Misinformation About COVID-19', Meta, 8 February 2021
11. 'Promoting Authoritative Information About Covid-19 Vaccines', Meta, 2021
12. Culloty, Eileen, 'CovidCheck report highlights inconsistencies in platforms' response to disinformation', Fujo Media, 16 December 2021
13. 'The Disinformation Dozen: Why platforms must act on twelve leading online anti-vaxxers', Centre for Countering Digital Hate, 21 March 2021
14. Maguire, Stephen, 'Gardaí suspect fires at 5G masts were deliberate after coal found', The Journal, 13 April 2020
15. 'False claim: Video shows 5G telecoms equipment stamped with "COV-19" ready to be installed into a mast', Reuters, 15 May 2020
16. Isaac, Mike, and Frankel, Sheera, 'Facebook Braces Itself for Trump to Cast Doubt on Election Results', *The New York Times*, 21 August 2020
17. Clegg, Nick, 'In Response to Oversight Board, Trump Suspended for Two Years; Will Only Be Reinstated if Conditions Permit', Meta, 4 June 2021
18. 'Permanent suspension of @realDonaldTrump', Twitter, 8 January 2021
19. @MarkLTighe [tweet], 'Have been tracking the Irish Covid conspiracy theories online for months. Got to meet some today. Interviewed these protesters outside the GPO. Details in tomorrow's @SunTimes Ireland. Fairly wild and scary what people believe.' 7:09 pm, 27 February 2021

20. Bracken, Ali, 'No criminal charges for anti-vaxxer over death of Donegal man Joe McCarron', *The Irish Independent*, 1 May 2022

21. Edwards, Rodney, '"My husband was killed by a disease he didn't believe was real" – Joe McCarron's widow on his death from Covid', *The Irish Independent*, 27 March 2022

GHOSTS IN THE MACHINE

The Other Side of the Screen

1. Perraudin, Frances, 'Shamima Begum tells of fate since joining Isis during half-term', *The Guardian*, 14 February 2019

2. Kachroo, Rohit, 'Kadiza Sultana Has Been Killed in ISIS Stronghold: Family', NBC News, 12 August 2015

3. Sandberg, Sheryl, 'Facebook Chief Operating Officer Sheryl Sandberg's letter to New Zealand', *The New Zealand Herald*, 30 March 2019

4. Zuckerberg, Mark, post describing Minnesota woman Diamond Reynolds' Facebook live immediately after the shooting of her fiancé, Philando Castile, and a message of condolence to her family, Facebook, 7 July 2016

5. Fassrainer, Victoria, 'Tweeting Terror Live: Al-Shabaab's Use of Twitter during the Westgate Attack and Implications for Counterterrorism Communications', *Military Review*, March 2020

6. Clegg, Nick, 'Meta Launches New Content Moderation Tool as It Takes Chair of Counter-Terrorism NGO', Meta, 13 December 2022

7. 'Sharing Our Actions on Stopping Hate', Meta, 17 June 2021

8. Stone, Brad, 'Policing the Web's Lurid Precincts', *The New York Times*, 18 July 2010

9. Cassidy, Ciaran, and Chen, Adrian, *The Moderators*, Field of Vision, 17 April 2017

10. Block, Hans, and Riesewieck, Moritz, *The Cleaners*, Periscoop, 2018

11. Isaac, Mike and Satariano, Adam, 'The Silent Partner Cleaning Up Facebook for $500 Million a Year', *The New York Times*, 31 August 2021

12. Roberts, Sarah T., *Behind the Screen: Content Moderation in the Shadows of Social Media* (Yale University Press: 2021)

13. Boran, Marie, 'Life as a Facebook moderator: "People are awful. This is what my job has taught me"', *The Irish Times*, 27 February 2020

14. O'Connell, Jennifer, 'Facebook's dirty work in Ireland: "I had to watch footage of a person being beaten to death"', *The Irish Times*, 30 March 2019

15. Gray, Chris, *The Moderator: Inside Facebook's Dirty Work in Ireland* (Gill: 2022)

16. Reynaldo Gonzalez et al. vs Google LLC, Supreme Court, No. 21-1333, 21 February 2023

17. Loh, Michelle, 'Facebook sorry for gay "censorship"', *The Courier Mail*, 20 April 2011

18. 'Oversight Board overturns original Facebook decision: Case 2020-004-IG-UA', Oversight Board, January 2021

The Future of Moderation

1. Newton, Casey, 'All Hands On Deck', The Verge, 1 October 2019

2. De Hoyos Hart, Angela, et al., 'Open letter from content moderators re: pandemic', Foxglove, November 2020

3. Shead, Sam, 'Facebook moderators say company has risked their lives by forcing them back to the office', CNBC, 18 November 2020

4. Iyengar, Rishi, 'Facebook is giving $1,000 to all of its 45,000 employees', CNN Business, 19 March, 2020

5. 'Online Content Moderation: Discussion', Joint Committee on Enterprise Trade and Employee Debate, Houses of the Oireachtas, 12 May 2021

6. '"It took me ages to sleep": Facebook moderators on the things they can't unsee', RTÉ.ie, 29 January 2021

7. Masnick, Mike, 'Masnick's Impossibility Theorem: Content Moderation At Scale Is Impossible To Do Well', TechDirt, 29 November 2019
8. Masnick, Mike, 'There Is No Magic Bullet For Moderating A Social Media Platform', TechDirt, 18 May 2018

TECH AND THE CITY

Big Tech Constellation

1. 'Collapse of Tenements 1963', Dublin City Council, 3 September 2019
2. Hosford, Paul, 'The silos at Boland's Mill have been fully demolished', The Journal, 19 July 2016
3. Morgan, Edel, 'Barrow Street booms as south docklands schemes take off', *The Irish Times*, 24 November 2020
4. 'Bord Gáis Energy Theatre and Grand Canal Commercial Development', Libeskind, 2010
5. 'Planning Permission Granted For New Liffey Bridge', RTÉ Archives, 2001
6. 'Ambitious Plans For Dublin Docks', RTÉ Archives, 1997
7. 'Dublin Docks Development Plans', RTÉ Archives, 3 December 1987
8. Mulvey, Kieran, 'Dublin North East Inner City, Creating A Brighter Future', Health Research Board National Drugs Library, February 2017
9. Reilly, Owen, The Docklands Residential Report 2021, 2021
10. 'What's In A Wall?', *The Irish Times*, 30 September 1997
11. CR's Video Vaults, 'Growing Up In Sheriff Street, Dublin City, Ireland 1970', YouTube, 28 August 2021
12. '"It Was All a Bit of a Joke" – the Isle of Dogs' Unilateral Declaration of Independence', Isle of Dogs, Past Life, Past Lives, 7 December 2013
13. Sustainable Urban Housing: Design Standards for New Apartments, Guidelines for Planning Authorities (December 2020), Department of Housing, Local Government and Heritage

Acknowledgements

Writing a book is both a solo and team effort – I might have spent hours writing alone but I couldn't have done it without a large number of people.

For starters, thank you to Conor Nagle and Catherine Gough of HarperCollins Ireland for giving me this opportunity and allowing me to write about such an endlessly fascinating topic. Huge thanks also to Stephen Reid, Patricia McVeigh for publicity, and in particular to Flora Moreau, who helped me whip the draft into shape and bring it to fruition.

Thanks to all of my interviewees for being so generous with your time, and honest in your thoughts – I hope I have done your stories justice.

To my great colleagues at The Journal, thanks for your support and the time I needed to take to work on this book.

Big thanks to my friends who supported and cheered me on, especially E & C for the Sunday lunches; the Bad Bitches for the WhatsApp cheer-leading, the Frog Gang for the writing help and inspiration; my Jazz Gals for being so supportive.

A huge thank you to my family, especially my mum, Mags, for her brilliant editorial eye and never-ending encouragement: I think Kieran would have had plenty of feedback to give us on the book.

And finally, thanks to Cormac for being a constant support and sounding board through it all.